Rashida Z. Shaw McMahon's exhaustive investigation of the history and ongoing appeal of the theatrical "Chitlin Circuit" sheds light on a crucial component of contemporary Black popular culture that continues to be ignored by most scholars. In her masterful movement across time, geographies, and source materials, she offers an unparalleled gift and resource to African American Studies and Performance Studies.

> **—GerShun Avilez**, University of Maryland, author of *Radical Aesthetics and Modern Black Nationalism*

Rashida Z. Shaw McMahon provides a first-hand, comprehensive history of the "Chitlin Circuit," or what the author calls the "Black Circuit," a popular entertainment potpourri consisting of drama, comedy, gospel music, Christian faith, family, romance, melodrama, hair salons, barber shops, and vaudeville. Methodically researched, *The Black Circuit* illuminates the plays, performers, and audience responses rooted in the African American cultural experience. Building on the theme of "Chitlins," an African American "soul food" that slaves cooked primarily from swine leftovers, McMahon tracks the development of this eclectic genre, from artists like Langston Hughes to notable contemporaries Tyler Perry, David Talbert, the team of Johnson and Guidry, and many others. This groundbreaking work will be the standard study of this unique subject for years to come.

> **—David Krasner**, Five Towns College, author of *Resistance, Parody, and Double Consciousness in African American Theatre, 1895–1910* and *A Beautiful Pageant: African American Theatre, Drama, and Performance in the Harlem Renaissance, 1910–1927*

Rashida Z. Shaw McMahon ambitiously takes on the challenge of chronicling and conveying Black theatrical pleasure in the "Chitlin Circuit," deftly nuancing black performance and reception, beyond easy scripts. Using rigorous methods and analyses, *The Black Circuit* taps into an original, rich, and dynamic archive of performances—to tell a beautifully complex story of another side of black theatre history and world-making.

> —**Jeffrey Q. McCune, Jr**, Associate Professor of Women, Gender, Sexuality Studies and African and African American Studies, Washington University in St. Louis, author of *Sexual Discretion: Black Masculinity and the Politics of Passing*

Whether you call it the "Chitlin Circuit," the "Urban Theater Circuit," or, as Rashida Z. Shaw McMahon does in her important and timely book, the "Black Circuit," you will want to know all that she can tell you and more about this effervescent scene of African-American popular entertainment.

> —**Joseph Roach**, Sterling Professor Emeritus of Theater and English, Professor Emeritus of American Studies and African American Studies, Yale University, author of *Cities of the Dead: Circum-Atlantic Performance*

The Black Circuit is the first sustained examination of "Chitlin Circuit" theatre, best exemplified, perhaps, by Tyler Perry and "Madea." Rashida Z. Shaw McMahon skillfully debunks accusations that this theatre simply recycles stereotypes to unsophisticated, African American audiences willing to ignore low production values. Instead she unearths historical links not only to poet Langston Hughes' gospel plays of the 1950s but equally importantly, to the sermonic and other performative strategies crafted over centuries by the Black Church. Indeed, the reader sees how this theatre offers a secular Christianity, steeped in contemporary popular culture yet aimed at enabling spectators to surmount, with grace, challenges facing black communities.

> —**Sandra L. Richards**, Professor Emerita of African American Studies, Theatre, and Performance Studies, Northwestern University, author of *Ancient Songs Set Ablaze: The Theatre of Femi Osofisan*

A smart, sophisticated blend of ethnography, cultural criticism, and historical writing. *The Black Circuit* spotlights one of the most important but critically overlooked branches of contemporary American theatre: independently produced urban circuit Black theatre a.k.a "the Chitlin Circuit." Examining the works of Tyler Perry among numerous other innovative theatre artists, Rashida Z. Shaw McMahon explores the past and present, politics and economics, and the dynamic live experience of this massively popular genre.

> —**Harvey Young**, Boston University, author of *Embodying Black Experience: Stillness, Critical Memory, and the Black Body*

THE BLACK CIRCUIT

The Black Circuit: Race, Performance, and Spectatorship in Black Popular Theatre presents the first book-length study of Chitlin Circuit theatre, the most popular and controversial form of Black theatre to exist outside the purview of Broadway since the 1980s. Through historical and sociological research, Rashida Z. Shaw McMahon links the fraught racial histories in American slave plantations and early African American cuisine to the performance sites of nineteenth-century minstrelsy, early-twentieth-century vaudeville, and mid-twentieth-century gospel musicals. *The Black Circuit* traces this rise of a Black theatrical popular culture that exemplifies W. E. B. Du Bois's 1926 parameters of "for us, near us, by us, and about us," with critical differences that, McMahon argues, complicate our understanding of performance and spectatorship in African American theatre. McMahon shows how an integrated and evolving network of consumerism, culture, circulation, exchange, ideologies, and meaning making has emerged in the performance environments of Chitlin Circuit theatre that is reflective of the broader influences at play in acts of minority spectatorship. She labels this network *the Black Circuit.*

Rashida Z. Shaw McMahon is an Associate Professor of English and Affiliated Faculty of African American Studies at Wesleyan University. Her research uses interdisciplinary methodologies and collaborative approaches toward examining the dramatic and performance traditions of Africa and the African diaspora. Professor Shaw McMahon is originally from the island of St. Croix in the US Virgin Islands.

Sociology Re-Wired

Edited by Jodi O'Brien, Seattle University, and Marcus Hunter, University of California, Los Angeles

Sociology Re-Wired captures this combustible moment in American and global societies with new books that innovate and reconfigure social and political issues. This hybrid series publishes timely, relevant, original research and textbooks that address significant social issues informed by critical race theory, Black feminism and queer studies traditions. Series books are written in a publicly accessible, multi-vocal style broadening the reach and impact of significant scholarly contributions beyond traditional academic audiences.

Some titles published in this series were published under an earlier series name and a different editorship.

Published:

The New Black Sociologists
Historical and Contemporary Perspectives
edited by Marcus A. Hunter

The Black Circuit
Race, Performance, and Spectatorship in Black Popular Theatre
Rashida Z. Shaw McMahon

All Media are Social
Sociological Perspectives on Mass Media
Andrew Lindner and Stephen R. Barnard

For a full list of titles in this series, please visit: www.routledge.com

THE BLACK CIRCUIT

Race, Performance, and Spectatorship in Black Popular Theatre

Rashida Z. Shaw McMahon

Routledge
Taylor & Francis Group

NEW YORK AND LONDON

First published 2020
by Routledge
52 Vanderbilt Avenue, New York, NY 10017

and by Routledge
2 Park Square, Milton Park, Abingdon, Oxon, OX14 4RN

Routledge is an imprint of the Taylor & Francis Group, an informa business

Library of Congress Cataloging-in-Publication Data
A catalog record for this title has been requested

ISBN: 978-1-138-04673-3 (hbk)
ISBN: 978-1-138-04674-0 (pbk)
ISBN: 978-0-203-73244-1 (ebk)

Typeset in Bembo
by Apex CoVantage, LLC

Dedicated in gratitude to the ancestors, the living, and the not yet born of my familial circle who continue to bear fruit and conjure wonder across the Atlantic. With special attention to the blessings of magic, light, and freedom, granted to your daughters Zadie and Zuri.
Ashe.

CONTENTS

ACKNOWLEDGMENTS

The soul of this book pays homage to the great mothers of my ancestral line who birthed, nourished, and emboldened those who came before me. They are the Great Mothers of my great-grandmother Daisy, of my grandmothers Gaynel and Julia, and of my mother Beryl, the wondrous woman who birthed me and then selflessly set herself on a path to support and sharpen my curiosities. They are the foremothers to Shakuwra, my light-bearing sister who continues to bestow on me the lifelong gifts of friendship, foundation, and play. And they are the life force that burns inside my daughters, Zadie and Zuri. Fire stirs, embers aglow, and paths lit.

The spine of this book has been made straight by the unwavering support of my husband, Odari, yet another gift from the ancestors, who lovingly reminds me that I am enough and that my reach is infinite. My love supreme. My sun. In my stepson, Odarion, I am reminded of the limitless imaginary of youth and to keep the wonders of discovery and first encounters close at hand. My father, Gary, presciently gifted me with a *World Book Encyclopedia* set on the day I was born, thereby ordaining my path toward research, exploration, and questions and cementing a loving association with books.

The typeface on each page of this book is indelibly marked by my editor/ kindred spirit, Marcus Anthony Hunter, whose friendship and mind have made a profound impact on my personal and professional selves.

The design, development, and completion of this project is a testament to the collective brilliance possessed by the four members of my dissertation committee, who ceaselessly dedicated their time, energy, and insight in support of my ideas. As chair of my dissertation and advisor of my graduate studies, Dr. Sandra Lee Richards challenged me to think deeply and critically about Black theatre in ways that will forever impact my research, scholarship, teaching, and voice. The nascent stages of this project benefited from her careful eye, expansive knowledge, limitless investment, and exemplary guidance. Dr. Gary Alan Fine nurtured my combined interests in Sociology and Theatre from the beginning of my graduate career, with unlimited confidence and encouragement. The scholarship, perspectives, and resourcefulness of Dr. Margaret Drewal have impacted the scope and execution of this project immeasurably. In no small terms, many aspects of this project would not have been possible without the feedback and the investment of Dr. Richard Iton. In memoriam, I continue to thank him for enthusiastically participating in a theatre studies project and for granting me access to his critical insight, intellectual interests, and arsenal of cultural studies resources. His presence and friendship are sorely missed.

Across the interdisciplinary fields of English, Theatre, and African American studies, I have been supported, guided, and reinforced by a critical mass of colleagues at Wesleyan University. I thank Dr. Claudia Nascimento for her mentorship and resounding support of this project and my intellectual path during my time in the Theater Department. A perfect alignment in the universe at Wesleyan's Center for Humanities brought me in close proximity to the brilliance and generosity of Dr. Natasha Korda, who has wholly invested in my academic growth and the development of this project, as my mentor, my colleague, and my friend. I give thanks to the following members of my intellectual community across Wesleyan's academic expanse whose scholarship and praxis have reinforced my intellectual spirit as professor and undergraduate: Robyn Autry, Sally Bachner, Marina Bilbija, Amy Bloom, Kathryn Brewer Ball, Lois Brown, Lisa Cohen, Mary Ann Clawson, Christina Crosby, Jonathan Cutler, Andrew Curran, Ann duCille, Kimberly DaCosta-Holton, Alex Dupuy, Demetrius Eudell, Joseph J. Fitzpatrick, Harris Friedberg, Anne Garcia-Romero, Leah C. Gardiner, Matthew Garrett, Greg Goldberg, Alice Hadler, Anthony Hatch, Jay Hoggard, J. Kehaulani Kauanui, Ethan Kleinberg, Georgianne Leone, Jerome Long, Douglas Martin, Sean McCann, Kristin McQueeney, John Murillo, Ren Ellis Neyra, Ruth Nisse, Marguerite Nguyen, Erin Ogrean, Marcela Oteiza, Courtney Patterson-Faye, Joel Pfister, Michael Armstrong Roche, Robert Rosenthal, Ashraf Rushdy, Kate Rushin, Hirsh Sawhney, Lily Saint, Erinn Savage, Andrew Szegedy-Maszak, Nicole Stanton, William Stowe, Amy Tang, Cliff Thornton, Renee Johnston Thornton, Elizabeth Tinker, Gina Ulysse, Mark Wade, Leslie Weinberg, Stephanie Weiner, and Leah Wright Rigeur.

I remain forever indebted to Northwestern University's interdisciplinary PhD in theatre and drama (IPTD) program. I extend a heartfelt thank-you to Dr. Tracy C. Davis, Dr. Susan Manning, Dr. Ana Puga, and Dr. Harvey Young for their mentoring, teaching, and training in support of my career development and success. Over the years, I have been humbled by the collective support that is extended to me by my IPTD peers, with special gratitude to Adrian Curtin, La Donna Forsgren, Jacob Juntunen, Oona Kersey Hatton, Keith Byron Kirk, Christina McMahon, Stefka Mihaylova, Jesse Njus, Samuel O'Connell, Emily Sahakian, Jon Sherman, Daniel Smith, Ann Folino White, and Katherine Zien.

Recognition and appreciation is also owed to the various institutions, organizations, and individuals who generously provided space, financial support, and resources to the research and writing of this project: Arie Crown Theater (Chicago, IL), Black Women's Playwright Group, Center for Humanities at Wesleyan University, *Chicago Time Out* magazine, Christopher Piatt, Consortium for Faculty Diversity in Liberal Arts Colleges, Grinnell College, Murat Theatre (Indianapolis, IN), Northwestern University, and Windsor Public Library (Windsor, CT). At all times, the contours of my work benefit from the students I engage with within classroom environs that are attuned to African American and African diaspora theatre and performance. I thank the countless students I have encountered at Northwestern University, Grinnell College, and Wesleyan University for leaving an indelible mark on my intellectual conjuring.

My appreciation for the abundant doses of encouragement, inspiration, love, and patience bestowed on me at various intervals throughout my professional career is more than can be contained in this brief statement. I owe sincere gratitude to numerous unmentioned advisors, colleagues, family, and friends across numerous states and bodies of water, who have bestowed me with unwavering support. I extend notable gratitude to Otis Alexander, Melody Baker, Lori Baptista, Aunt Joycelyn Baptiste, Jean Beaman, Shana Benjamin, Joyan Belle, Lisa Biggs, Krista Bywater, Lesley Delmenico, Zinga Fraser, Racquel Gates, the Grant family, Tyson Hall, Aunt Annette Henry, Michelle Nasser, Javon Johnson, Lakeisha Johnson, Mario Johnson, Nina Johnson, La TaSha Levy, Great Aunt Alice Maynard and family, the McMahon family, Falani Piggott and family, Caroline King, Uncle George Lopez, Uncle Luis Lopez, Camisha Lynch, Joseph Neisser, Kerry Odom, Thomas Ossowski, Damani Phillips, Charnelle Raphael and family, Cherise Richards, Breagin Riley, Zandria Robinson, Thandekile Shange, Dante Taylor, and Queen Meccasia Zabriskie. *Thank you.*

> *"However long the night, the dawn will break"*
> —*African proverb, author unknown*

Rashida Z. Shaw McMahon
Middletown, CT

Then everybody laughed. And laughed! We almost had hysterics. All at once we dropped our professionally self-conscious "Negro" manners, became natural, ate fish, and talked and kidded freely like colored folks do when there are no white folks around. We really had fun then, joking about that red-haired guy who mistook a fair-colored woman for white. After the fish we went to two or three more night spots and drank until five o'clock in the morning.

—Langston Hughes, *Laughing to Keep from Crying*
(New York: Aeonian Press, 1976), 6

1

THE BLACK CIRCUIT

> This is not a counter-discourse but a counterculture that defiantly reconstructs
> its own critical, intellectual, and moral genealogy in a partially hidden sphere
> of its own.
>
> —Paul Gilroy, *The Black Atlantic: Modernity and*
> *Double Consciousness* (1993)[1]

As history will document, the 2017 Academy Awards season will be memorialized not only for its politically charged environment, coming at the dawn of the Donald J. Trump presidency, but also for the range of racially and ethnically diverse nominations that arrived two years after the academy had been severely criticized for repeatedly ignoring the filmic contributions of people of color. The hashtag #OscarsSoWhite, credited as being started by the attorney, writer, and media personality April Reign in 2015,[2] gained traction on Twitter due to its poignant encapsulation of minority outrage that spoke to the heart of the matter. Reign and those who heeded her call directed attention toward the academy's relentless tradition of excluding minority artistry and toward their simultaneous and ironic praise for white nominees who collaborated with Black artists on motion pictures that were topically about Black lives. Case in point, during the 2015 awards season, *Creed* (Ryan Coogler, 2015), the contemporary extension of the popular *Rocky* (John G. Avildsen, 1979) films, garnered a nomination for Sylvester Stallone in the best supporting actor category yet ignored the acting performance of the African American actor Michael B. Jordan in the lead role and the directing feats of Coogler, also African American. A similar racially charged specter followed the original screenplay category in which an all-white screenwriting team was nominated for the blockbuster narrative *Straight Outta Compton* (F. Gary Gray, 2015); a film that chronicled the rise of the 1980s African American hip hop group N.W.A.[3]

The 2016 Academy Award season became a catalyst for even more outrage and coalition against more of the same. The January 2016 article in *The Economist* "How racially skewed are the Oscars?" documented the fact that the twentieth century had seen "95% of [all] Oscar nominations" awarded to "white film stars."[4] The February 27, 2016, *Star Tribune* article "Whitewashing the Oscars: How did Hollywood get in this predicament?" shed contemporary light on the issue:

> For the second year in a row, each and every actor in the 2016 Oscar nominations is white. That's 20 best actor, actress, supporting actor and supporting actress candidates in Sunday's telecast, with zero people of color.[5]

This bold-faced and long-standing lack of diversity in Academy Award nominations seared fresh wounds into a fraught condition of erasure and disregard, specifically as experienced by African American artists and audiences. Very much in line with the sociopolitical, governmental, and economic structures that many Americans were protesting in the streets outside of cinemas across the country, the Academy Awards seemed to be the artistic wing of a larger hegemonic structure that was boldly and unapologetically reflecting and reinforcing that Black lives, Black narratives, and Black artistry do not matter here.

However, in 2017, a cultural and representational healing seemed to walk in and reconcile the academy's almost century-long history of alienation and dismissal of artists and artistry of color. Positioned at the helm of this diversity was theatre, specifically African American theatre. The still unforgettable surprise wins for *Moonlight* (Barry Jenkins, 2016) in the categories of best picture, best supporting actor, and best adapted screenplay alongside Viola Davis's momentous win for best supporting actress in *Fences* (Denzel Washington, 2016), sought to redress the academy's past violations. Yet for those whose interests lie in theatre more pointedly, the awards also heralded the celebration of playwrights and their devoted attention to the theatre and the narratives that have existed and thrived there for centuries. The plot of *Moonlight* derives from the original play *In Moonlight Black Boys Look Blue*, written by African American playwright Tarell Alvin McCraney. Set in a contemporary neighborhood in Liberty City, Miami, *Moonlight* presents the life of Chiron, a gay African American man, as he navigates his sexuality and parental abandonment within an environment that is simultaneously filled with violence, crime, drugs, and nontraditional love. *Fences*, the 1987 Pulitzer Prize–winning play authored by African American playwright August Wilson and set in Pittsburgh's Hill District, explores love, betrayal, resilience, and faith in an African American family led by Troy and Rose Maxson. While Wilson and *Fences*, in particular, have received worldwide acclaim, McCraney is a name that only theatregoers interested in African American drama and performance may have readily recognized despite the fact that he was awarded a McArthur Genius Grant in 2013.

As film and theatre historians easily recognize, of course, this is not the first year in which films rooted in the stage have gained entry and garnered accolades from the academy. Included in a list of these lauded stage-to-screen adaptations are Tennessee Williams's *A Streetcar Named Desire* (Elia Kazan, 1951), William Gibson's *The Miracle Worker* (Arthur Penn, 1962), Edward Albee's *Who's Afraid of Virginia Woolf* (Mike Nichols, 1966), and James Golden's *The Lion in Winter* (Anthony Harvey, 1968).[6] Yet as a scholar devoted to the study and practice of Black theatre and performance, I see the marked significance not in the commendation that theatre has once again received from the film industry but in the landmark achievement and recognition of Black playwrights, Black theater artists, and Black dramatic narratives in this contemporary moment. For those interested in when and where African American theatre is granted access into the mainstream, the 2017 Academy Awards season would signal a moment of confirmation, celebration, and first-time recognition. The 2017 Academy Awards also direct interests toward probing the options, possibilities, limitations, advantages, and conditions in which Black theater and performance have thrived without or in spite of acknowledgment from the mainstream.

The Black Circuit: Race, Performance, and Spectatorship in Black Popular Theatre complicates our understanding of this mainstream by presenting the first book-length study of Chitlin Circuit theatre, the most popular form of contemporary Black theatre outside the purview of Broadway since the 1980s. In so doing, Black theatrical productions and their audiences move from the margins to the center of focus, and thus, a notable shift of vantage point and power occurs. Instead of African American theatre artists, like McCraney and Wilson, being situated as wholly (economically and artistically) dependent on accolades, legibility, and acknowledgment from the large, outside, and white-oriented mainstream, a small cadre of artists and spectators have built their own theatrical empire complete with their own category of standards, content, aesthetics, performance spaces, and interests. The result is that this community of artists and audiences looks inward for merits of success and acknowledgment rather than outward, as has been the case with most traditional African American theatrical fare. The impact of their choices, in the creation of a theatre world that is, I argue, by and for a segment of the Black American community whose interests have been devalued and marginalized, even by other Black Americans, has caused cataclysmic representational and aesthetic shockwaves across the national frontier of the so-called American mainstream. *The Black Circuit* therefore maps the politics of Black theatrical pleasure in these performance enclaves. In what follows, I examine the making, the performing, the spectating, and articulation of contemporary Chitlin Circuit theatre and performance as political acts that have far-reaching implications both inside and beyond the terrain of theatre and performance studies.

Chitlin Circuit theatre (also known as gospel musicals, gospel plays, urban musicals, urban theatre[7] or more recently as the urban circuit), emerged from a varied theatrical lineage encompassing influences such as nineteenth-century melodramatic theatre,[8] early-twentieth-century vaudeville and theatre performance, the 1950s gospel musicals of Langston Hughes, and a practitioner-produced tradition of African American musicals of the 1980s in which Black dramatists infused religion, comedy, gospel, jazz, and R&B into contemporary narratives about urban African American life, set in fictional, inner city environments. The productions also contain African American popular culture elements found in music, television, film, and literature. Many productions also feature African American entertainers who perform their celebrity identities in the context of the play. Early circuit playwrights, such as Vy Higgensen and Ken Wydro, creators of the popular musical *Mama, I Want to Sing* (1983), and Shelly Garrett, author of *Beauty Shop* (1989), set a number of important precedents for the more recent wave studied in this book, achieving commercial success, wide recognition, and loyalty among African American audiences, extended runs, and consistent tour bookings. They likewise laid the groundwork for the independent, community-based nature of these productions, in which playwrights continue to serve as their own directors and producers. Financial support, then as it does now, came largely from the pockets of the playwrights themselves and from family, friends, and interested community members. Similar to the environments that are found in today's circuit events, Higgensen, Wydro, Garrett, and other early circuit artists created highly interactive theatre environments in which audiences were seen singing, dancing, and engaging in dialogue with performers, from their seats.

Typically, circuit productions are staged in large performance spaces that cater to touring entertainment such as popular music concerts, conventions, or motivational speakers. The plays share particular themes of love, loss, lust, moral intervention, spiritual redemption, and faith inspiration. Popular narrative topics include, but are not limited to, stories about adultery, domestic violence, mental abuse, marriage, and divorce. An average production runs between two and three hours, depending on the amount of audience interaction and onstage improvisation on any given performance night. After engaging with a varied presentation of play-related materials and merchandise in the theater's lobby, ticket holders are welcomed into a well-lit auditorium and usually take their seats while popular R&B and/or gospel music is played overhead. Once the curtain rises, audiences are introduced to the unfolding drama that is interwoven with songs, comedic routines, and musical accompaniment provided by the band members and sometimes vocalists who play and/or sing from the theater's orchestra pit (a sunken area located at the front of the stage that is usually out of view and separated from the auditorium seats). At curtain call, all of the actors traditionally appear onstage one by one for audience applause, and if the playwright is in attendance, they come onstage for applause and thank the spectators directly for attending the show.

Tracing this historical and aesthetic lineage, *The Black Circuit* focuses on the contemporary wave of Chitlin Circuit theatre that emerged in the 1990s. In doing so, I acknowledge how the efforts of its practitioners and the loyal and engaged support of its spectators have impacted American theatre and culture more broadly. Religion, comedy, music, and African American culture still loom large in this second generation, and yet, unlike their predecessors, these younger playwrights are interested in creating an entire repertoire of block-buster productions rather than relying solely on the success of one or two box office hits. Although many African American playwrights and producers have staged Chitlin Circuit productions throughout the country, four men—David Talbert, Tyler Perry, and the playwriting duo of Je'Caryous Johnson and Gary Guidry—have respectively gained commercial success and millionaire status by writing, producing, and directing their own circuit plays. Their financial and cultural achievements mark a turning point in the relationship between Black theatre and Black audiences that have left many American critics, academics, and practitioners, many of whom are also African American, wondering how the circuit has developed such a loyal Black fan base when it is brimming with stereotypes and controversial content about African Americans and given that theatre producers have historically struggled to get Black patrons into seats even for Black/African American–oriented theatrical fare. The artistry of these men, the techniques of their performers, the content of their productions, and the loyalty of their spectators serve as the main focus of the book. Their theatrical environments become the launching pads from which I make larger cultural, historical, economic, and ideological connections that speak to a dismissed arena of theatre and performance that has been misunderstood by many and actively ignored by most.

Within this framework, *The Black Circuit* positions contemporary circuit artists and audiences as national and global citizens whose dreams and desires have been marginalized even in the already marginalized context that is African American. How might an examination of the relationship between theatre and the popular, in this Black-on-Black performance audience context shed light on new, alienated, and/or differently constituted Black subjectivities, expressions of "blackness," political ideologies, historical underpinnings, and sociocultural leanings? In asking this question, I argue that the reception processes of contemporary circuit audiences signal the emergence of a Black theatrical public sphere.

Houston A. Baker, Jr, in his essay "Critical Memory and the Black Public Sphere," critiques Habermas's white and bourgeois designation of the public sphere and asks whether such a socially and economically driven collective could emerge in contemporary America and be composed of African Americans:

> Habermas's bourgeois public sphere, *in situ*, is a beautiful idea. It is grounded in a historiography that claims universal men were once golden citizens, rationally exchanging arguments in a realm between the family and the market—regardless of race, creed, color, annual income or national origin. But insofar as the emergence and energy of Habermas's public sphere were generated by property ownership and literacy, how can black Americans, who like many others have traditionally been excluded from these domains of modernity, endorse Habermas's beautiful idea?"[9]

As Baker points out, as utopic and inclusive as Habermas's public sphere may overtly read, in truth, it produces a coalition and a subjectivity that are driven by white and male intimacy, political action, economic interests, intellectual discourse (in social and public contexts), and commercialism. On the basis of these characteristics and wholly in spite of how incongruous the notion of a Black public sphere, of Habermas's origins, is for African Americans who have collectively been outside of these realms of power, as Baker asserts, African Americans are still "drawn to the possibilities of structurally and affectively transforming the founding notion of the bourgeois public sphere into an expressive and empowering self-fashioning."[10] Indeed, Baker's essay emboldens the refrain that has been sung by many recent cultural critics of Black America: there are and have always been segments, locations, and refuges in everyday Black public life in which coalitions, safety, debate, and mobilizing thought are encouraged, birthed, and sustained. The opening chapter of historian Robin D. G. Kelley's *Race Rebels: Culture, Politics, and the Black Working Class* reinforces this vantage point, in a study dedicated to the same population that this book is partially concerned with, the Black working class:

> A lot of black working people struggled and survived without direct links to the kinds of organizations that dominate historical accounts of African American or U.S. working-class resistance. The so-called margins of struggle, whether it is the unorganized, often spontaneous battles with authority or social movements thought to be inauthentic or unrepresentative of the "community interests," are really a fundamental part of the larger story waiting to be told.[11]

Following this trajectory, Baker, Kelley, and others have privileged Black political action and mobilization in such spaces as African American churches, public transportation, US prisons during the Civil Rights Movement, African American colleges and universities, and rap lyrics.

Richard Iton's *In the Search of the Black Fantastic: Politics and Popular Culture in the Post-Civil Rights Era* critically enlightens our understanding of the longstanding union between art and politics in the sphere of the African American public. For Iton and counterparts such as Baker, Kelley, Stuart Hall, Tricia Rose, Paul Gilroy, Todd Boyd, Zandria Robinson, and Patricia Hill Collins,[12] to name a few, doing Black art is always-already doing Black politics. He reminds us that,

> For African Americans, partly because of their marginal status and often violent exclusion from the realms of formal politics, popular culture was an integral and important aspect of the making of politics throughout the pre-civil rights and the civil rights era itself. . . . Indeed, in the absence of any significant space for black participation in the institutionalized realm (outside of, perhaps, the machine politics associated with the city of Chicago),

the notion that politics and art might not be intimately connected was rarely suggested.[13]

Yet divorcing problematic Black representations from the always-already bound and valued relationship that Black politics and Black art hold has become an altogether easy project for those who are unwilling to think through the complexity of these representations, particularly when they are made by and presented before African Americans who are socially, intellectually, and economically deemed to come from the wrong side of the tracks. *The Black Circuit* is indebted to tracking and tracing these complexities, taking its charge from Iton's declaration:

> If we are to understand Black politics fully, from an empirical or academic perspective, we cannot overlook those spaces that generate difficult data. Similarly, those committed to progressive change must also engage with those arenas and voices that promote regressive and discomforting narratives.[14]

As a Black-produced and Black-consumed artistic product that emerged during the Reagan presidential era, thrived in the background of both Bush presidencies, persisted during the eight years in office held by Bill Clinton and Barack Obama, respectively, and, continued and continues to bloom even now amid the Trump administration, I see the significances in the parentage of Chitlin Circuit theatre as being multiple and vast, as are the trajectories of its life course, which has developed amid a changing cultural, environmental, economic, and political American landscape. Despite how incongruous (and perhaps incomprehensible) the popular demand for the circuit has been in spite of its complicated portrayals of African American lives, it has been the site in which millions of Black artists and spectators have affirmed and confirmed particular ideologies, practices, narratives, and histories. It is this *Black Circuit*, this integrated network of consumerism, culture, circulation, exchange, ideologies, and meaning making that meets at the nexus of Black theatre-making, performance, and reception that I am concerned with. I see this Black Circuit as being itinerant, knowledge based, critically engaged, and historically rooted yet focused on the present. This Black Circuit not only identifies particular performative modes of exchange and reveals specific methods of reception in African American theatre but also establishes important routes of circulation in and for Black popular culture. More importantly, this Black Circuit is not limited to or confined by Black performance spaces. Instead, it should be understood as being activated by and ignited in Chitlin Circuit theatrical spaces, because they produce safe meeting and testing grounds in which Black artistic, cultural, ideological, and spiritual thoughts and imaginings can be expressed, confirmed, and/or rejected by and among African American practitioners and audiences with shared priorities and interests.

The Black Circuit, as concept and praxis, is indebted to Gilroy's seminal work in *The Black Atlantic: Modernity and Double Consciousness* in its inquiries, foci, and framing. Gilroy reminds us to acknowledge—at all times—that the American-rooted Chitlin Circuit theatre is foremost an African diasporic expressive culture. Standing firmly as both a counterculture[15] and subculture in the African American performance landscape and the broader American cultural sphere, my discoveries and assessments on Chitlin Circuit theatre are influenced by not only Gilroy's attention to the aesthetic content of Black music in his study but also his understanding of Black art—in all of its cultivated forms—as being always-already historically, socially, and politically brimming with significant merit and meaning. The theories and methodologies that undergird *The Black Circuit* are thus indelibly marked by Gilroy's attention to the production, consumption, and sociology of Black artistic expression.

The Black Circuit therefore traces the rise of a Black theatrical popular culture that has created a Black theatrical public sphere that exemplifies W. E. B. Du Bois's 1926 parameters of "for us," "near us," "by us," and "about us,"[16] with a critical difference. This project qualifies, historicizes, and recalibrates exactly who the "us" is in the contemporary Chitlin Circuit theatre context. Additionally, rather than ignoring the fact that these productions have been criticized for circulating negative stereotypes and damaging representations of African Americans, I put these contradictions front and center, by asking, how do these circuit events appeal to thousands of African American audiences in consideration of the assumed negative content and, of equal note, in light of the fact that theatre attendance in America has been historically underrepresented by Black spectators?

In answering these and other questions relating to theatre, performance, and spectatorship, as well as consumption, history, culture, and tastes, *The Black Circuit* enters into dialogue with theatre and performance scholars, such as Annmarie Bean, Susan Bennett, Catherine Cole, Harry J. Elam, Jr., David Krasner, David Savran, and Larry Stempel;[17] media scholars, including Jacqueline Bobo, Nelson George, Robert W. Snyder, and Jacqueline N. Stewart;[18] and, importantly, social scientists and cultural theorists such as Pierre Bourdieu, Herbert J. Gans, Lawrence W. Levine, Peter Stallybrass, and Allon White[19]—along with those already mentioned. As many of these scholars have noted, the content, appeal, and longevity of popular culture forms should be recognized as inherently political precisely because of how they produce pleasure for citizens whose interests lie outside of the dominant cultural order.

As Elam has stated, "Consequently, African American theatre and performance have been and remain powerful sites for the creation, application, and even the subversion of notions of blackness and of concepts of African American identity."[20] When critically viewed, the content and audience preferences found in Chitlin Circuit theatre subvert dominant *notions of blackness and of concepts of African American identity*. However, their continued criticism, seclusion, and separatism in an era marked by social and civic protests in support of Black (read: African

American) visibility in an American context shed light on the fact that in the realm of theatre and performance, like perhaps, the greater environs of the country, all Black lives—or, specifically, all Black theatrical and performance output—do not matter. Part of what is taken into consideration throughout the book is how this artform's designation as popular and musical contributes to its lowly and stigmatized designation. Focusing on the musicals produced on Broadway in various scholarship, Savran has done extensive work tracking the prejudice that musical theatre has historically endured both culturally and in the academy, as he says, "since the 1920s."[21]

> American musical theatre offers an important site for an analysis of antitheatricality. For it has been ignored or scorned not only by most theatre historians but also literary scholars, musicologists, dance scholars, and cultural-studies specialists. Neither as exalted as literary drama nor as working-class as cinema, musical theatre since the 1920s has epitomized middlebrow culture, the most loathed category for those with the leisure and ambition to map American cultural production. And even for many devotees of the so-called straight theatre, musical theatre remains (at best) a guilty pleasure—a little too gay, too popular, too Jewish, and too much damned fun.[22]

As part of my mission to historically contextualize Chitlin Circuit theatre and the Black Circuit, Chapter Two and Chapter Three delve deeply into the specific blend of discrimination, stereotype, and alienation that have consistently marked these performances, performers, and attending audiences as *a little too* and *not enough*. For now, I ask my readers to be attentive to how the theatrical genre of choice—dramatic narratives told via integrated musical expression, dance, and performance—has also cast a prejudiced shadow on the work and interests of circuit artists and their loyal audiences. This study also investigates the troubled incorporation of comedy in circuit productions with specific attention given to the ways much of the humor found in these plays relies on stereotypes that further complicate the circuit's ability to engender appeal and disdain simultaneously. A focus on the religious elements and aspects of the productions brings faith, ideology, and performativity to the forefront. Meanwhile, an attention to history is maintained throughout, calling attention to the ways much of what is presented on circuit stages is part and parcel of what Henry Louis Gates, Jr. refers to as repetition with a "critical difference," and in the context of these performances, that critical difference also has a new focus.[23]

In large part, the project of *The Black Circuit* is one of reconciling the past with an eye on the present and an acknowledgment of the indeterminacies of the future. It is a study that is foremost interested in how contemporary representations of Black bodies, Black theatrical audience consumption, Black nostalgia, Black imaginings, and Black dreams are entangled in representational precedents, long-standing class and taste wars, larger pursuits of freedom and independence, and, as often is the case, innovation that comes from places where none is assumed to exist. Instead of analyzing each of the plays, produced by Talbert, Johnson, Guidry, and Perry in their entirety, I present *snapshots* from each playwright's oeuvre that I then use as the case studies to analyze how each playwright uniquely achieves Black spectatorial engagement and singularly contributes to the matrix that is the Black Circuit. I am particularly attuned to how Black audience reception has been conditioned by the inventiveness of the respective circuit playwrights who, throughout this entire study, serve as their own director and producer. I argue that these playwright-director-producers strategically use elements in their productions to entertain and engage with their audiences. In interrogating the parameters of Black theatrical pleasure within contemporary Chitlin Circuit theatre environments, I aim to uncover how these specific practitioners have introduced new aesthetic models and aim to identify how and why spectators engage with the presented stage material. In all cases, I suggest that Black audiences position themselves as critical spectators who reject, sanction, and/or confirm onstage content based on their own standards of evaluation that are historically and contemporaneously marked. To be sure, the making, doing, and viewing of Chitlin Circuit theatre is revealed to be a dynamic, interactive, and evolving process in which African American practitioners and spectators collaboratively engage in the evolution of contemporary Black theatre-making.

Ethnographic Pathways to Methodology and Theory

In the summer of 2004, a few months before I was to start graduate school at Northwestern University, I casually popped in a DVD copy of Tyler Perry's 2001 play *Diary of a Mad Black Woman*, purchased from a street vendor in Brooklyn, NY, out of curiosity. As the production unfolded, I soon realized that this play was not as bad as I had thought or had heard. Moreover, upon viewing the recordings of multiple productions, purchased online, and written by a range of playwrights, I realized that while it was true that the characterizations, themes, and representations in these plays were remarkably different from the dramatic work produced by critically acclaimed African American playwrights like Suzan-Lori Parks or August Wilson, it was also evident that these artists had developed a cohesive and thriving form of theatre that conformed to its own standards. What I witnessed on that bootleg DVD copy completely altered my previous assumptions about these productions and my intended area of focus while in school: an analysis of color-blind casting in American theatre via a sociological lens. In those early days, my repetitive video watching was geared toward understanding the mechanics of this theatre and how particular components were integrated. However, I soon realized that above all else, these DVDs documented a commonality that could not be ignored: the continuous laughter and cheers of pleased spectators. This awareness quickly sparked my curiosity in the audiences who attended these plays and their relationship with the onstage performances. Although the eye of the camera never turned its attention toward these spectators, their felt presence was remarkable. I began to wonder about the characteristics of this fanbase and became interested in their experiences at these productions and their genuine attraction to these performances. Even in those nascent stages of inquiry, I suspected that there was a complicated and direct correlation between the efforts of the artists and the enthusiasm of the spectators.

Once in graduate school, under the tutelage of convinced and supportive advisors, I charged myself with examining how the circuit play was changing the face of contemporary Black theatre and making an impact on millions of African American audiences. During a roughly four-year period, I researched Chitlin Circuit theatrical events by attending live productions in Chicago, Illinois, and neighboring Indianapolis, Indiana, and viewed DVD recordings of past productions that were made available for retail purchase by the playwrights themselves. As a representative example, the following excerpt, assembled from field notes, recalls an early pre-show moment during an evening of ethnographic exploration. Scenes such as the one below became significant, not only for their dynamism and vibrancy but also for how they illuminated necessary methodological and theoretical pathways to decoding the circuit.

My watch reads 7:00p.m. on a cool May night in downtown Chicago. I have just arrived inside of the large and cavernous McCormick Place that houses the 4,239 seat Arie Crown Theater. Chicago's Arie Crown is unlike many traditional, stand-alone theaters across the country, primarily due to the fact that it is situated within the lakeside wing of a 2.7 million square foot convention center. Over the years, the theater has emerged as the premiere destination for African American–centered touring shows that run the gamut from plays and comedy shows to concert events and dance performances. Tonight's sold-out show is the Chicago debut of the latest play produced by the popular African American playwright, producer, director, and actor: Tyler Perry. As evidence of this, I note that the underground parking lot is overflowing with numerous parked and arriving cars. Once upstairs, I see even more cars and charter buses pulling up alongside the building's front entrance. Each unloads well-dressed and excited African American ticket holders. I try to squeeze through the crowd and am immediately lost within a sea of coats, tailored suits, dresses, and casually attired patrons. Once inside the convention hall-like lobby, I try to quickly take note of the people and the environment. Across the expanse, I see assorted groups of ticket holders who I assume to be inclusive of family and friends. Over along the main walkway, I see numerous elderly African American women sitting patiently on Arie Crown–provided folding chairs. As I continue walking, I reach beyond a floor-to-ceiling partition and notice that there are fifteen large, circle-top tables that have been set up with white table cloths. The seats surrounding the tables are filled with eating ticket holders. There is also a separate section containing stand-alone circular bar tables. The smell of BBQ chicken and rib dinners is now thick in the air. In addition to a red-clothed covered alcohol and beverage bar that one would normally encounter in many regional and Broadway theaters, there is a vendor who is selling warm pretzels and the booth of one of the most popular rib restaurants on the South Side: JJ Robinson's. As I continue to walk, I observe an increasing crowd of Black patrons of all ages laughing, talking, eating, and greeting each other familiarly from afar. The small portable boom box that belongs to the workers of the shoeshine stand blasts popular R&B and Soul classics. When I listen closely, I think I recognize a refrain from a James Brown song. At this point, there are almost forty-five minutes to go before show time. I continue walking and begin to wonder which one of these patrons will be friendly enough to share their theatergoing experiences with me.

In this project, I take what I am labeling as an *audience-centered research approach* to examine and uncover how theatre and performance operate in relation to audiences. This audience-centered focus offers a way of evaluating theatrical audiences through primarily qualitative and embodied forms of research. In so doing, I move away from methods of investigation that reduce these spectators to "the passivity of demographics" or consider them simply as part of a certain taste culture, in Bourdieu's sense.[24] As Willmar Sauter has discovered when analyzing theatrical events, methods that seek to uncover how tastes are related to economics and social practices alone do not account for how "a performance [is] actually enjoyed and understood."[25] Instead, I use methods of traditional, historical, and performance ethnography,[26] respectively, alongside semiotics, to capture the experience, meaning making and identification practices of spectators in these theatrical spaces. I therefore evaluate individual responses and group responses to the production, and when analyzing the performances that I have witnessed as live events, I acknowledge my own experiences in the theatrical space. By these standards, I am able to interrogate numerous factors within the confines of this study. From the perspective of the practitioner, I uncover how production techniques (e.g., dramaturgical process and performance objectives) are conditioned to garner audience response and identification. From the perspective of spectators, I identify and determine their horizons of expectation when coming to a show and consider how these relate to their subsequent engagement with the theatrical product.

To provide a thorough account, I employ interdisciplinary methods of research that span across theatre studies, performance studies, sociology, film studies, and dance studies. In analyzing the live theatrical event from a contemporary vantage point and a historical vantage point, I use Ric Knowles's and Marvin Carlson's methods of evaluating theatre semiotics in theatrical events. Knowles's triangle allows me to focus on three aspects in the event: the conditions of production, the performance text, and the conditions of reception. In this model, meaning is dependently produced as each aspect of the event (or corner of the triangle) works interactively in relation with the others. Thus, the *production* affects the *text*, which affects *reception*—in a continuous and reflexive manner. Yet because this project is centered on the live event in the theatre as experienced by the spectator, I focus more on the performance text ("script, mise-en-scène, design, actors' bodies, movement and gestures, etc.") and the conditions of reception ("publicity/review discourse, front-of-house, auditorium, and audience ameni-ties, neighborhood, transportation, ticket prices, historical/cultural moment of reception, etc.").[27] I supplement my application of Knowles's triangle with Carl-son's attention to the semiotics achieved through iconicity, predictable narrative structures, casting (i.e., actors in recurring or familiar roles), and architectural space.[28]

I unite these methods with those of Stewart, as advanced in her book *Migrating to the Movies: Cinema and Black Urban Modernity* and her article "Negroes Laughing at Themselves? Black Spectatorship and the Performance of Urban Modernity," in an effort to reconstruct spectatorship in the chosen theatrical events. Although I am not using literary accounts of Black spectatorship as Stewart did in her study, I do use nonfictional accounts as collected in interviews, articles, reviews (from Internet, mainstream, and Black press sources), and personal observations in a similar manner to interrogate Black spectating practices.[29] When available, I also use performance videos (taped and distributed by the producers of the plays) and audio recordings of the performance (taped by myself when attend-ing live productions) to supplement my analyses.[30] In the case studies that I was able to view live, I combined the traditional ethnographic methods listed earlier with performance ethnography methods as advanced by Dwight Conquergood and D. Soyini Madison. Throughout the course of my research, I was interested in achieving "another way of knowing that [was] grounded in active, intimate, hands-on participation and personal connection within the theatrical event."[31] As a scholar relaying my interpretation of these events, I therefore acknowledge my own participatory role as a spectator in the space, engaging in "critical reflection" and "thinking about, through, and with [my own] performance" as a Black specta-tor. In so doing, I situate in my examination of the circuit theatre what Conquer-good calls the "knowledge that comes from doing, participatory understanding, [and] practical consciousness."[32]

My analysis of Chitlin Circuit theatre events activates a coalition of interdisci-plinary theories which underscore the importance of examining the implications of race, class, culture, and place in performance and audience reception studies. Although considerable work has been done on American theatre audiences and their reception of various kinds of cultural performances,[33] existing large-scale analyses of American theatre audiences are incomplete due to their failure to consider race alongside other dominant factors. As a result, African American the-atrical productions and African American spectators, in particular, remain ignored and seldom acknowledged in the field. In fact, although this project engages most with Susan Bennett's and Sauter's work on culture and sociopolitical contexts in theatrical events, neither scholar considers how race complicates or modifies their analysis.[34] Alternatively, included among notable scholarship concerned with analyzing African American spectators are Margaret Wilkerson's articles "Black Theater in California" and "Redefining Black Theatre"; Mimi Gisolfi D'Aponte's "*The Gospel at Colonus* (and Other Black Morality Plays)"; Floyd Gaffney's "A Hand is On the Gate in Athens"; and Rhett Jones's "Orderly and Disorderly: Why Church and Sports Appeal to Black Americans and Theatre Does Not."[35] Additionally, in "Writing the Absent Potential: Drama, Performance, and the Canon of African American Literature," Sandra L. Richards suggests, in consideration of Zora Neale Hurston's 1926 play *Color Struck*, that we "reconfigur[e] the analysis of African American drama" in ways that bring the "spectator (or reader) more into the foreground." Among possible strategies available to the researcher, Richards lists the potential of considering "the reactions of spectators in the auditorium."[36] Moreover, Susan Manning's *Modern Dance, Negro Dance: Race in Motion* critically evaluates how Black and white spectators of Black dance "read theatrical constructs of blackness and whiteness" along multiple frames, including race, class, gender and sexuality in the theatre.[37]

Developing out of this trajectory, this study is one of the first to discuss the dynamics of Black theatrical spectatorship and events at length. Notable publications that have discussed Chitlin Circuit theatre from varied vantage points include the oft-cited Warren Burdine and Gates essays, both of which serve as foundational texts for my analyses. In his study of the "semiotics of the entire theatre experience," Carlson defines the theatrical event as the spectator's experience in the entire physical space of the theatre, which includes the lobby and halls of the theatre. He states that the sign system embedded in the information that the spectator receives (e.g., programs, displays, pamphlets, etc.) is integral to meaning making. Carlson reminds us that "when we begin to consider the audience experience of the theatrical event, we should soon come to realize that the actual performance is only a part . . . of an entire social and cultural experience."[38] My preliminary observations revealed that the lobbies, auditoria, and halls of contemporary circuit events were filled with music, displays, and activities (e.g., picture taking and selling merchandise) that occurred before the production started and then continued during intermission and after the show. Therefore, in the full-length study presented here, I unite Carlson with Richard Schechner's definition of performance in theatrical events. For Schechner, performance is the "whole constellation of events, most of them passing unnoticed, that take place in/among both performers and audience from the time the spectator enters the field of performance . . . to the time the last spectator leaves."[39] Therefore, this study relies on the premise that theatrical events are conditioned by spectators' engagement with onstage *and* offstage performances, elements, and social factors contained in the physical theatre building during the time of the production. Consequently, for each spectator in this project, the theatrical event begins when they enter the physical theatre building and ends with their subsequent departure.

My focus on theatrical events engages Sauter's call for "theoretical reorientation" in theatre studies.[40] For Sauter, theatrical analyses that place all of their emphasis on the text and performance suffer from being "dated and far too limited for a serious discussion of theoretical issues as well as for the discourses of intercultural perspectives."[41] Instead, a reoriented theatrical analysis is one that "reconsider[s] the entire theatrical event as the intersection of production and reception . . . or presentation and perception."[42] Using this model, the researcher, whether working from a historical vantage point or a contemporary vantage point, will always "bring into focus the contextual events as objects of [theatre] studies, the live interaction between stage and auditorium."[43] From this direction, Sauter emphasizes theatricality or "actions and reactions" in the event as the performer uses "encoded actions" that are "determined not only by individual and cultural condition, but also by the aesthetic norms of the particular performance."[44] By examining the encoded actions of both the performers *and* the spectators in the theatrical event, I build on and simultaneously expand on Sauter's critical theoretical model. I illustrate how spectators and performers are able to communicate dialogically and thereby interactively produce meaning.

I combine Sauter's theoretical perspective with that of Bennett in her attempt to unite the study of theatre audiences with that of cultural studies. I acknowledge, with Bennett, that theatre has a mutually constitutive relationship with culture. I therefore accept her argument that "establishing cultural markers are important in pre-activating a certain anticipation, a horizon of expectations, in the audience drawn to any particular event."[45] From this theoretical perspective, I am able to treat culture as exhibited in contemporary circuit events as being dynamic not static, meaning then that culture is "necessarily flexible and inevitably rewritten on a daily basis."[46] This is a crucial theoretical perspective to incorporate into this project, particularly because, as I will argue, this form of theatre relies on current elements and historic elements and practices in Black culture to create its representations in the hopes of fostering spectatorial engagement. Thus, an understanding of how the dynamic nature of culture may affect an audience's literacy and engagement with a text allows me to consider how spectators may interact differently to different performances of the same production (on the basis of the changing dimensions of their day-to-day experiences) and also how spectators may have differing levels of engagement in the same production (bringing their individual experiences to bear on the text). In so doing, I advance a cultural studies perspective to audience studies that "resists the view of art and life as autonomous experiences and insists, instead that they are inextricably entangled in history and that they are both products of and productive of cultural processes."[47]

Aiding me in this line of reasoning is Carlson's discussion of the relationship between theatre and cultural memory in *The Haunted Stage: The Theatre as Memory Machine*. Carlson builds on Joseph Roach's concept of surrogation and argues that theatre serves as the "repository of cultural memory" in which every play operates as a "memory play."[48] First, "the present experience [of live spectating] is always ghosted by previous experiences and associations," and second, the "ghosts are simultaneously shifted and modified by the processes of recycling and recollection."[49] I use this to suggest that the responses and levels of engagement in circuit events are conditioned by the audiences' experiences in everyday life and past circuit events. I argue that as a result of the proliferation of popular culture images and references in performances, spectators' reception is also governed by the spectators' exposure to such media as literature, film, television, Internet, print, and radio.

I also apply Schechner's broad definition of performance to my theoretical analysis to consider the cultural and the theatrical in the theatre event. I thereby extend my analysis of performance to include not only the onstage occurrences but also the multiple and simultaneous performances that can manifest anywhere in the physical theatre building, as performed by spectators or practitioners, that are related to the theatrical event. Because as a researcher I have not been privy to every manifestation of performance, I use Schechner's perspective to broaden my interrogation of performance and allow myself to consider both the theatrical performances and the performances of everyday life as they may be enacted by the spectators I observe.

My interest in spectatorship practices in the theatrical event is supplemented by the theories advanced by Nelson Goodman, Rose, Hall, and Michel de Certeau. Goodman argues in his *Languages of Art* that the aesthetic experience is never separate from cognition or knowing. I use this to suggest that when spectators are attending these theatrical events, they are "discriminating and relating them in order to gauge and grasp the work and integrate it with the rest of [their] experience and the world."[50] I assert that Black spectators respond on the basis of shared knowledge and do so in ways that perform not only their cultural but also their raced, classed, gendered, and sociopolitical status inside the theatre as well as outside. Treating circuit productions as a part-manifestation of popular culture, I fuse Goodman's discussion of cognition and knowing with Rose's parameters for any interrogation into aesthetics in Black popular culture. Primarily, Rose argues, "historical contextualization," must be undertaken in these projects because without it "certain cultural practices are made to appear essential to a given group of people."[51] Second, "without aesthetic considerations, Black cultural practices are reduced to extensions of sociohistorical circumstances."[52] I unite Rose's perspective with that of Hall's, concerning the authenticity of Black popular culture representations. Hall reminds us that "[h]owever deformed, incorporated, and inauthentic are the forms in which Black people and Black communities and traditions appear and are represented in popular culture, [African Americans] continue to see, in the figures and the repertoires on which popular culture draws, the experiences that stand behind them."[53] I use Hall's position to acknowledge the agency of circuit spectators and in so doing am able to consider spectators' ability to view and relate these mediatized images to their own knowledge. Thus, my study takes into consideration what spectators know (analyzing how this knowledge affects their engagement), how and why they know what they know (examining the conditions that create this knowledge), and what their knowledge and concurrent engagement say about what they value. De Certeau's discussion of consumption practices in popular culture urges me to consider how spectators and practitioners of circuit events "make . . . innumerable and infinitesimal transformations of and within the dominant cultural economy in order to adapt it to their own interest and their own rules."[54] This theoretical perspective allows me to take into consideration the objectives of both practitioners and spectators when they design, produce, and consume circuit theatre.

An emphasis on aesthetics also allows me to examine what Ian Hunter refers to as the "'self-supporting ensemble of techniques and practices [. . . that complicate] conduct and events.'"[55] I approach the development of theatrical aesthetic paradigms through a critical method of investigation that unites the study of aesthetics with cultural studies interests, resulting in what Gena Dagel Caponi refers to as "cultural aesthetics."[56] This approach allows me to investigate the "structure of the cultural expression" in these events and determine how it "reflects and supports the ethics of the society [and] reinforces its values and philosophy."[57] In fact, in their respective studies of theatre audiences and aesthetics, Janet Wolff and Bennett both agree that "'[a]s the artist works within the technical means available and within the scope of aesthetic convention, so audiences read according to the scope and means of culturally and aesthetically constituted interpretive processes.'"[58] I therefore argue that in my case studies, cultural expression is revealed through dialogic interactions or what some scholars refer to as call and response. Ceola Ross Barber defines call and response as "a communicative process that involves an active interchange between speaker and listener. The speaker's observations are met with spontaneous verbal and nonverbal responses from the listeners," which can manifest in the form of "talking and [in] more symbolic forms of communication, such as singing [and] dancing."[59] I employ Barber's definition in this study as a starting point from which to investigate spectators' embodied responses which include talking back or responding directly to theatrical material when receiving no response from the production/actor/element and engaging in moments of direct interaction with theatrical material during moments of improvisation (i.e., when characters onstage engage in conversation with specific audience members as part of the performance).

Lastly, my theoretical investigation into identity formation is framed by the discussions presented by Charles Taylor, Gilroy and E. Patrick Johnson. In "Politics of Recognition," Taylor states that one's "identity crucially depends on [one's] dialogical relations with others."[60] He argues that through conversations and exchanges with those around us, an "inwardly generated identity is formed."[61] I am interested in how Chitlin Circuit theatre provides a space and a context for these dialogic, identity-forming exchanges to occur. In these dialogic exchanges,

I interrogate what Gilroy calls the "outcome of practical activity: language, gestures, bodily significations, [and] desires," which in the context of performance "produce the imaginary effect of an internal racial core or essence by acting on the body through the specific means of identification and recognition that are produced in the intimate inter-action of performer and crowd."[62] In this process, Gilroy is referring to how identity manifests in performance. Linking Gilroy's perspective with that of Taylor's, I investigate the group dynamics of identity formation in performance events. In so doing, I also strive for an anti-essentialist conception of how Black identity is formulated, by adhering to Johnson's contention that the "signification" of blackness varies "materially, politically, socially, and culturally depending on the body upon which it settles."[63]

Black Circuit Routes

In what follows, I present the results of a detailed study of the popularly labeled *Chitlin Circuit theatre* that aims to go beyond the general speculation of what this theatre is assumed to be about, in order to definitively state what it is and imagine what it might become. Through an interdisciplinary approach to theatre studies that incorporates performance studies, sociology, African American studies, cultural studies, and religion, this project turns the seemingly makeshift fabric of the circuit inside out and uncovers not only the depth and dimensions of its productions but also the motivations of its playwrights and the allure that it holds with its spectators. The productions of David Talbert, the playwriting duo Je'Caryous Johnson and Gary Guidry, and Tyler Perry were respectfully chosen in part because their work was readily available during my research but also because their long-standing and successful relationship with African American audiences afforded me the opportunity to observe the unique ways that they consistently created an interdependent relationship between their work and their audience during live productions.

The chapters of this book will take most of its readers on what might be considered by some to be an unconventional journey. The productions of the circuit fall squarely on the terrain of the popular, and again without apology, as is the nature of the popular, they carry with them the ephemeral traces of contemporary life that are recognizable only to those who happened to be tuned in or *in the know* at the time of circulation, dispersion, and/or saturation.[64] As a result, these plays contain references that may be almost unknown to those who are less attuned to the always-already changing popular culture references in American culture and even stranger to those who are unfamiliar with the plethora of American and/or globally constituted references that have found temporal significance in African American culture. In general, the references used in circuit productions alternate between those that are contemporary and those that are historical in nature. This study advances the notion that the average circuit audience during the time of my research shared common experiences before their theatrical attendance that in turn enabled them to readily identify specific popular cultural references and comprehend, as a collective, a reference's utility within a given performance. As an interpreter of this form and a tour guide into these events, I do not assume that all of my readers will have had access to these particular experiences and/or even that they will be able to recollect a reference's cultural significance with ease. For these reasons, I have provided detailed descriptions of the popular culture references used in my examples and in some cases have included outside source information. However, the task for my reader is not to determine whether a given reference is as significant as I say it is but instead to discover how circuit audiences identify with, respond to, and comprehend said references on their own terms. In turn, by the book's end, readers will have gained a deeper understanding of how these particular playwrights make use of their audience's experiences and employ specific and strategic techniques to create identification, meaning making, and engagement during their productions.

In Chapter Two, "Slow-Roasted Chitterlings," I read critical scholarship on American cuisine and American slave culture alongside American performance histories in order to trace the specific developments that I identify as giving rise to Chitlin Circuit musical theatre in the late twentieth and early twenty-first centuries. Attention is first paid to rooting the term *chitlin* in the fraught racial histories of American slave plantations wherein the culinary inventiveness that produced pork chitterling fare was a byproduct of dehumanizing conditions, oppression, waste, and economy. The setting of the slave plantation also enables an examination of how Black bodies produced pleasure, not for themselves but for their white captors. From there, I journey to late nineteenth-century minstrel performance spaces, where the pursuit of white pleasure through the controlling mimetic grasp of "black fun"[65] produced enduring African American stereotypes that I genealogically link to the execution of forms, characters, and aesthetics on circuit stages. The related history enveloping the emergence of segregated performance spaces and artistic routes in the first half of the twentieth century is then uncovered. As Black artists entertained countless African American crowds in towns and cities across the country, I mark these African American—*only* venues and the Black performance trails that they gave rise to as the places and spaces in which Black theatrical pleasure first coalesces in response to Black mainstream entertainment. Weaving together scholarship on African American food, cultural practices, slavery, performance, and mass entertainment, this chapter's mindset of redirection and recovery weds the terrain of "the popular" with African American theatre and performance history.

Chapter Three, "Looking for Langston," turns to the mid-twentieth-century musicals of Langston Hughes and positions this dramatist of African American musicals, during the late 1950s and early 1960s, as the father and architect of contemporary Chitlin Circuit musical theatre. Here I rely on documented histories on the production contexts, critical reception, and artistic motivations that enveloped the musicals *Simply Heavenly: A Comedy* (1957), *Black Nativity: A Gospel*

Song-Play for a Variable Cast (1961), and *Tambourines to Glory: A Comedy* (1963). In each, I view the politics of Hughes's Black theatre-making and performance alongside the contours of Black spectatorship, as they existed during, what I argue is, a formative period of Black popular musical theatre. As it unfolds, this chapter unveils the parentage and, perhaps, ill-fated historical unions, that gave birth to Chitlin Circuit theatre.

Chapter Four, "David Talbert: Resurrecting Langston," focuses on the plays and theatrical events crafted by playwright, producer, and director David Talbert since the 1990s. Referred to by some as the "original Tyler Perry," Talbert has developed a patented product with a loyal and nationwide fanbase by rendering dramatic presentations of African American heterosexual relationships. These theatrical events and their reception, I argue, are conditioned by three interrelated factors. First, Talbert cultivates every aspect of the writing, directing, music, and acting in his productions according to the tenets of what he terms *inspirational theatre*. The spiritual and religious associations of this term, I argue, are self-consciously deployed by the playwright to move Chitlin Circuit theatre away from historically racialized and presently stigmatized associations in order to advance the artistic merit of the entire gamut of circuit productions and to elevate the perception and tastes of all circuit audiences. Second, I argue that Talbert's incorporation of relatable faith-based ideologies and experiences into fictionalized onstage presentations of contemporary urban environments build on Hughes's musical theatre efforts during the 1950s and 1960s, a lineage illuminated by my comparative analysis of Hughes's 1963 play *Tambourines to Glory* and Talbert's 1996 play *He Say . . . She Say . . . But What Does God Say?* Here I suggest that Talbert, like Hughes, engages with African American spectators via theatrical events that exemplify the specific characteristics of the Black Circuit. In Talbert's case, he directly plays upon his audience's expectations through the use of culturally specific storylines, strategic modes of African American cultural representation, and African American vernacular–based performance content. Finally, this chapter investigates Talbert's reception process, which transforms uninhibited circuit spectators into controlled *character*-like participants whose dialogue, responses, and actions are largely predetermined by Talbert. This chapter reveals both the originality of Talbert's theatre-making and how he strategically uses elements of his productions to entertain and engage African American audiences.

In Chapter Five, "Johnson and Guidry: Vaudeville 2.0," I focus on the plays and theatrical events of the nephew and uncle duo Je'Caryous Johnson and Gary Guidry. Their unique contribution to the genre of Chitlin Circuit theatre since 2000 comes in the form of full-length African American musical dramas that contain narrative plotlines and characters that were adapted from popular African American novels. It offers a nuanced investigation of both the form and content of their theatrical models alongside analyses of the performance and reception practices associated with their theatrical events. The Johnson–Guidry model, I argue, infuses secular and popular African American novels with religious and/

or sacred content and then (re)presents these same narratives in a theatrical and performance frame. The inclusion of this material infuses the narratives of popular novels with religious content, while the performances mimetically re-create the physical, spiritual, and emotional dimensions of African American religious experiences and environments onstage. The theatre fare presented by Johnson and Guidry, I argue, grants audiences a more varied form of entertainment than that of their peers due to their insertion of vaudeville-style variety acts that intentionally interrupt and manipulate the plot as a means of audience engagement. With an eye toward the history of Black vaudeville, I examine the controversial, stereotypical, and negative representations of blackness in these settings but, importantly, also signal the historical dimensions of my Black Circuit concept. With an understanding of the Black Circuit as an integrated network of consumerism, culture, circulation, exchange, and meaning making that meet at the nexus of Black theatre-making, performance, and reception, the theatre-making of Johnson and Guidry, as detailed in this chapter, expands our critical understanding of the politics of aesthetics, consumption, and representation in contemporary Black culture and how these terrains are historically and spiritually rooted.

Chapter Six, "Tyler Perry: Minstrelsy Inverted," turns to the plays, performances, audiences, and theatrical environments of the Chitlin Circuit's most successful theatre artist to date: Tyler Perry. Since 1998, this actor, director, producer, and writer has produced sold-out live shows across the country and made profits from DVD sales of these same touring productions. Previous scholarship on Perry has focused on the negative class-based portrayals of African Americans presented in his work while making assumptions about the kinds of people who attend his productions and how their viewing is derived. This chapter probes the complexities of the "Perry brand" in an effort to push back and against these assumptions and to reconsider the relationship between African American art, culture, representation, consumption, and intellect. Reducing the wide appeal of Perry's productions to easily consumable, low-aesthetic standards or to its assumed gender or class appeal simplifies what are in fact more-complex acts of minority spectatorship and minority consumption of equally complex performances that concern and/or feature minorities. In working through these complexities, I argue that the Black Circuit concept enables a balanced critique of Perry's work, theatrical environments, and spectators, one that is grounded in ethnographic data collection and "historical contextualization."[66] As the title of this chapter suggests, I see Perry's project as one that inverts, rather than merely replaces, minstrelsy. Undeniably, Perry's productions circulate stereotypes that dangerously reduce African Americans to loud-talking, childlike, adulterous, greedy, abusive, violent, rude, delinquent, and sexually promiscuous characteristics that harken back to nineteenth-century American minstrel performances. Yet drawing on Gates's "signifying monkey" and on revisionist scholarship on minstrelsy, I argue that there is repetition with a critical difference occurring here. As Bobo discovered in her study of African American women who found pleasure in the violent and negative depictions of African American womanhood in Steven Spielberg's 1982 film *The Color Purple*, I find that Perry's minority spectators similarly bring their personal, communal, group histories and their interpretive skills to bear on his performance texts.[67] Perry's theatrical presentations of spirituality, blackness, and crossdressing, I argue, reveal the complex dynamics involved in how his African American spectators find subversive pleasure in markedly stereotypical and negative images and, in their place, relate to and identify with the more positive and useful material left behind.[68] As the last and final case study chapter in the project, the revelation of cognizant and purposeful reception practices undertaken by minority spectators are at the heart of the political utility, import, implications, and dynamics of the Black Circuit.

The concluding chapter, "Small Acts: The Politics of Black Theatrical Pleasure" further emphasizes the pervasiveness, importance, and durability of the Black Circuit as an interpretive method and as a theoretical concept based on the collective findings of the entire project. On the basis of the analysis in previous chapters, the politics of minority spectatorship, broadly constituted, is put into dialogue with—what has now emerged as a result of this study—a politics of Black theatrical pleasure. Of utmost interest in this summative discussion is a consideration of how minority spectatorship and Black theatrical pleasure are conditioned by choice, access, space, temporality, history, innovation, identification, and healing. Advancing a call to action rooted in Black feminist and womanist ideologies and praxis, the chapter closes with a call for including theatre in the study of popular culture, Black politics, and race and intraracial relations in the United States.

From start to finish, I aim to present the intricacies of Chitlin Circuit theatrical events from the vantage point of its producers and consumers. Admittedly then, this project could not have been undertaken without the help of the people whom it is about: the artists and spectators of Chitlin Circuit theatre. However, this project has also necessitated that I acknowledge upfront my participatory role as a spectator in these spaces. During my research, I entered theatres and engaged with these productions by using cultural and personal experiences that were at times similar and at other times different than those around me. My racial and gender statuses as Black and as a woman allowed me to enter into many spaces with ease, and I was often a welcomed receiver of privileged information. However, my cultural status as a West Indian from the Caribbean island of St. Croix in the US Virgin Islands meant that I was at times unfamiliar with particular references or that my experiences triggered associations that were at times different than those received by my fellow spectators. The experiences of my island upbringing were always in dialogue with my experiences gained from living in various parts of the United States over the past two decades. Yet as a United States territory, St. Croix is not altogether removed from the vast cultural terrain of America, so the first 16 years of my life were highly influenced by "the mainland." To this day, all but a small few of our television shows are from the United States, and most of those are brought to us by New York City satellite stations. As a result,

I grew up in a culture that was bombarded with American and especially African American cultural products via radio, television, and magazines. Moreover, as the daughter of a West Indian mother and an African American father, my childhood can best be described as a cultural fusion. All of these factors were brought to bear on this study as I set out to personally engage with the plays, productions, and people that I came into contact with on their own terms, but with an awareness of how my eyes and ears were receiving and interpreting information.

With optimism, I hope that what I have assembled here will not only shed light on this salient moment in American theatre but also help to promote dialogue between the separate worlds of the popular and the established in African American theatre and performance. I ask readers to consider this project as one that aims to promote dialogue, bridge unnecessary gaps, and foster new insights, alliances, reciprocity, and respect on either side.

Notes

1 Paul Gilroy, *The Black Atlantic: Modernity and Double Consciousness* (Cambridge, MA: Harvard University Press, 1993), 37–38.
2 Lily Workneh, "Meet April Reign: The Activist Who Created #OscarsSoWhite," *The Huffington Post*, February 27, 2016, www.huffingtonpost.com/entry/april-reign-oscarssowhite_us_56d21088e4b03260bf771018#, accessed April 2, 2017.
3 Colin Covert, "Whitewashing the Oscars: How Did Hollywood Get into This Predicament?" *The Star Tribune*, February 27, 2016, www.startribune.com/whitewashing-the-oscars-how-history-of-exclusion-led-to-academy-awards-controversy/370185841/, accessed April 2, 2017.
4 J. T., "How Racially Skewed Are the Oscars?" *The Economist*, January 21, 2016, www.economist.com/blogs/prospero/2016/01/film-and-race, accessed April 2, 2017.
5 Covert, "Whitewashing the Oscars."
6 Katherine Blauvelt, "BWWW Exclusive: A History of Tony Award Winning Plays," *Broadwayworld.com*, March 11, 2017, www.broadwayworld.com/article/BWW-Exclusive-A-History-of-Tony-Award-Winning-Plays-Becoming-Oscar-Award-Winning-Movies-20170311, accessed April 2, 2017.
7 In the summer of 2006, I interviewed Malik Yoba, a well-known African American actor, who was playing a lead role in a circuit production entitled *Work It Out* (written and directed by Eric Rico Nance) at Chicago's Arie Crown Theater at the time of our conversation. In the interview Yoba was asked directly about the "Chitlin Circuit" label given to this category of African American theatre. In his response Yoba disparaged the moniker in favor of the term "Urban Theatre." As I will unpack in the unfolding chapters, it is important that we acknowledge the agency of the African American practitioners who are choosing to move away from the term "Chitlin Circuit" because of the negative associations it carries. To read the interview in its entirety, please see, Rashida Z. Shaw McMahon, "Urban Development," Theater, *Time Out Chicago*, 73 (2006): 137.
8 This popular theatrical form displays a combination of qualities that are akin to both late-nineteenth-century and contemporary standards of melodramatic theatre, such as evocative music, stereotypical character portrayals, exaggerated physical gestures, and excessive character emotions. Please see David Mayer, "Nineteenth Century Theatre Music," *Theatre Notebook* 30, no. 3 (1976): 115–22; and Michael Booth, *English Melodrama* (London: Herbert Jenkins, 1965). Both authors discuss the use of exaggerated gestures and movement displayed in late nineteenth Century melodramatic

acting. Although the highly stylized form that Booth describes is albeit different when compared to the acting standards exhibited on contemporary Chitlin Circuit stages, I am suggesting that this modern form of melodramatic acting contains traces of its nineteenth-century predecessor in the form of stylized gestures and exaggerated movements.

9 Houston A. Baker, Jr., "Critical Memory and the Black Public Sphere," in *The Black Public Sphere: A Public Culture Book*, ed. The Black Public Sphere Collective (Chicago and London: The University of Chicago Press, 1995), 13.

10 Baker, "Critical Memory and the Black Public Sphere," 13.

11 Robin D. G. Kelley, *Race Rebels: Culture, Politics, and the Black Working Class* (New York: The Free Press, 1994), 4.

12 Baker, "Critical Memory and the Black Public Sphere"; Todd Boyd, *Am I Black Enough for You? Popular Culture from the 'Hood and Beyond'* (Bloomington, IN: Indiana University Press, 1997); Patricia Hill Collins, *Black Sexual Politics: African Americans, Gender, and the New Racism* (New York and London: Routledge, 2005); Gilroy, *The Black Atlantic*; Stuart Hall, "What Is This 'Black' in Black Popular Culture?" in *Black Popular Culture: A Project by Michelle Wallace*, ed. Gina Dent (New York: The New Press, 1988), 21–33; Richard Iton, *In Search of the Black Fantastic: Politics and Popular Culture in the Post-Civil Rights Era* (Oxford and New York: Oxford University Press, 2008); Kelley, *Race Rebels*; Zandria F. Robinson, *This Ain't Chicago: Race, Class, and Regional Identity in the Post-Soul South* (Chapel Hill: The University of North Carolina Press, 2014); and Tricia Rose, "Black Texts/Black Contexts," in *Black Popular Culture, a Project by Michelle Wallace*, ed. Gina Dent (New York: The New Press, 1983), 223–27.

13 Iton, *In Search of the Black Fantastic*, 6.

14 Iton, *In Search of the Black Fantastic*, 18–19.

15 Gilroy, *The Black Atlantic*, 37.

16 W. E. B. Du Bois, "Krigwa Players Little Negro Theatre," *Crisis* 32, no. 3 (July 1926): 134.

17 As representative examples of their related scholarship, please see Annmarie Bean, "Blackface Minstrelsy and Double Inversion, Circa 1890," in *African American Performance and Theater History*, ed. Harry J. Elam, Jr. and David Krasner (Oxford and New York: Oxford University Press, 2001), 171–90; Susan Bennett, *Theatre Audiences: A Theory of Production and Reception* (New York and London: Routledge, 1997); Catherine Cole, *Ghana's Concert Party Theatre* (Bloomington and Indianapolis: Indiana University Press, 2001); Harry J. Elam, Jr., "The Device of Race: An Introduction," in *African American Performance and Theater History: A Critical Reader*, ed. Harry J. Elam, Jr. and David Krasner (Oxford and New York: Oxford University Press, 2001), 3–16; David Krasner, *A Beautiful Pageant: African American Theatre, 1910–1927* (New York: Palgrave Macmillan, 2002); David Krasner, *Resistance, Parody, and Double-Consciousness in African American Theatre, 1895–1910* (New York: St. Martin's Press, 1997); David Savran, *Highbrow/Lowdown: Theater, Jazz, and the Making of a New Middle Class* (Ann Arbor: The University of Michigan Press, 2009); David Savran, "Toward a Historiography of the Popular," *Theatre Survey* 45, no. 2 (2004): 211–17; and Larry Stempel, *Showtime: A History of the Broadway Musical Theatre* (New York: W. W. Norton & Company, 2010).

18 Please refer to Jacqueline Bobo, *Black Women as Cultural Readers* (New York: Columbia University Press, 1995); Nelson George, *Buppies, B-boys, Baps & Bohos: Notes on Post-Soul Black Culture* (New York: HarperCollins Publishers, 1992); Robert W. Snyder, "The Vaudeville Circuit: A Prehistory of the Mass Audience," in *Audiencemaking: How the Media Create the Audience*, ed. James S. Ettema and D. Charles Whitney (Thousand Oaks, CA: Sage Publications, 1994), 215–31; and Jacqueline N. Stewart, "Negroes Laughing at Themselves? Black Spectatorship and the Performance of Urban Modernity," *Critical Inquiry* 29 (Summer 2003): 650–77.

19 Here I refer readers to Pierre Bourdieu, *Distinction: A Social Critique of the Judgment of Taste*, trans. Richard Nice (Cambridge: Harvard University Press, 1984); Herbert J. Gans, *Popular Culture & High Culture: An Analysis and Evaluation of Taste* (New York: Basic Books, 1999); Lawrence W. Levine, *Black Culture and Black Consciousness: Afro-American Folk Thought from Slavery to Freedom* (New York: Oxford University Press, 1978); and Peter Stallybrass and Allon White, *The Politics and Poetics of Transgression* (Ithaca, NY: Cornell University Press, 1986).

20 Elam, "The Device of Race," 5–6.

21 Savran, "Toward a Historiography of the Popular," 212.

22 Savran, "Toward a Historiography of the Popular," 216.

23 Henry Louis Gates, Jr., *The Signifying Monkey: A Theory of African-American Literary Criticism* (New York and Oxford: Oxford University Press, 1988), 134. Although Gates directly uses the phrase "critical difference" in this particular moment of his discussion, the nuanced and multiple ways in which African American literature, culture, and meaning making relies on the consistent (re)application and renewal of African and African diasporic culture, traditions, significations, etc. is explicated throughout the entirety of Gates's seminal text.

24 John Tulloch, *Shakespeare and Chekhov in Production and Reception: Theatrical Events and Their Audiences* (Iowa City: University of Iowa Press, 2005). For more on the limitations of Bourdieu's methodology on the study of theatrical events, see Willmar Sauter, *The Theatrical Event: Dynamics of Performance and Perception* (Iowa City: University of Iowa Press, 2000), 3.

25 Sauter, *The Theatrical Event*, 3.

26 By "traditional" ethnography methods, I am referring here to my immersion in my field study sites, Chicago's Arie Crown Theater and Indianapolis' Murat Theatre, over a sustained period of time in which I studied the people, theatrical events, occurrences, and the material conditions present in these locations. When I use the term *historical* in the earlier sentence, I am first referencing the work of sociologists such as John and Jean Comaroff as detailed in *Ethnography and the Historical Imagination* (Boulder, CO: Westview Press, 1992); Michael Burawoy's work as presented in "Revisits: An Outline of a Theory of Reflexive Ethnography," *American Sociological Review* 68, no. 5 (2003): 645–79; and Diane Vaughan's discussion of the term in "Theorizing Disaster: Analogy, Historical Ethnography, and the Challenger Accident," *Ethnography* 5, no. 3 (2004): 315–47. Referencing Burawoy, Vaughan writes that

> Exploring the variety of revisits, Burawoy identifies the archeological revisit: the ethnographic practice of digging into the past, deliberately reconstructing history in order to identify and then track the processes connecting past and present. Distanced from action by time and space, the ethnographer working in this mode relies, to a greater or lesser extent, on documentary records.
>
> (Vaughan 316)

Second, my use of the term refers to my own efforts in this project to reconstruct past performances and theatrical events that I did not see and participate in through the use of DVDs, images, programs, and other forms of historical evidence.

27 Ric Knowles, *Reading the Material Theatre* (Cambridge: Cambridge University Press, 2004), 19.

28 Marvin Carlson, *Theatre Semiotics: Signs of Life* (Indianapolis, IN: Indiana University Press, 1990).

29 Stewart, "Negroes Laughing at Themselves?" 654.

30 Here scripts or play texts of circuit plays are rarely available. To date, only David Talbert has published any of his plays.

31 Dwight Conquergood, "Performance Studies Interventions and Radical Research," *The Drama Review* 46, no. 2 (Summer 2002): 146.

32 Conquergood, "Performance Studies Interventions and Radical Research," 151–52.

33 Please see Bennett, *Theatre Audiences*; John Russell Brown, *Shakespeare and the Theatrical Event* (New York: Palgrave MacMillan, 2002); A. Maria Van Erp Taalman Kip, *Reader and Spectator: Problems in the Interpretation of Greek Tragedy* (Amsterdam: J. C. Gieben, 1990); Sauter, *The Theatrical Event*; and Tulloch, *Shakespeare and Chekhov in Production and Reception*.

34 I will explain my engagement with these texts in my upcoming discussion of theory. For now, the particular texts that I am referring to are Bennett, *Theatre Audiences*; and Sauter, *The Theatrical Event*.

35 Please refer to Margaret Wilkerson, "Black Theater in California," *The Drama Review* 16, no. 4 (December 1972): 25–38; Margaret Wilkerson, "Redefining Black Theatre," *The Black Scholar* 10, no. 10 (July–August 1979): 32–42; Mimi Gisolfi D'Aponte, "*The Gospel at Colonus* (and Other Black Morality Plays)," Special Issue: The Black Church and the Black Theatre, *Black American Literature Forum* 25, no. 1 (Spring 1991): 101–11; Floyd Gaffney, "A Hand Is on the Gate in Athens," Special Issue: The Black Church and the Black Theatre, *Black American Literature Forum* 25, no. 1 (Spring 1991): 196–201; and Rhett Jones, "Orderly and Disorderly: Why Church and Sports Appeal to Black Americans and Theatre Does Not," Special Issue: The Black Church and the Black Theatre, *Black American Literature Forum* 25, no. 1 (Spring 1991): 43–52.

36 Sandra L. Richards, "Writing the Absent Potential: Drama, Performance, and the Canon of African-American Literature," in *Performativity and Performance*, ed. Andrew Parker and Eve Kosofsky Sedgwick (New York and London: Routledge, 1995), 72.

37 Susan Manning, *Modern Dance, Negro Dance: Race in Motion* (Minneapolis, MN: University of Minnesota Press, 2004), xvi.

38 Carlson, *Theatre Semiotics*, xiii.

39 Richard Schechner, *Performance Theory* (New York and London: Routledge, 2003), 71.

40 Sauter, *The Theatrical Event*, 47.

41 Sauter, *The Theatrical Event*, 48.

42 Sauter, *The Theatrical Event*, 48.

43 Sauter, *The Theatrical Event*, 49.

44 Sauter, *The Theatrical Event*, 53–54.

45 Bennett, *Theatre Audiences*, 106.

46 Bennett, *Theatre Audiences*, 106.

47 Joseph Roach, "Introduction," in *Critical Theory and Performance*, ed. Janelle G. Reinelt and Joseph R. Roach (Ann Arbor: The University of Michigan Press, 1992), 10.

48 Marvin Carlson, *The Haunted Stage: The Theatre as Memory Machine* (Ann Arbor: The University of Michigan Press, 2001), 2.

49 Carlson, *The Haunted Stage*, 2.

50 Nelson Goodman, *Languages of Art: An Approach to a Theory of Symbols* (Indianapolis: Hackett Publishing Company, Inc., 1976), 248.

51 Rose, "Black Texts/Black Contexts," 223.

52 Rose, "Black Texts/Black Contexts," 223.

53 Hall, "What Is This 'Black' in Black Popular Culture?" 27.

54 Michel de Certeau, *The Practice of Everyday Life* (Berkeley: University of California Press, 1988), xii–xiv.

55 Ian Hunter, "Aesthetics and Cultural Studies," in *Cultural Studies*, ed. Lawrence Grossberg, Gary Nelson, and Paul Treichler (New York and London: Routledge, Chapman and Hall, 1992), 348; quoted in Caponi, "Introduction: The Case for an African American Aesthetic," in *Signifyin(g), Sanctifyin', & Slam Dunking: A Reader in African American Expressive Culture*, ed. Gena Dagel Caponi (Amherst, MA: The University of Massachusetts Press, 1999), 8.

56 Caponi, "Introduction: The Case for an African American Aesthetic," 7.

57 Caponi, "Introduction: The Case for an African American Aesthetic," 8.

58 Janet Wolff, *The Social Production of Art* (London: Macmillan, 1981), 65; quoted in Bennett, *Theatre Audiences*, 92.

59 Ceola Ross Barber, "The Artistry of Black Communication," in *Expressively Black: The Cultural Basis of Ethnic Identity*, ed. Geneva Gay and Willie L. Barber (New York: Praeger Publishers, 1987), 95.

60 Charles Taylor, "The Politics of Recognition," in *Multiculturalism: A Critical Reader*, ed. David Theo Goldberg (Cambridge, MA: Blackwell Publishers, 1994), 80.

61 Taylor, "The Politics of Recognition," 80.

62 Paul Gilroy, "Sounds Authentic: Black Music: Ethnicity, and the Challenge of a Changing Same," in *Imagining Home: Class, Culture, and Nationalism in the Black Diaspora* (New York: Verso, 1994), 108–9; quoted in E. Patrick Johnson's "Performing Blackness Down Under: Gospel Music in Australia," in *Black Cultural Traffic: Crossroads in Global Performance and Popular Culture*, ed. Harry J. Elam, Jr. and Kennell Jackson (Ann Arbor: University of Michigan Press, 2005), 70–71.

63 Johnson, "Performing Blackness Down Under," 80.

64 Rashida Z. Shaw McMahon, "From the Margins to Center Stage: Tyler Perry's Popular African American Theatre," in *From Madea to Media Mogul: Theorizing Tyler Perry*, ed. TreaAndrea M. Russworm, Samantha N. Sheppard, and Karen M. Bowdre (Jackson: University Press of Mississippi, 2016), 30.

65 The quoted phrase "black fun" is taken from a longer quote in Eric Lott's seminal essay on blackface minstrelsy. The speaker is an unidentified white minstrel performer. The full quote in Lott's publication reads, "I shall be rich in black fun." Please refer to Eric Lott, "Love and Theft: The Racial Unconscious of Blackface Minstrelsy," *Representations* 39 (Summer 1992): 25. In his accompanying notes, Lott refers readers to the source text, see Mrs. Anne Matthews, *A Continuation of the Memoirs of Charles Matthews, Comedian*, 2 vols. (Philadelphia, PA: Lea & Blanchard, 1839), vol. 1, 239.

66 Rose, "Black Texts/Black Contexts," 223.

67 Bobo, *Black Women as Cultural Readers*, 96.

68 Bobo, *Black Women as Cultural Readers*, 96.

2

SLOW-ROASTED CHITTERLINGS

Pork—and the fatter the better—is the only proper substance of animal food for Negroes.

—Anonymous man from Alabama cited in Kenneth Stampp,
The Peculiar Institution: Slavery in the Ante-bellum South (1956)[1]

Maws are things ofays seldom get to peck, nor are you likely ever to hear about Charlie eating a chitterling. Sweet potato pies, a good friend of mine asked recently, "Do they taste anything like pumpkin?" Negative. They taste more like memory if you are not uptown.

—Amiri Baraka, "Soul Food," *Home: Social Essays* (1962)[2]

Jeri's Chitterlings

Mrs. Jeri Headley of New York makes this delicious dish for company dinner. Chitterlings are often spelled "chitlins" and are always pronounced that way.

5 pounds frozen chitterlings, thawed	*1 teaspoon salt*
5 cups water	*2 tablespoons cornstarch*
½ cups vinegar	*½ teaspoon Gravy Master or*
3 large onions, chopped	*Kitchen Bouquet*

1. Wash the meat, making sure it is entirely free of dirt. Cut meat into small pieces (approximately 1 inch).
2. Soak it in 2 cups water and ½ cup vinegar for 15 minutes. Drain. Place in a large pot.
3. Add onions, salt, and remaining 3 cups of water. Bring to a boil. Lower heat. Cover and simmer 2½–3 hours or until meat is fork tender. Thicken gravy

with cornstarch. Season gravy with Gravy Master. Cook another 5 minutes. Serve hot. [*Serves 4–6*]

—Helen Mendes, *The African Heritage Cookbook* (1971)[3]

Any investigation into the controversial yet resilient longevity of Chitlin Circuit theatre must focus on the history of popular Black representation in the United States. It is expected then, that not only do these analyses contend with the expanse and complexity of tracing the history of Black performed and produced representations, genres, modes, and aesthetics that have been commercially successful in a diverse array of performance and audience contexts, but they must also consider the history of lucrative performance practices of alleged blackness, as produced and performed by non-Black artists. Whereas traditional scholarship may pinpoint the origins of popular Black representation history in an American context on the latter, minstrelsy, I root the history of Chitlin Circuit musicals in the perhaps unorthodox soil of slave plantations and the culinary and dietary practices, ideologies, and cultural assumptions and associations that they have produced. In other words, before we can comprehend the *circuit*, we must first understand the *chitlin*. In this chapter, I unpack the foundational theatrical precedents to Chitlin Circuit theatre, all with an eye toward how Black pleasure has been cultivated and maintained therein. *Slow roasting*, as signaled in this chapter's title, both signifies a method of cooking applied to chitlins or chitterlings and descriptively calls attention to a complex history, one that is bound in the cultural and culinary relationship between chitlins and the African American experience. When seen as Black cuisine, a cultural symbol, and a performance-rooted descriptor of touring African American performance environments, the roots and mechanics of the circuit are more precisely artistically, culturally, and politically marked. We begin with the food.

Stated plainly, chitlins are pig intestines that have been laboriously cleaned, washed, seasoned, and cooked in ways similar to Mrs. Jeri's famous recipe. The enterprising creation of chitlins was conjured by Black cooks tasked with the basic human need to feed themselves and their families with the unwanted and wasted food scraps of plantation owners (and the harvest of their own small gardens, if they were so fortunate[4]). This creative use of the unwanted and the undesirable has launched strains of positive and negative cultural associations and stereotypes for and about African Americans with food that has lasted for centuries. Importantly, and as will be discussed in the coming pages, the moniker *chitlin* has also housed generative fields of performance and Black artistry that encompass multiple genres, aesthetics, and performance contexts across the twentieth and twenty-first centuries.

While at first glance the choice to distribute the entrails of pigs to slaves may appear to be one of convenience as well as a purposeful demonstration of power that reinforced status and hierarchal differences, historians have also made a connection between the medical and scientific ideologies and practices of the time and the nutritional and dietary allowances enforced on slaves by their owners. As Stampp and Mendes, for example, recount in their respective publications, *The Peculiar Institution: Slavery in the Ante-bellum South* (1956) and *The African Heritage Cookbook* (1971), many nineteenth-century physicians, influenced by the scientific work of Charles Darwin and others who advanced theories of biological Black inferiority and difference,[5] believed that pigs were effective nutritional catalysts for producing healthy Black workforces. As evidence of this, Stampp cites the medical opinion of Dr. John H. Wilson of Georgia in 1859, who Mendes also references in her book:[6]

> It was a common notion, he observed, "that fat bacon and pork are highly nutritious; but almost everything, even the lightest amount of watery vegetables, contain more nutritive muscle-building elements. Yet these fatty articles of diet are peculiarly appropriate on account of their heat-producing properties; they generate sufficient heat to cause the wheels of life to move glibly and smoothly, . . . and hence negroes who are freely supplied with them grow plump, sleek and shiny."[7]

Moreover, Stampp also cites the recollections of a former cotton plantation slave who confirms that bacon and corn made up the majority of the food that he and his fellow slaves received.

> All that is allowed . . . is corn and bacon, which is given out of the corncrib and smoke-house every Sunday morning. Each one receives, as his weekly allowance, three and a half pounds of bacon, and corn enough to make a peck of meal.[8]

Wilson cautions, however, that a diet high in pork is not recommended for slave owners due to the fact that they "are different [from their slaves] in their habits and constitutions, and that while fat meat is the life of the negro. . . . it is a prolific source of disease and death among the whites."[9] As a result of such dictates, plantation owners, many of whom were also consumers of pork, spared and distributed "the feet, snout, tail, intestines, stomach, etc.,"[10] of the pig, along with bacon, in an effort to adequately maintain their human property and increase the likelihood of high crop yields.

Medical principles on the health and nutritional needs of slave populations not only generated dangerous health consequences for Black slave populations but also helped to cement dangerous cultural and biological stereotypes and perceptions about African Americans that have remained through generations. These stereotypes and perceptions continue to impact how generations of Black Americans select, prepare, and choose to eat or not eat dishes laced with negative associations to slavery and also influence how non-Black observers associate African Americans with food that share the same fraught plantation history with pork. Herein lies the root origin of the ironies, stereotypes, and complexities in the term *chitlins* that bleed from past and present African American dinner plates, graced with these cultivated intestinal delicacies, onto and into Chitlin Circuit musical theatre and its predominantly African American audience. Yes, one side of the culinary history of chitlins brims with innovation, artistry, and the resilient ability of African Americans to make a way out of no way in the biblical sense of Isaiah 43:16. Yet the other side of this historical food context contains elements of oppression, cultural shame, distrust, and mockery, because chitlins symbolically represent an engineered hindrance to Black progress that was literally force-fed to Black populations. As we will see, not even the inventive platform of African American musical theatre has been able to escape these associations.

Making a Way Out of No Way, in Search of Black Pleasure

While the pleasure of Black audiences is well positioned to be a subject of inquiry in the late twentieth century and into the early twenty-first century, as Saidiya Hartman reminds us in *Scenes of Subjection: Terror, Slavery, and Self-making in Nineteenth-Century America*, when Africans first arrived on the North American continent as chattel slaves, the powerful reins of pleasure were held by the white slave masters, not the slaves who became the human objects on which white pleasure was desired, elicited, projected, and maintained, at the will and behest of the pleasure seeker. She writes,

> The relation between pleasure and the possession of slave property, in both the figurative and literal sense, can be explained in part by the fungibility of the slave—that is, the joy made possible by virtue of the replaceability and interchangeability endemic to the commodity—and by extensive capacities of property—that is, the augmentation of the master subject through his embodiment in external objects and persons. Put differently, the fungibility of the commodity makes the captive body an abstract vessel vulnerable to the projection of others' feelings, ideas, desires, and values; and, as property, the dispossessed body of the enslaved is the surrogate for the master's body since it guarantees his disembodied universality and acts as the sign of power and dominion. Thus, while the beaten and mutilated body presumably establishes the brute materiality of existence, the materiality of suffering regularly eludes (re)cognition by virtue of the body's being replaced by other signs of value, as well as other bodies. Thus, the desire to don, occupy, or possess blackness or the black body as a sentimental resource and/or locus of excess enjoyment is both founded upon and enabled by the material relations of chattel slavery.[11]

Like Hartman, Eric Lott, Bean, and numerous scholars have demonstrated, the white performance minstrel walked or literally jigged, sang, mocked, and laughed into place as an embodied actualization of white pleasure honed at the expense of Black people.[12] The white minstrel performer dons the façade of blackness through the use of cosmetics, costumes, physical and verbal mockery, and slapstick humor sharpened in violent, racist, and misogynistic ideologies. In its original manifestation, blackface minstrelsy performances involved a blend of pantomime, parody, dialogue, song, dance, and musical accompaniments. Yet what is of utmost importance in thinking through racially immersed pleasure histories and how they directly influence how Black pleasure is enacted in contemporary circuit musical theatre environments is an understanding that in white performances of minstrelsy, white pleasure clung to Black bodies against Black people's will or enjoyment.

Moreover, pleasure making, as it occurred in these performance contexts, was the sole domain of white bodies on either side of the figurative and literal performance curtain. A case in point is the now oft-cited historical account of the popular white minstrel performer Thomas D. Rice and his racist creation of the Jump Jim Crow character—costuming, physicality, song and dance—in 1830. Lott reminds us of the conditions under which Rice's theft and appropriation of blackness was birthed:

> Confronted one day with the dazzling spectacle of black singing, the story goes, Rice saw his "opportunity" and determined to take advantage of his talent for mimicry. Fortunately, intones *Atlantic* writer Robert P. Nevin, "There was a negro in attendance at Griffith's Hotel, on Wood Street, named Cuff,—an exquisite specimen of his sort,—who won a precarious subsistence by letting his open mouth as a mark for boys to pitch pennies into, at three paces, and by carrying the trunks of passengers from the steamboats to the hotels." After some persuasion, "Cuff" agrees to accompany the actor to the theater. There Rice blacks his face, orders Cuff to disrobe, and "invest[s] himself in the cast-off apparel." As Nevin puts it, on stage "the extraordinary apparition produced an instant effect."[13]

While Rice was onstage capitalizing on his packaged presentation of seeming authenticity in full artifice, an offstage Cuff, still mindful of his duties, heard an approaching steamboat and called out to the performing Rice for his shoes and clothing. Rice, fully immersed in his performance and unable to hear Cuff's plea for his belongings, was soon joined onstage by Cuff, who was in an unclear state of nudity. As the *Atlantic Monthly* journalist notes, Cuff's authenticating walk-on provided "'the touch, in the mirthful experience of that night, that passed endurance.'"[14] Lott credits this report as being "probably the least trustworthy and most accurate account of American's minstrelsy's appropriation of black culture."[15]

The narrative of Rice and Cuff is provided here to draw attention to how Cuff's personhood, humanity, and needs were cast aside by Rice in pursuit of white pleasure and white profit. Moreover, even when a dismantled and anxious

Cuff tried to secure his property by interrupting Rice's fraudulent imitation of his blackness in performance, the intrusion only resulted in the displayed "blackness" of both Cuffs, the fake and the real, doubling the respective entertainment returns for the performer and his thrilled audience.

This theatrical and visual dissonance was not lost on the field. Indeed, as Daphne Brooks demonstrates in *Bodies in Dissent: Spectacular Performances of Race and Freedom, 1850–1910*, such dissonance would paradoxically give rise to an increasing investment in authenticity:

> audiences of the Atlantic world would indeed gradually turn their attention to black performers who redirected conventional performance practices in the nineteenth century, who mastered the art of spectacle, (representational) excess, and duality, and who signified on the politics of racial "imitation" in order to reinvent the transatlantic cultural playing field from abolition forward.[16]

Along these lines, Krasner uses the terms *reinscription* and *reversal*, as he provides representative case studies of Brooks's redirection, found in the blackface performances of Bert Williams and George Walker, producer Sam T. Jack's "The Creole Show," producer Nat Salsbury's "Black America," and the whiteface performance of Bob Cole as Willie the Wayside in "A Trip to Coontown"—against the backdrop of the advent of modernism in the late nineteenth century and the foundation of the New Negro Movement at the turn of the twentieth century.[17]

According to Krasner, reinscription occurred when Black performers, like Williams and Walker, donned blackface and performed an altered presentation of established minstrel representations to both Black and white audiences.[18] Krasner cites Williams and Walker's "Two Real Coons" show as an example of this. He notes that

> [a]lthough Bert Williams did employ blackface techniques, his partner, George Walker, countered Williams' appearance. Walker was articulate, wore stylish clothes, and succeeded in presenting himself as a foil to Williams' slow and hapless character.[19]

He goes on to say, "Operating within the presentation cycle of minstrel stereotyping, Williams and Walker capitalized on the concept of authenticity making use of white performer's vernacular."[20]

In such instances of reinscription, Black minstrels were forced to contend with the troubled reception and critique of their performances and the choices therein, by Black audiences who watched with critical eyes. Yuval Taylor and Jake Austen remind us that whereas late-nineteenth-century Black minstrel shows performed largely before white audiences and some Black audiences, in the early twentieth century, Black minstrels regularly performed for all-Black audiences in southern tent shows.[21] Marvin McAlister, in *White People Do Not Know How to Behave at Entertainments Designed for Ladies and Gentlemen of Colour: William Brown's African and African American Theater*, calls attention to the Black theatrical contexts of New York City during the early 1820s, in which Black performers, like Bob Cole, donned the minstrel mask and performed before majority-Black audiences at the African Company, the African Grove Theater, the American Theatre, and the Minor Theatre.[22] Krasner positions such performances as projects of recovery aimed at countering the "darky image" through methods of "refashion[ing]" and "refinement."[23] In that vein, Bob Cole's whiteface performance accomplished a "reversal strategy" of this image through the use of "repetitive parody," "double meaning," "strategic verbal indirection," and "disguised irony." Not only did Cole's performance "suggest that parody can work both ways,"[24] but it also made a political intervention in the public sphere. This intervention was one that although it was based on a racist original, it had the potential to cause white spectators to turn their gaze inward and, contrarily, engender Black spectators to find new pleasure, albeit in a theatrical event context. If only for a moment, Cole's African American spectators were granted the opportunity to witness and legibly read the performance innards of Willie the Wayside. In such a spectatorial process of identification, coding, differentiation, and cognition, Cole didactically gave his Black spectators the potential to reflexively see how their own bodies were being oppressively subjected to prejudice, stereotype, and exaggeration, inside and outside of existing and historical popular performance contexts, since the inception of chattel slavery.[25] Thus, even in this early African American performance and reception context, involving comedic narratives and impersonation, Black pleasure and Black merriment reveal themselves to be always-already bound in clarity, discernment, thought, and a long-view of historical precedents, on both sides of the proscenium.

Significantly in these histories, Black audiences of popular performance become accomplishments. Enactments of Black popular spectating are unveiled as acts of viewing that are actively informed by the white supremacist and colonizing foundation on which Black caricatures, Black representation, and Black comedy are built. In spite and perhaps because of this fact, Black spectators reveal themselves as folk capable of understanding and distinguishing between the comingled presentations of positive and negative images of blackness. In these Black popular performance contexts, the pleasure-inducing modes of meaning making, such as comedy, parody, irony, and stereotype portrayals, are uncovered as collaboratively working alongside aesthetic, narrative, and representational choices, all geared toward Black audience identification and engagement and, moreover, relying on the Black utility and application of this same historical and reflexive cognition while spectating. Accounts such as those found in the performance histories of Walker, Williams, Cole, and Black female performers—many of whom brought male impersonation through crossdressing into the Black minstrel performance arena—like Florence Hines, Ada Overton Walker, the Hyer Sisters, and the Whitman Sisters, also celebrate the birthing of gendered diversity and agency in Black popular performance contexts.[26]

In the progressive atmosphere of the New Negro, Black artists worked with the intention of carving their own images and visions into the American imaginary even if it meant first having to work in the confines of the minstrel image. With the agency of Black performers comes the discerning agency of Black spectators who were tasked with decoding the numerous layers of a given performance. These early Black audiences emerged as skillful spectators capable of deep discernment, rejection, and prioritizing that, I argue in subsequent chapters, contemporary Black audiences of Chitlin Circuit musical theatre have inherited and equally mastered.

On the Circuit: Black Enterprising Since Vaudeville

Historically speaking, the origins of the name "Chitlin Circuit" began as popular shorthand for the segregated Black routes of American vaudeville circuit tours that originated during the 1920s.[27] Like other vaudeville productions of the time, early Chitlin Circuit shows covered the gamut of popular entertainment: circus acts, melodrama, comedy, minstrelsy, and song and dance routines.[28] To date, sparse academic research has been done on these segregated performance routes, although in recent years, more work has begun to emerge on individual artists. With that being said, one of the historically salient effects of American vaudeville and its subsequently smaller segregated African American strain are how they contributed to the development of a heretofore nonexistent mass American audience. Media scholar Robert W. Snyder, in "The Vaudeville Circuit: A Prehistory of the Mass Audience," identifies vaudeville theatre, popular during the late nineteenth century through the early twentieth century, as the originator of the American mass audience. According to Snyder, vaudeville booking agents B. F. Keith and E. F. Albee created an organized, regulated, and lucrative theatrical enterprise that focused on "mass marketing . . . leisure" to a nationwide audience. Their mass theatrical system prospered for a few decades until newer forms of entertainment and media gained more audience popularity.[29]

During this time, vaudeville theatre was able to capture the attention of a nationwide and heterogeneous audience that was divided along class, ethnic, gender and racial lines. Before the inception of vaudeville in the 1880s, American entertainment was performed in multifarious venues across the country—anywhere from saloons and burlesque houses to small theatres and music halls. These performance spaces did not cater to diverse audiences; nor were acts able to move to new locations with any consistency or wide recognition.[30]

However, with the introduction of Keith and Albee's vaudeville theatre agency, vaudevillian spectators were figuratively "lifted . . . out of [their] intimate communities and placed . . . in a mass audience."[31] For Snyder, Keith and Albee were the pioneers who created this mega-enterprise by centralizing their booking agencies in two major locations—Chicago and New York—which gave them access to areas of the United States such as the East Coast and the West Coast and parts of the South. These circuits catered to almost all subgroups of the US population and divided themselves between top-billing and beginner venues and routes. Out of these two major offices flowed acts originating from variety theatre,[32] blackface minstrelsy, dramatic theatre houses,[33] and circuses. With these major components covering the gamut of nineteenth-century popular entertainment, vaudeville soon became the most successful and the first form of mainstream entertainment.[34]

In recent years, scholars have begun to revisit vaudeville's history and make the claim that this diverse form of traveling entertainment is in fact the precursor to contemporary mass media. Vaudeville performers pursued audience involvement relentlessly, by using unabashed methods and techniques. The more the audience showed appreciation for the show by laughing, clapping, singing along, whistling, etc., the greater the odds that the show would be performed again and continue along the circuit route.[35] Richard Butsch highlights in *The Making of American Audiences: From Stage to Television, 1750–1990* the importance of vaudeville theatre in the creation of American audiences. Similar to Snyder, Butsch acknowledges that this was an entertainment form that was controlled in large part by the likes and dislikes of its spectators.

One popular tactic for securing audience response was to seat actors posing as regular spectators amid an unsuspecting audience. These decoys would laugh, sing, heckle, and sometimes cause disruptions in an effort to incite audience participation. As Butsch notes, these tactics should be considered the precursors to the methods by which today's media advertising agencies employ strategies to secure audience spectatorship.[36] While admittedly helpful in providing us with a context for understanding how audience-maneuvering schemes were applied to a wide-scale entertainment market, Butsch and Snyder's scholarship is less so when it comes to understanding how audience participation methods were deployed within African American–specific touring entertainment of the time. Aiding in this effort of recovery is Krasner's scholarship in *A Beautiful Pageant: African American Theatre Drama and Performance in the Harlem Renaissance 1910–1927*, which importantly introduces us to two overlooked areas in Black-specific US vaudeville history: Black producers and Black entrepreneurship. Specifically, Krasner's discussion of the entrepreneurship embarked on by actor, producer, and writer Sherman (S. H.) Dudley is of particular interest because of how Dudley's legacy marks him as a predecessor to the pleasure-crafting writer-producer-director teams of the contemporary circuit discussed in this book:

> Dudley realized that African American performers were at the mercy of white booking agents. Theaters across the country depended on them to arrange for playhouses and tours. By controlling these bookings and their routes, managers essentially dictated which shows would perform and in

what locales. In addition, black actors and shows had to contend with two problems: a difficult time with Jim Crow segregation and the burden of dealing with corrupt and bigoted agents who refused to pay or pay adequately. Actors were frequently warned in the black newspapers that particular towns along the booking routes had few accommodations for them. . . . In other instances actors were confronted by overt hostility and even Ku Klux Klan demonstrations. . . . The complexities of running a show in various parts of the nation caught up with both the desire for vaudeville theatre and segregation, creating difficulties beyond the usual ones of scheduling, lodging, salaries and transportation. Dudley addresse[d] the matter by buying up theatres across the country.[37]

By 1916, Dudley had created his own company, the Dudley Theatrical Enterprise, and owned several theatres across the South and Midwest and in Washington, DC; Virginia; and Philadelphia.[38] Soon after, Dudley and his partners created the Southern Consolidated Circuit, or the SCC, which had a far-reaching impact on Black American touring entertainment in the South, the Southeast, the Northeast (excluding New York City), and Midwestern portions of the country.[39] According to Krasner's and co-authors Errol Hill and James Hatch's respective discussions in *A History of African American Theatre*, it was around this time, in the early 1920s, that the previously referenced white-owned touring entertainment corporation, Theater Owners Booking Association (TOBA), became interested in Black performers and performance routes.[40]

Hill and Hatch explain that the TOBA did not always cater to Black entertainment. Although created in 1909, the TOBA owners' business came to a halt a few years later. Once they realized that there was a competitive market for Black entertainment, they decided to revive their agency again in the 1920s, declaring that they would "save the colored theatrical industry."[41] With the return of TOBA, Black theatre producers, booking agents, and managers were now forced to reckon with this competitive entertainment giant.

As a result, the National Managers Protective Agency was organized on May 26–27, 1920, and Dudley created the Colored Actors Union, which focused on the rights of African American artists.[42] Unfortunately, none of these efforts were able to withstand the eventual takeover of smaller booking agencies by TOBA:

> Dudley was included; however, by the mid-1920s, the size of TOBA and its subsidiaries had rendered Dudley less important. He was simply one of several producers, some trying to protect black performers from unscrupulous agents and managers, others seeking only self-interest and profit. He was still a force working for the best interests of black artists, but his power had been diminished by the onslaught of new agents and the multifarious needs of the entertainment industry. . . . The enormity of TOBA made it

impossible for any individual to protect the rights of all artists working in this fast-paced environment.[43]

As Krasner notes, although Dudley's own musicals and performances catered to white audiences and Black audiences (because Black audiences were less accessible) and the modes of many of his performances were blackface minstrelsy and comedy, his work and touring routes should be considered "forerunners of the Chitlin Circuit" that we are still encountering today.[44] Krasner's unearthing of Dudley's entrepreneurial legacy therefore provides an important foundational fragment in the history of how African Americans produced and created performances in the racialized confines of early Chitlin Circuit entertainment.

In an American context, the history of the Chitlin Circuit musical theatre is also intertwined with the genealogy of Black musical theatre. Warren Burdine's 1991 article "Let the Theatre Say 'Amen'" is the first academic article to take note of these productions and bracket them under the category of gospel musicals.[45] He subsequently published a second article in 1999 titled "The Gospel Musical and its Place in the Black American Theatre."[46] In both articles, Burdine maps the evolution of the subgenre, along with his own changing perceptions about the form.

Although Burdine criticizes the producers and audiences in 1991 for being unsophisticated, by the 1999 publication, he reconsiders the genre's significance due to what he calls its recognizable impact on audiences and on the development of Black theatre. The last sentences in the final paragraph of the latter publication read:

> Whatever some may see as the theatrical "purity" of the gospel musical (in terms, of course, of Eurocentric dictates on drama), that genre's popularity resides in the universal truth upon which it touches. Those truths will never change, and the impact of the gospel musical on the overall scene in the black theatre, though it may ebb and reach a crest, will never disappear.[47]

Between Burdine's publications, the conversation continued in a 1997 article published in *The New Yorker* by Gates. In the article, Gates discusses Chitlin Circuit musical theatre in the context of African American playwright August Wilson's rally for more funding initiatives in support of all-Black theatres. In his now oft-cited keynote address, "The Ground on Which I Stand," presented before a crowd of assembled theatre artists at the 1996 Theatre Communications Group's eleventh biannual conference, Wilson demanded funding for the support and the development of Black theatres that would cater to the work of Black artists:

> We do not need colorblind casting. We need some theatres to develop our playwrights. We need those misguided financial resources to be put to better use. We cannot develop our playwrights with the meager resources at our disposal.[48]

He also condemned the League of Resident Theatre (LORT) system for having only one member theatre (out of 66) dedicated to the production of Black plays and performance—the now-unaffiliated Crossroads Theatre of New Brunswick, New Jersey. For Wilson, the disproportionate privileging of the work of white artists over those produced by minorities did not end there. He also denounced what he calls the "assimilation[ist]" objectives of color-blind casting.[49] While many praised Wilson for shedding light on a history of discrimination and privilege in the US professional theatre system, Gates found his commentary particularly ironic given that Wilson was and, arguably, remains "the most celebrated American playwright . . . [and] certainly the most accomplished black playwright in the nation's history."[50]

Wilson's views and the groundbreaking color-blind casting debates that it generated notwithstanding, Gates's essay makes a critical revelation and contribution to African American theatre and performance that is granted full import in the unfolding chapters of this book. He importantly identifies Chitlin Circuit musical theatre as an example of self-supported Black theatre, ignored by Wilson, during a critical historical moment when such undertakings were rare and, most often, unsustainable. After attending a performance and witnessing the peculiar, yet special, dynamism himself, he reflects, "It's true that black audiences have always had a predilection for talking back at performances. But more than that is going on in this theatre: the intensity of engagement is palpable."[51] The contemporary Black American theatre of the Chitlin Circuit that Gates witnessed brimmed with Black spectators, centered Black lives in dramatic narratives, incorporated Black cultural references and content, and employed Black artists. In all certainty, the Black theatrical enterprising and onstage and offstage Black performance revelry of a bygone era of segregated Black stage shows were alive and thriving once again. As Gates revealed, some Black audiences were not only welcoming but also attuned to the aesthetic, ideological, and representational content, methods, and references of the Chitlin Circuit. Black pleasure, roasted in a history of enslavement, misrepresentation, ingenuity, enterprising, and risk-taking, was once again made lucrative, this time by Black artists presenting Black, yet controversial, narratives and representations within perhaps the most unlikely environs of American theatre.

Notes

1 Kenneth Stampp, *The Peculiar Institution: Slavery in the Ante-bellum South* (New York: Knopf, 1956), 285.
2 Amiri Baraka, *Home: Social Essays* (New York: Akashic Books, 2009), 121.
3 Helen Mendes, *The African Heritage Cookbook* (New York: The Macmillan Company, 1971), 103.
4 Jessica B. Harris makes mention of American slave plantations that allowed slaves to grow and harvest their own crops in either individual or shared garden spaces. Please see Jessica B. Harris, *Welcome Table: African-American Heritage Cooking* (New York: Fireside, 1995), 26.

5 Mendes, *The African Heritage Cookbook*; and Stampp, *The Peculiar Institution.*

6 Mendes, *The African Heritage Cookbook*, 59.

7 Stampp, *The Peculiar Institution,* 283.

8 Stampp, *The Peculiar Institution,* 285.

9 Stampp, *The Peculiar Institution,* 283.

10 Baraka, *Home*, 122.

11 Saidiya Hartman, *Scenes of Subjection: Terror, Slavery, and Self-Making in Nineteenth Century America* (Oxford: Oxford University Press, 2016), 21.

12 For more history on white performers of blackface minstrelsy, see Hartman, *Scenes of Subjection*; Lott, "Love and Theft," 23–50; and Bean, "Blackface Minstrelsy and Double Inversion, Circa 1890," 171–90.

13 Lott, "Love and Theft," 24; with quoted reference to Robert P. Nevin, "Stephen C. Foster and Negro Minstrelsy," *Atlantic Monthly* 20, no. 121 (1867): 608–16.

14 Lott, "Love and Theft," 24; as quoted in Nevin, "Stephen C. Foster and Negro Minstrelsy," 609–10.

15 Lott, "Love and Theft," 24.

16 Daphne Brooks, *Bodies in Dissent: Spectacular Performances of Race and Freedom, 1850–1910* (Durham and London: Oxford University Press, 2006).

17 Krasner, *Resistance, Parody, and Double-Consciousness in African American Theatre, 1895–1910* (New York: St. Martin's Press, 1997), 26.

18 Krasner, *Resistance, Parody, and Double-Consciousness in African American Theatre, 1895–1910*, 26.

19 Krasner, *Resistance, Parody, and Double-Consciousness in African American Theatre, 1895–1910*, 28.

20 Krasner, *Resistance, Parody, and Double-Consciousness in African American Theatre, 1895–1910*, 29.

21 Taylor Yuval and Jake Austen, *Darkest America: Black Minstrelsy from Slavery to Hip-Hop* (New York and London: W. W. Norton and Company and Austen, 2012), 73. For more on the performance history of African American tent shows, please consult Paige McGinley, *Staging the Blues: From Tent Shows to Tourism* (Durham, NC: Duke University Press, 2014).

22 Marvin McAllister, *White People Do Not Know How to Behave at Entertainments Designed for Ladies and Gentlemen of Colour: William Brown's African and African American Theater* (Chapel Hill: The University of North Carolina Press, 2003).

23 Krasner, *Resistance, Parody, and Double-Consciousness in African American Theatre, 1895–1910*, 26–27.

24 Krasner, *Resistance, Parody, and Double-Consciousness in African American Theatre, 1895–1910*, 29, 32.

25 For more details on Black performance during chattel slavery, please refer to Hartman, *Scenes of Subjection*; and Douglas A. Jones, Jr., *The Captive Stage: Performance and the Post-Slavery Imagination of the Antebellum North* (Ann Arbor: University of Michigan Press, 2014).

26 Bean, "Blackface Minstrelsy and Double Inversion, Circa 1890"; Nadine George-Graves, *The Royalty of Negro Vaudeville: The Whitman Sisters and the Negotiation of Race, Gender, and Class in African American Theatre, 1900–1940* (New York: St. Martin's Press, 2000).

27 For more information on touring African American vaudeville on Chitlin Circuit performance routes, see Henry Louis Gates, Jr., "Dept. of Disputation: The Chitlin Circuit," *The New Yorker*, February 3, 1997, 44–55; and Errol Hill and James Hatch, *A History of African American Theatre* (Cambridge: Cambridge University Press, 2003).

28 On any given night, performers presented an array of small shows in no particular order. These shows were unrelated in form, content, style, and performance quality. For more information, please see Robert W. Snyder, "The Vaudeville Circuit: A Prehistory

of the Mass Audience," in *Audiencemaking: How the Media Create the Audience*, ed. James S. Ettema and D. Charles Whitney (Thousand Oaks, CA: Sage Publications, 1994), 215–31; and Richard Butsch, *The Making of American Audiences: From Stage to Television, 1750–1990* (Cambridge: Cambridge University Press, 2001).

29 Snyder, "The Vaudeville Circuit," 228.
30 Snyder, "The Vaudeville Circuit," 222.
31 Snyder, "The Vaudeville Circuit," 228.
32 According to Butsch, variety theatre was most popular during the early to mid nineteenth century. On any given night, variety theatre performers would perform an array of small shows—in no particular order—that were all unrelated in form, content, style, and performance quality. The venues that housed variety shows ranged from saloons and music halls to middle- and upper-class society theatres. For additional details, please see Butsch, *The Making of American Audiences*, 95.
33 Butsch also discusses the existence of theatre houses during this time that catered to middle- and upper-class clientele who were interested in seeing melodrama. Plays such as *Richard III, Uncle Tom's Cabin*, and *Macbeth* were popular productions on these stages. Museums also created museum theatres during this time, which also became popular venues for these melodramatic productions, often catering to largely middle- and upper-class female audiences. Please see Butsch, *The Making of American Audiences*, 69, 72, 81.
34 Butsch, *The Making of American Audiences*, 108.
35 Snyder, "The Vaudeville Circuit," 226; Butsch, *The Making of American Audiences*, 116.
36 Butsch, *The Making of American Audiences*, 116–17.
37 Krasner, *Resistance, Parody, and Double-Consciousness in African American Theatre, 1895–1910*, 272.
38 Krasner, *Resistance, Parody, and Double-Consciousness in African American Theatre, 1895–1910*, 272.
39 For example, a theatrical booking agency called the Quality Amusement Corporation was formed in 1919 to cater to Midwestern cities. Although founded by white producer Robert Levi, the short-lived company was eventually comanaged by African American theatre critic Lester A. Walton and African American banker and theater owner E. C. Brown. Please see Krasner, *Resistance, Parody, and Double-Consciousness in African American Theatre, 1895–*1910, 273.
40 Please see Hill and Hatch, *A History of African American Theatre*; and David Krasner, *A Beautiful Pageant: African American Theatre, 1910–1927* (New York: Palgrave Macmillan, 2002).
41 Hill and Hatch, *A History of African American Theatre*, 206.
42 Krasner, *A Beautiful Pageant*, 274–75.
43 Krasner, *A Beautiful Pageant*, 274.
44 Krasner, *A Beautiful Pageant*, 275.
45 Warren Burdine, "Let the Theatre Say 'Amen'," *Black American Literature Forum* 25, no. 1 (1991): 76.
46 Warren Burdine, "The Gospel Musical and Its Place in the Black American Theatre," in *A Sourcebook of African-American Performance: Plays, People, Movements*, ed. Annmarie Bean (London and New York: Routledge, 1999), 190–203.
47 Burdine, "The Gospel Musical and Its Place in the Black American Theatre," 202.
48 August Wilson, "The Ground on Which I Stand," *Callaloo* 20, no. 3 (1998): 499.
49 Wilson, "The Ground on Which I Stand," 499.
50 Gates, "Dept. of Disputation," 44.
51 Gates, "Dept. of Disputation," 52; Rashida Z. Shaw McMahon, "Insert [Chitlin Circuit] Here: Teaching an *Inclusive* African American Theatre Course," Special Issue: Teaching African American Theatre, *Theatre Topics* 19, no. 1 (March 2009): 67–76.

3

LOOKING FOR LANGSTON

If, as Krasner has stated, Sherman Dudley entered the historical record of segregated Black touring entertainment as an entrepreneurial "forerunner"[1] to today's Chitlin Circuit theatre, I propose that we understand Hughes as its architect. In assigning Hughes the role of architect, I am asserting not only that he determined the ideological framework of this theatre but also that he shaped the political dimensions of its productions, its reception, and its performance venues. Hughes must also be recognized for defining the aesthetic terrain of circuit productions, including its necessary incorporation of gospel music, religion, and popular culture. As evidenced by the scripts, representations, and performances of his mid-century musicals, I read Hughes as engineering the performance environments and dramatic narratives that eventually gave rise to the theatrical fare of the contemporary Chitlin Circuit theatre.

In the twenty-first century, African American artists continued and continue to prove that they possess a penchant for dramatic voicing and a fearless command of imagination. At the same time, producers and performing artists persistently craft and execute stage presentations that pay homage to Black lives and Black art. And it is in the musical theatre productions of author and activist Langston Hughes during the late 1950s and early 1960s where this form was pioneered alongside the contours of contemporary circuit narratives, performances, spectatorship, and venues.

For Hughes, drama, like all of Black art, had the capacity to serve as both a mirrored reflection of Black experiences and a catalyst capable of igniting, disseminating, and celebrating Black culture. Yet as a younger Hughes lamented in his 1926 essay "The Negro Artist and the Racial Mountain," many of his peers refused to present a full spectrum of blackness in their work. They chose instead to focus on the elite and educated of the race. Hughes recalls a conversation that he had with an unidentified African American poet who proclaimed, "I want to be a poet—not a Negro poet."[2]

In response, Hughes reflects, "But this is the mountain standing in the way of any true Negro art in America—this urge in the race toward whiteness, the desire to pour racial individuality into the mold of American standardization, and to be as little Negro and as much American as possible."[3] From a contemporary vantage point, such preferences sound a figurative alarm and point a knowing finger toward how racism, Eurocentrism, and classism have coexisted alongside assimilationist and social mobility objectives in past and present African American realities. For Hughes, this blatant disregard and erasure of Negro life was negligent, if not also morally and politically unjust. The result of which was a glaring misrepresentation of Black lives and the loss of rich culture in developing African American art worlds. As the essay unfolds, Hall's "ordinary folks," who, notably, are the same "leftovers of history" featured in the work of August Wilson,[4] are identified by Hughes as the "low-down folks."[5]

Even more significant, however, are Hughes's allegiance with the "low-down folks"[6] and his equally public condemnation, as presented in this same essay, of his fellow artists for their inability to see the beauty and dimensionality of Black lives. He champions this ignored segment of the African American population in this representative passage:

> The people who have their nip of gin on Saturday nights and are not too important to themselves or the community, or too well fed, or too learned to watch the lazy world go round. They live on Seventh Street in Washington or State Street in Chicago and they do not particularly care whether they are like white folks or anybody else. Their joy runs, bang! into ecstasy. Their religion soars to a shout. Work maybe a little today, rest a little tomorrow. Play awhile. Sing awhile. O, let's dance! These common people are not afraid of spirituals, as for a long time their more intellectual brethren were, and jazz is their child. They furnish a wealth of colorful, distinctive material for any artist because they still hold their own individuality in the face of American standardizations.[7]

Without apology, Hughes found value in (re)presenting blackness, Black spaces, and Black expressions in narratives that were far removed from the noble environs of Du Bois's talented tenth[8] and his European-centric pageant play of 1911, *The Star of Ethiopia*.[9] Written in the context and climate of the New Negro Movement, Hughes's essay assertively positioned him as an artist interested in critiquing the sociological, psychological, and political contours of the representations crafted by him and others. Presented here as a critical precursor, Hughes's "low-down folks"[10] were enacting what Hall and other scholars would later refer to as "black cultural vernacular traditions."[11]

Rising to the surface of Hughes's ethnographically thick and dramatically rich description of everyday African Americans is the glaring revelation that he was documenting activities and cultural interests that would become legible signposts, among others, of African American popular expression, well beyond the time of his writing. Nesting in this passage are Hughes's descriptive associations of African American working-class community members. Free of the encumbrances of decorum, respectability politics,[12] and wealth, these are the Black Americans who are willing and capable of enjoying life to the fullest. Saturday nights feature alcohol, music, dance, and merriment. Their lives appear to be uncomplicatedly divided between work, play, and religious worship. Their limited education and economy seem to grant them full immersion into the world without pretense or barriers.

As typified by the placement of exclamation points in such sentences as "Their joy runs, bang! into ecstasy" and "O, let's dance!" Hughes aims to capture their movements, impulses, heightened emotions and jubilant celebrations. Yet Hughes's intentional use of punctuation adds visual and sonic dimensions to his textually bound tableaux. At the same time, Hughes's language also problematically caricatures and activates dominant stereotypes about African American bodies and aspects of African American culture that he so reveres.

While Hughes comes dangerously close to outright declaring that these African Americans inherently possess all that is authentic and real in the race, he does make sure to clearly assert their agency and purposefulness. Positing a political dimension to their ways of being and moving through the world, he adds that "they still hold their own individuality in the face of American standardizations."[13] Here, an African American demographic that is falsely assumed to be without worth, motivations, or awareness, even in Black spaces, are importantly read by Hughes to be folk who are clear about their preferences and priorities.

The interests, experiences, and liberties possessed by Hughes's "low-down folks" of the New Negro Movement era are enmeshed in the Black popular culture championed by Hall in the twentieth century. In his essay, "What is this 'Black' in Black Popular Culture?" Hall reminds us that

> popular culture always has its base in the experiences, the pleasures, the memories, the traditions of the people. It has connections with local hopes and local aspirations, local tragedies and local scenarios that are the everyday practices and the everyday experiences of ordinary folks.[14]

For both artist and scholar, there is a shared acknowledgment of the hierarchical stratification that affects the production, consumption, and categorization of African American art.

This genealogy, however, is not without its complications and complexities. Across and beyond the history and time of these publications, complicated questions concerned with the marked distinctions and blurred edges between "black,"

American, and popular culture continue to emerge. Here, Donald Byrd's essay "Twenty Questions," in Elam's and Kennell Jackson's edited anthology *Black Cultural Traffic: Crossroads in Global Performance and Popular Culture,* that begins with the following question comes to mind: "Today when we say 'black popular culture' do we really mean American popular culture?"[15] Indeed, when and under what conditions of granted and/or absent permission does "black" culture become American culture? Along this vein of parsing out the specifics, Byrd continues:

5. Is there a singular black culture or a singular black popular culture?
6. Which black are we talking about? Black Americans, black Caribbean, black African, black European . . . black . . . black black . . . black?
7. Can people of black African descent be the only ones to contribute to black culture? Would it still be black if nonblacks contributed?[16]

Hughes, Hall, and Byrd explicate stories of race, class, representation, consumption, and the consequences of each in the larger hegemonic framework of mass culture that selectively and consistently consumes Black culture.

Langston Hughes's musical theatre of the 1950s and 1960s served as a repository, progenitor, and catalyst for Black popular culture. Hughes's long-standing and sometimes fraught relationship with professional American theatre and the marked value that he placed on drama as a creative and political artform has been well documented by numerous biographers and scholars.[17] What rises to the surface in these documented histories and critiques is Hughes's insistence that the theatre created by, for, and about African Americans be one that stands on its own terms and reflects the diverse tableaux of African American lives.

Before Hughes embarked on his own blend of mid-century African American musical theatre, he had recently gained commercial and brief economic success as the African American writer who penned the operatic lyrics of *Street Scene*—Kurt Weill and Elmer Rice's 1947 Broadway adaptation of Rice's 1929 Pulitzer Prize winning play of the same name. Biographer Arnold Rampersad notes Hughes's historically cognizant excitement about being asked to be a part of the project as an African American artist, noting that their choice was "so remarkable as to be virtually without parallel in recent decades." Gone were the days when artists of color were readily employed on The Great White Way.[18]

> "That I, an American Negro, should be chosen to write the lyrics of *Street Scene* did not seem strange to Kurt Weil and Elmer Rice," he wrote. "They wanted someone who understood the problems of the common people. . . . They wanted someone who wrote simply. . . . I did not need to ask them why they thought of me for the task. I knew."[19]

Rampersad contextualizes further: "The two men wanted someone who knew all the aspects of the city but emphasized most with its working poor, whose humanity *Street Scene* would attempt to honor."[20] In this instance, Hughes's advocacy for the "low-down" and the ignored had qualified him to cross the color barrier on Broadway; this was a historically salient moment of inclusion and irony that should not be forgotten, particularly as we look forward to how Broadway would become a contested space for his own musicals, on racist and classist grounds.

Indeed, the glory of *Street Scene* would prove short-lived since Hughes struggled to secure African American dimensionality in mainstream theatrical fare due to a lack of creative and financial support. Just about one year after *Street Scene* embarked on Broadway, he sent a cautionary warning to his friend Arna Bontemps: "I WARN YOU ONE MORE TIME ABOUT FOOLING AROUND WITH THE THEATRE. . . . It does more than cripple your legs. It cripples your soul."[21] The soul crippling that Hughes would endure on Broadway, while debilitating in the moment, would lead to his theatrical awakening. The visionary dramatist would soon look beyond white frameworks and white contexts for his theatre.

Before Hughes's African American–centered musical theatre, the landscape of African American musicals held important precedents that should also be understood as informing and conditioning Hughes's theatrical innovations and their reception by Off-Broadway and Broadway audiences. Burdine reminds us that the winding history of what we now label *Chitlin Circuit theatre* is rooted in the milieu of Black and white stage performances that reach back to early-twentieth-century ragtime musicals of such companies as Cole & Johnson and Williams & Walker. Importantly, Burdine credits these "seemingly incongruous hybrids of the blackface minstrel shows and Gilbert & Sullivan operettas"[22] with "help[ing] to define the structure of the Broadway musical as we know it."[23] By the 1921 debut of *Shuffle Along*, the following 16 years of Broadway featured a wave of African American musicals that either were modeled after the song and dance routines of *Shuffle Along* or favored the operetta formats of the Cole & Johnson and Williams & Walker shows. These productions included the respective 1930s dramas *Green Pastures* (1930) and *Run, Little Chillun* (1933), both of which featured moments of embedded songs and music;[24] the 1940 production of *Cabin in the Sky*, which later became the first major Hollywood feature film based on a Broadway musical with an African American cast;[25] and the 1950s Caribbean-centric musicals *House of Flowers* (1954) and *Jamaica* (1957), which notably featured performances by African American performers Pearl Bailey, Diahann Carroll, and Lena Horne. It was not, however, until the productions of Hughes's musicals, beginning with *Simply Heavenly: A Comedy* that the gospel musical—or, what I am calling the Chitlin Circuit musical—was born.

Throughout Hughes's career, he produced numerous Black musicals, inclusive of operas, with varying success, beginning with *Troubled Island: An Opera in Three Acts* (1937) and culminating in *The Prodigal Son: A Song-Play with Traditional*

Spirituals, Gospel Hymns, and Songs Illuminating the Bible Story Retold (1965). Along the way, he penned numerous librettos, lyrics, and cantatas for other artists.[26] However, of utmost importance in establishing a historical lineage and foundation for contemporary Chitlin Circuit musical theatre are three productions of the late 1950s and early 1960s that were respectively produced on Broadway and Off-Broadway: *Simply Heavenly: A Comedy* (1957), *Black Nativity: A Gospel Song-Play for a Variable Cast* (1961) and *Tambourines to Glory: A Comedy* (1963).

Appearing eventually on Broadway,[27] *Simply Heavenly* added another chapter to the adventures of his fictional African American protagonist Jesse B. Semple, who came to life in 1943 as a fictional character in Hughes's weekly *Chicago Defender* column.[28] In 1954, Arthur P. Davis provided a vivid characterization of Hughes's creation in an article titled "Jesse B. Semple: Negro American."

> Mr. Jesse B. Semple, or Simple for short, is an uneducated Harlem man-about-town who speaks a delightful brand of English and who, from his stool at Paddy's Bar, comments both wisely and hilariously on many things, but principally on women and race. An unusual character in several respects, Simple's most appealing trait is that he is a Negro comic figure at whom Negroes themselves can laugh without being ashamed. Simple is so human, so believable, and so much like each of us that we are drawn to him; and our laughter is therapeutic because it tends to make us aware of our own cliché thinking on the race question, a shortcoming which we all evidence at one time or another.[29]

By the time Hughes wrote and produced *Simply Heavenly*, Simple's dialogues were no longer confined to the *Defender*. In total, five books were published before and after the musical that further chronicled the life, thoughts, and misadventures of Simple: *Simple Speaks His Mind* (1950), *Simple Takes a Wife* (1953), *Simple Stakes a Claim* (1957), *The Best of Simple* (1961), and *Simple's Uncle Sam* (1965).[30] Exactly who Simple was and what he represented was perhaps described best by the author himself. Taken from a 1945 article published in the journal *Phylon* titled "Simple and Me," Hughes described Simple plainly as "[J]ust myself talking to me. Or else me talking to myself."[31] Scholar James Smethurst, in his writings on the artist, considered Simple to be emblematic of Hughes's purposeful use of and attention to African American culture:

> For decades, Hughes had theorized, polemicized for, and practiced in his work broadly defined, but distinctly African-American literary forms, for decades drawing on a broad range of folk and popular genres: jazz, the blues, gospel, r&b, toasting, badman stories and songs, tall tales, black vaudeville humor, the dozens, and other forms of "signifying" street corner and barbershop conversations, sermons.[32]

With this in mind, it is no surprise that Simple's musical debut captured Hughes's interest in African American folk life presented in an urban locale filled with African American music and comedy. As Allen Woll notes,

> Hughes endeavored to transform the current state of Black entertainment on Broadway virtually on his own. While most "black" musicals of the 1950s featured a few prominent black performers in shows created by whites, Hughes attempted to forge a new black musical entertainment based on black sources with black casts and for black audiences.[33]

Although *Simply Heavenly*, a musical adaptation of the 1953 book *Simple Takes a Wife*, set in Paddy's Bar,[34] did not contain gospel music, it did contain brief references to African American religion, church life, and worshiping practices. Examples of this include, Joyce's reference to "communion Sunday" as a reason why she cannot drink a beer with Simple[35] and Simple's lengthy recollections of his devout, yet strict, Aunt Lucy.[36] Critically, as Woll notes, *Simply Heavenly* should be recognized as the "first of a series of Langston Hughes musicals that attempted to revive black musical theatre."[37] Indeed, Hughes's plot and representational content are significant to thinking through the historical foundation that it builds for contemporary Chitlin Circuit musicals; however, even more significant are the reviews and reception the musical received.

In the backdrop of a strengthening Civil Rights Movement, biographers and historians have noted that many of Hughes's most ardent supporters felt that the musical presented a dangerous emphasis on the kind of African American comedy that ventured too close to stereotype. Hughes's protagonist, Jesse B. Semple, bore the brunt of the negative critique. Identified in the play's list of characters as a Harlemite,[38] Semple was criticized as being a "far cry from the deeply humorous and brilliantly satirical denizen of Hughes's columns."[39] Rampersad recounts notable responses to the production that opened at the 85th Street Playhouse on May 21, 1957:

> At least two critics noted that blacks in the audience seemed to enjoy the play, its jokes and allusions and situations, more than their white fellow patrons did. But some blacks did not care at all for Simple in this theatrical guise. [African American playwright] Alice Childress, who had declined Langston's invitation to direct the show, was openly "disturbed and bewildered" by aspects of *Simply Heavenly*, especially its apparent scorn of the middle class and its contempt for integration; the play "did not ring true as a real reflection of Negro life." Still a major leader in the Communist Party, William L. Patterson, who saw the play with his equally committed wife, Louise Thompson Patterson, was blunt: "I cannot say that I liked it." Dismayed at the hedonism of Langston's characters who seemed to live only for food, dance, and sex, he quietly chastised the author: "To me, Lang, the

play was political. But the politics suited my enemy's—Simple's enemy's—aims and purposes in describing the Negro."[40]

Throughout the various incantations and revivals of *Simply Heavenly*, including its summer run at Manhattan's 85th Street Playhouse, its move to Broadway's 48th Street Playhouse for 62 shows; its brief production run at the Renata Theater on Bleeker Street; its debut performances in London's West End; its multiple restagings at historically Black colleges and universities in Washington, DC, and Florida; and, finally, its run before military audiences of the USO, Hughes witnessed how most practitioners and audiences, regardless of race, were unable to grasp the complex simplicity of Jesse P. Semple and his fictional counterparts.

> From various sources, Langston deduced that the enormous potential danger in dramatizing the Simple character—the tendency for the cast to lapse into farce and even burlesque, rather than offer a comic but dignified human being—had been realized. Apparently, [he reflected,] "in being restaged, Simple's original simplicity must have become real simple, and the accent shifted from a character study to entertainment—which doesn't quite come off."[41]

When mining the production, representation, and reception history of *Simply Heavenly*, it is important to remind ourselves of Rose's directives for examinations of Black popular culture. For Rose, any analysis of Black popular culture must investigate the text alongside the context:

> When we speak about the production of Black popular culture, we need to keep at least two kinds of questions in the foreground: the first has to do with Black aesthetics, style, and articulation, and the hybridization of Black practices; and the second involves the historical context for the creation, dissemination, and reception of Black popular forms.[42]

In thinking through the "aesthetics, style, and articulation" of *Simply Heavenly* Hughes's musical on its surface reads perhaps customarily as a play in two acts. Each act contains multiple short scenes with titles that succinctly name a scene's given location, such as Act 1 Scene 1 "Simple's room" or Act II Scene 6 "Lenox Avenue."[43]

Based on the 1959 Dramatists Play Service Acting Edition republished by Sanders,[44] Hughes spends careful time presenting purposeful character descriptions at the front of the text, displaying a vibrant range of Black Harlem across gender, age, status, interests, and personas. He carefully includes a general note at the top of the character descriptions that reads as follows:

> GENERAL The characters in "Simply Heavenly" are, on the whole, ordinary, hard-working lower-income bracket Harlemites, Paddy's Bar is like

a neighborhood club, and most of its patrons are not drunkards or bums. Their small kitchenette rooms or overcrowded apartments cause them to seek the space and company of the bar. Just as others seek the church as a social center, or the poolhall, or dancehall, these talkative ones seek the bar.[45]

In total, Act 1 contains seven scenes, and Act II contains 11. Harlem musician David Martin served as the composer of *Simply Heavenly*'s 11 musical numbers, presented as either folk or blues compositions and improvisations. With the combined artistic sensibilities of Hughes and Martin, *Simply Heavenly* seemed poised for success from an aesthetic standpoint as a dynamic product of African American artistry.

Yet as Rampersad indicates, the failure of *Simply Heavenly* was perhaps predictable due to the non-Black frame in which Hughes and Martin inserted their Black world; this was an issue that had also plagued Hughes's previous dramatic work:

> Since 1947, [Hughes] had tried and failed to duplicate the artistic and financial success of *Street Scene*. . . . These failures all had one element in common. Even when the composer and the setting were black, the base form had been essentially foreign to his own best inspiration, which had always come from black mass culture. When the social setting was mainly white, Langston virtually eliminated his chances of creating striking theater. In working on *Simply Heavenly* with Dave Martin as composer, he had consciously followed the loose format of the innovative *Pal Joey*[46]—a play with a few songs added—to produce a work squarely in the Broadway tradition. Now, with an inspired, unprecedented fusion of black music, evangelical religion, and Harlem melodrama, his new venture in musical theater would take him closer to the black masses.[47]

This new venture became realized in *Black Nativity* (1961) and *Tambourines to Glory* (1963). Woll mentions that the 1960s, post–*Simply Heavenly*'s production run, ignited a thriving artistic period for Hughes who presented a musical "almost yearly on or Off-Broadway."[48] Significantly, Woll also notes that "each [of these musicals] caused a varying degree of controversy as they veered away from accepted patterns of black musical theatre."[49] *Black Nativity* and *Tambourines to Glory* took on Hughes's growing interests in dramatizing African American religiosity. According to Leslie Catherine Sanders, signs of Hughes's engagement with African American religion and spirituality first appeared in his 1937 play *Don't You Want to Be Free?* This interracial "music drama"[50] begins with a historical look at the struggles of African Americans since slavery and then narratively transforms into a staged documentation of the shared economic and labor troubles of low-wage Black workers and low-wage white workers in Harlem.

Hughes incorporates spiritual songs into early sections of the play and acknowledges the pervasive significance of religion and spirituality in the lives of African
Americans. Notably, in their edited collection of African American plays, theatre
scholars James Hatch and Ted Shine identify *Don't You Want to Be Free?* as a mark
of "Hughes's departure from conventional play structure" and characterize the
"style" of the play as also being "evident in his later gospel musical plays."[51]

In *Black Nativity*, Hughes's African American adaptation of the birth story of
Jesus Christ, the dramatist saturated the narrative with popular and original gospel
music. He recruited Alex Bradford of the Greater Abyssinian Church of Newark,
New Jersey, to assist him in crafting new gospel music. Bradford's experience as a
composer stemmed from his dual positions in his Newark church as both musical director and ordained minister.[52] The well-known songs in the musical were
freely accessed through the public domain.[53] Calling the show a success would be
an understatement by the standards of its critics. In his discussion of the musical,
Woll recalls the climate of enthusiasm surrounding its New York debut and makes
note of the significance of its success:

> Howard Taubman in the *New York Times* led the raves: "How these singers
> can belt out a religious tune! They sing with the afflatus of jazzmen in a
> frenzy of improvisation. The rhythms are so vibrant that they seem to lead
> an independent existence. The voices plunge into sudden dark growls like
> muted trombones and soar into ecstatic squeals like frantic clarinets." With
> such strong approval, *Black Nativity* had a successful New York run and then
> embarked on a European tour, which climaxed triumphantly at the Spoleto
> Festival. Back in America, *Black Nativity* appeared once again in New York
> and then toured twenty-two cities. The show had a major role in legitimiz-
> ing gospel and (actual) black music in general on Broadway.[54]

Of additional importance in the production history of *Black Nativity* is Rampersad's unveiling that Hughes hired "a dynamic young black director" by the name
of Vinnette Carroll to direct the musical.[55] Carroll's presence and participation are
deeply significant in the context of *Black Nativity*'s success and popularity, insofar
as her role as the musical's Broadway director critically inserts a woman into both
the history of African American musicals writ large and into the early developing
years of Chitlin Circuit musical theatre. In both arenas, there is seemingly invisible and glaringly limited documentation and recognition of the role and presence
of African American women beyond performance or spectating. Yet in the case
of Hughes's *Black Nativity*, Carroll's contribution reveals that the contribution of
women in this history may become more readily accessible if we closely mine the
existing dominant narratives.

To be sure, it is Carroll's landmark direction of Hughes's musical that served
as the template for numerous national and international offshoots of Hughes's
musical. In this regard, Carroll, who would later go on to have an acclaimed

career in American theatre,[56] stands out as a female pioneer in contemporary Chitlin Circuit theatre who should not be forgotten. While the next chapter will visit the impact of Carroll's widely popular musical of the 1980s, *Your Arms Too Short to Box with God*, as we track Hughes's artistic contributions to contemporary Chitlin Circuit theatre through his musicals, it is important to, albeit briefly, acknowledge how *Black Nativity* engendered and supported the voice and visions of women in its nascent stages. If Hughes's *Black Nativity*, made complete by Carroll's direction, served as the dramatist's polished template for evocatively and accurately depicting working-class dimensions of African American life, religion, and spirituality through song, then his 1963 production of *Tambourines to Glory* is an extension of the same formula. This time, however, Hughes was committed to presenting a musical that reflected all of his political, cultural, and artistic leanings.

Audiences of *Tambourines to Glory* were introduced to Hughes's full-fledged commitment to creating an urban musical drama that showcased both well-known and new play-specific gospel music. In Hughes's own words, this musical differed from his previous ones in that it used gospel music as "an actual part of the play itself."[57] Set in Harlem, the play begins with a money-scheming character named Laura convincing a pious woman by the name of Essie to restart a ministry on the streets of Harlem. The pair eventually gain enough followers to move into a storefront church. Throughout the course of the musical, the audience becomes well acquainted with the various street characters who frequent their church—hustlers, saints, sinners, fake prophets, and devout believers, to name a few—all of whom are attending services in the hopes of making "a way out of no way." By the play's end, good overcomes evil and God prevails. The last scene of the musical ends in testimonies and a riveting song sung by all cast members with lyrics that redirect us back to the title of the play: "Shake it to the glory of God! Tambourines! Tambourines! Tambourines to Glory!"[58]

Hughes began working on the musical he termed an "'urban-folk-Harlem-*genre*- melodrama' based squarely on the black gospel tradition" in 1956.[59] He completed *Tambourines to Glory* in rapid speed during a ten-day period and described it as a "singing, shouting, wailing drama . . . of the old conflict between blatant Evil and quiet Good, with the Devil driving a Cadillac."[60] In his hopeful imaginings for the production, he envisioned a star-studded cast of esteemed and popular African American artists of the time, including Pearl Bailey, Dorothy Dandridge, Mahalia Jackson, and Harry Belafonte.[61] By the time Hughes's artistry led him to create the musical version of *Tambourines to Glory*, he seemed to be keenly aware of the crucial and mutually beneficial relationship that the popular could have with the theatre. Before the musical's theatrical debut, a buzz had already generated about the material through Hughes's publication of a novel, a 70-page novella,[62] and an album release of 11 gospel songs.[63] These three offshoots were authored by Hughes after he finished writing the musical and were marketed under the same name.

Hughes appeared to be extremely cognizant of the mechanisms behind popular culture and the importance of the sociocultural environment and context in which his musical would be produced. The eight years between the writing of *Tambourines to Glory* in 1956 and its Broadway performance in 1963 are a moment wherein Hughes cultivated Broadway audiences in a deliberate and calibrated fashion. By publishing, producing, and distributing three media versions of *Tambourines to Glory*, Hughes single-handedly aimed to condition the horizons of expectations of his multipronged audience—the discerning everyday African Americans from Harlem, the representational-minded African American intelligentsia, and the unforgiving and unaccustomed white critics of American theatre. There is also an important marketing and economic dimension to this history. By pre-distributing musical-related material, before the show was even cast, Hughes founded the primary template for how contemporary gospel musicals—the kind created and produced by later playwrights in this study—create and garner multimedia and multi-genre appeal. Unfortunately, thus far, these approaches have falsely been assumed to be the brainchildren and/or manipulations of late-twentieth-century and early-twenty-first-century circuit artists.

Alas, in spite of its fresh innovations, *Tambourines to Glory* only lasted a few notable weeks on Broadway and received a plethora of negative reviews. Without recounting those reviews in their entirety,[64] critics questioned Hughes's representations of African Americans in ways that are notably similar to the stated problems and criticisms of *Simply Heavenly*. Soyica Diggs Colbert reminds us in her account of this history that performance and temporal context matter:

> Even though Hughes wrote the play in 1956, by the time it was staged in 1963 white theatregoers had lost interest in drama that overtly drew its idiom from vernacular culture without challenge, and black theatregoers were critical of the political implications of a play that critiqued the black church in a moment when the church served as a bedrock of political action. Nevertheless, two months after the historic March on Washington, in the midst of unease, *Tambourines to Glory* opened at the six-hundred seat Little Theater on Forty-Fourth Street near Broadway. And, as expected, the audience immediately interrogated the play's political position.[65]

One critic, Laurence Langer, the co-founder of the Theatre Guild, called the musical "Uncle Tommish and generally demeaning of blacks."[66] Other reviewers of *Tambourines to Glory* brought a unique aspect of intrigue into the foreground by questioning whether Broadway was a suitable venue for this kind of theatre. It appears that while Hughes seemed to be attuned to three of DuBois's dictates for African American theatre—authored *by*, produced *for*, and topically *about* African Americans—the innovative dramatist neglected to realize that legitimized Broadway and Off-Broadway venues were in no way *near* enough to the Harlem environs that he loved to depict in his work.[67] Theatre critic Martin Goddfried's comments stand out in this regard:

> warm, exuberant, modern Negro folk musical ... deeply rooted in the ethnic patterns of the Harlem Negro. And in that may lie the drawback of this musical for many non-Negroes, the attitudes, humor and personal flavor of a particular group hold an enormous amount of warmth and affection for its members ... [but] often become uninteresting and foolish to outsiders.[68]

Taubman also weighed in on the show and this time without the fanfare he had previously showered on *Black Nativity*:

> For this gospel singing play ... has the look of something slapped together. As drama it is embarrassing; it cannot make up its mind to a point of view, and it shifts carelessly from comedy to satire to melodrama to piety. Its characterizations is [*sic*] as casual as a comic strip's. And the story drags foolishly and gets in the way of the singing.[69]

Rampersad provides even more context from the vantage point of African Americans in a representative example from the esteemed Anna Arnold Hedgeman, a member of the National Council of Churches, the St. Marks Church, and YWCA, who described the production as "dreadful," among other choice words.

The production company received word that protests against the show were being organized to take place outside of the theatre. In kind, Hughes and Jobe Huntley, the show's composer, planned to respond with placards of their own. Hughes's declaration would proclaim "YOUR MAMA LIKES GOSPEL SONGS," and Huntley would be nearby with his emphatic closing statement: "AND I WRITE THEM."[70] African American playwright Loften Mitchell deduced that while dramas centered on African American churches and the corruption that can occur in them rings true to reality, these topics were not of interest to white consumers. He cautioned anyone who felt that *Tambourines to Glory* represented Hughes's disdain for African American religion. On the contrary, as a long-standing friend of Hughes, he stated that he knew first-hand about the artist's religious upbringing and personal dislike of immoral and illegal activities in the church.[71]

Taken together, this social and political history of *Simply Heavenly*, *Black Nativity*, and *Tambourines to Glory* opens the path toward deeply contextualizing contemporary Chitlin Circuit musical theatre. Despite the harsh criticisms that *Tambourines to Glory* received, aspects of the form, narrative content, aesthetics, and methods of audience engagement continue to be prevalent in future African American–written dramas and musicals of the 1960s, the white-produced musical adaptations of Black dramas of the 1970s and later in the resurgence of Black gospel musicals of the 1980s.[72]

What has also become readily apparent in this history is that Hughes's "failures" were in part due to his desire to be legitimized in the non-Black spaces of Broadway and Off-Broadway. After the harsh reviews of *Simply Heavenly*, he in fact lamented about the impossible task of pleasing all of his critics:

> it's the old story—and the problem I've been wrestling with for years—how to get everything to suit everybody in one piece. When it comes to plays, it's a miracle to end up with anything at all one wishes left in the play.[73]

In *Black Nativity*, Hughes not only achieved the successful integration of gospel music into the narrative but also succeeded in bringing the communal environment, revelry, and theological gravitas of Harlem's churches to the stage—a benefit of his ethnographic sojourns to local Harlem institutions of worship.[74]

While *Tambourines to Glory* has traditionally been read as a failure for the artist, the musical and its subsequent productions serve as an early signpost that urges us to critically think through the historical and contemporary import of Black and non-Black performance venues, post-segregation, alongside an attention to the complexity of Black representation, specifically the images and articulations of working-class African Americans, in comedic narratives. Moreover, the interconnected history of enslavement, cuisine, minstrelsy, and the cultivation of early African American agency and entrepreneurship in theatrical performance being read alongside the motivations, failures, and successes of Hughes's gospel musicals not only foment a history of Black theatrical pleasure but also, once again, illuminate how Black artistry, minority spectatorship, and Black theatrical pleasure have been conditioned by historical precedents en route to Chitlin Circuit theatre.

Perhaps as a testament to the difficult contexts and harsh consequences of this conditioning, Rampersad and other critics have documented Hughes's strong departure from comedy in his musicals after *Tambourines to Glory*. Returning to more respectable character depictions set in a politically grounded dramatic narrative, Hughes's next gospel musical, *Jericho-Jim Crow: A Song Play* (1964), departed from comedy, Harlem-based popular culture, the Black church as a central setting, and stereotype. Hughes's new gospel incantation revisited the pristine dialogues and representations of the well-received *Don't You Want to Be Free?* of 1937. In *Jericho-Jim Crow*, Hughes paid direct attention to the political and cultural climate of the 1960s that he had been working in, yet avoiding, in his previous musicals. *Jericho-Jim Crow* focused on the ongoing fight for equality during the Freedom Movement, with an eye on the proud heritage of African Americans, despite enslavement and persecution, and a forward sight toward a more positive and more progressive future. Notably, after *Black Nativity* and *Tambourines to Glory*, Hughes still sought audience identification and participation via popular cultural content. As an example of this, the musical's opening stage directions partly read the following: "*The songs may be sung in the gospel manner or as traditional spirituals. Audience participation is invited on familiar songs, particularly at the end of the play.*"[75]

As the archives document, Hughes's theatrical redirection, which debuted Off-Broadway in the Greenwich Mews Theater, worked! *Jericho-Jim Crow* is noted as being Hughes's most successful theatrical work at that point in his career, praised by one critic as "a major landmark in the history of American theatre."[76] Although Hughes's soul had been uncomfortably stirred by his major musical failures, it is clear that he was still determined to innovate and experiment with gospel musical content and presentation in Off-Broadway and Broadway settings. And it is Hughes's determination, sweat, grind, and aspiration that lay at the foundation of the contemporary Chitlin Circuit. Put simply, today's Chitlin Circuit lives in the house that Langston built.

Notes

1 Krasner, *A Beautiful Pageant: African American Performance, Drama, and Performance in the Harlem Renaissance, 1910–1927* (New York and Palgrave MacMillan, 2002), 275.

2 Langston Hughes, "The Negro Artist and the Racial Mountain," *The Nation* 122 (June 23, 1926): 692.

3 Hughes, "The Negro Artist and the Racial Mountain," 692.

4 The phrase "leftovers of history" is spoken by the character Toledo in August Wilson's 1984 play *Ma Rainey's Black Bottom*, set in a Chicago recording studio in 1927. In dialogue with Levee in Act 1, Toledo says, "That's what you is. That's what we all is. A leftover from history." Please see, August Wilson, *Ma Rainey's Black Bottom* (New York: Penguin Group USA Inc., 1985), 57.

5 Hall, "What Is This 'Black' in Black Popular Culture?" 25; Hughes, "The Negro Artist and the Racial Mountain," 692; and Wilson, *Ma Rainey's Black Bottom*, 57.

6 Hughes, "The Negro Artist and the Racial Mountain," 693.

7 Hughes, "The Negro Artist and the Racial Mountain," 693.

8 In 1903, W. E. B. Du Bois charged educated African Americans with the task of uplifting the entire race. By his estimation, 10 percent of African Americans fell into this fortunate and well-educated category. He continued to expand on this classification throughout the course of his life work.

9 For an in-depth critical history and theoretical analysis of Du Bois's turn-of-the-century pageant play, *The Star of Ethiopia*, please see Soyica Diggs Colbert, *The African American Theatrical Body: Reception, Performance, and the Stage* (New York and Cambridge: Cambridge University Press, 2011).

10 Hughes, "The Negro Artist and the Racial Mountain," 693.

11 Hall, "What Is This 'Black' in Black Popular Culture?" 22.

12 Darlene Clark Hine, *Hine Sight: Black Women and the Re-Construction of American History* (Brooklyn, NY: Carlson, Pub., 1994).

13 Hughes, "The Negro Artist and the Racial Mountain," 693.

14 Hall, "What Is This 'Black' in Black Popular Culture?" 25.

15 Donald Byrd, "Twenty Questions," in *Black Cultural Traffic: Crossroads in Global Performance and Popular Culture*, ed. Harry J. Elam, Jr. and Kennell Jackson (Ann Arbor: The University of Michigan Press, 2005), ix.

16 Byrd, "Twenty Questions," ix.

17 Notable works that discuss Hughes's artistic endeavors include, Colbert, *The African American Theatrical Body*; Harry J. Elam, Jr. and Michele Elam, "Blood Debt: Reparations in Langston Hughes's *Mulatto*," *Theatre Journal* 61, no. 1 (March 2009): 85–103; Leslie Catherine Sanders, *The Collected Works of Langston Hughes: Gospel Plays, Operas, and Later Dramatic Works*, ed. Leslie Catherine Sanders, vol. 6 (Columbia and London: University

of Missouri Press, 2004); and Arnold Rampersad, *The Life of Langston Hughes: Volume II: 1941–1967, I Dream a World*, 2nd ed. (Oxford and New York: Oxford University Press, 2002).

18 Rampersad, *The Life of Langston Hughes*, 109.

19 Rampersad, *The Life of Langston Hughes*, 109.

20 Rampersad, *The Life of Langston Hughes*, 109.

21 Rampersad, *The Life of Langston Hughes*, 157. Also requoted in Sanders, *The Collected Works of Langston Hughes*, 10.

22 Burdine, "Let the Theatre Say 'Amen'," 73.

23 Burdine, "The Gospel Musical and Its Place in the Black American Theatre," 191.

24 Burdine, "Let the Theatre Say 'Amen'," 74.

25 Allen L. Woll, *Black Musical Theatre: From Coontown to Dreamgirls* (New York: Da Capo Press, Inc., 1989), 195.

26 Sanders, *The Collected Works of Langston Hughes*, vii–ix.

27 Sanders, *The Collected Works of Langston Hughes*, 235.

28 Arthur P. Davis, "Jesse B. Semple: Negro American," *Phylon* 15, no. 1 (1st Quarter 1954): 21.

29 Davis, "Jesse B. Semple," 21.

30 Phillis R. Klotman, "Langston Hughes's Jesse B. Semple and the Blues," *Phylon* 36, no. 1 (1st Quarter 1975): 68.

31 Langston Hughes, "Simple and Me," *Phylon* 6, no. 4 (4th Quarter 1945): 349.

32 James P. Smethurst, "'Don't Say Goodbye to the Porkpie Hat': Langston Hughes, the Left, and the Black Arts Movement," *Callaloo* 25, no. 4 (Autumn 2002): 1229.

33 Woll, *Black Musical Theatre*, 235.

34 Leslie Catherine Sanders, "'I've Wrestled with Them All My Life': Langston Hughes's *Tambourines to Glory*," Special Issue: The Black Church and the Black Theatre, *Black American Literature Forum* 25, no. 1 (Spring 1991): 67.

35 Sanders, *The Collected Works of Langston Hughes*, 186.

36 Sanders, *The Collected Works of Langston Hughes*, 200–1.

37 Woll, *Black Musical Theatre*, 235.

38 Sanders, *The Collected Works of Langston Hughes*, 180.

39 Sanders, *The Collected Works of Langston Hughes*, 179.

40 Rampersad, *The Life of Langston Hughes*, 271–72.

41 Rampersad, *The Life of Langston Hughes*, 283.

42 Rose, "Black Texts/Black Contexts," 223.

43 Sanders, *The Collected Works of Langston Hughes*, 181.

44 Sanders, *The Collected Works of Langston Hughes* [provide citation info for 1959 Dramatists Play Service Acting Edition of Simply Heavenly used in Sanders' book].

45 Sanders, *The Collected Works of Langston Hughes*, 182.

46 *Pal Joey* is an original 1940 Broadway musical with current revivals and the subject of a 1957 film adaptation. John O'Hara penned the book and Richard Rodgers and Lorenz Hart wrote and produced the music. For a broader history of the musical, please see Stempel, *Showtime*.

47 Rampersad, *The Life of Langston Hughes*, 254–55.

48 Woll, *Black Musical Theatre*, 237.

49 Woll, *Black Musical Theatre*, 237.

50 Sanders, *The Collected Works of Langston Hughes*, 63.

51 James V. Hatch and Ted Shine, *Black Theatre, U. S. A.: The Early Period 1847–1938, Revised and Expanded Edition* (New York: The Free Press, 1996), 266.

52 Hatch and Shine, *Black Theatre, U. S. A.*, 346.

53 Hatch and Shine, *Black Theatre, U. S. A.*, 345.

54 Woll, *Black Musical Theatre*, 238.

55 Rampersad, *The Life of Langston Hughes*, 346.

56 Calvin A. McClinton, *The Work of Vinnette Carroll: An African American Theatre Artist* (Lewiston, NY: Edwin Mellen Press, 2000).

57 Woll, *Black Musical Theatre*, 239.

58 Sanders, "I've Wrestled with Them All My Life," 349.

59 Rampersad, *The Life of Langston Hughes*, 255.

60 Rampersad, *The Life of Langston Hughes*, 255.

61 Rampersad, *The Life of Langston Hughes*, 256.

62 Rampersad, *The Life of Langston Hughes*, 256.

63 Rampersad, *The Life of Langston Hughes*, 290–91.

64 Rampersad, *The Life of Langston Hughes*; and Woll, *Black Musical Theatre* are great starting points for unearthing these inquiries.

65 Colbert, *The African American Theatrical Body*, 158.

66 Rampersad, *The Life of Langston Hughes*, 322.

67 In the 1926 publication of *The Crisis* magazine, W. E. B. Du Bois proclaimed that African American theatre should adhere to four "fundamental principles." This theatre should be "about us," "by us," "for us," and "near us." Notably, Du Bois contextualizes "near us," in ways that are critical to understanding the importance he was placing on performance space and its proximity to "ordinary" blackness. He writes, "The theatre must be in a Negro neighborhood near the mass of ordinary Negro people." Please see Du Bois, "Krigwa Players Little Negro Theatre," 134; quoted in Krasner, *A Beautiful Pageant*, 214.

68 Sanders, *The Collected Works of Langston Hughes*, 65–66.

69 Howard Taubman, "Tambourines: 'Gospel Singing Play' Is at Little Theater," *New York Times*, November 1963, 46, Sec. 4.

70 Rampersad, *The Life of Langston Hughes*, 370.

71 Rampersad, *The Life of Langston Hughes*, 370.

72 For a chronologically driven discussion and analysis of African American musicals during this time period, which includes the broader history of Black gospel musicals, please see Woll, *Black Musical Theatre*; Burdine, "Let the Theatre Say 'Amen'"; and Burdine, "The Gospel Musical and its Place in the Black American Theatre."

73 Rampersad, *The Life of Langston Hughes*, 272.

74 Rampersad, *The Life of Langston Hughes*, 345.

75 Sanders, *The Collected Works of Langston Hughes*, 256.

76 Rampersad, *The Life of Langston Hughes*, 372.

4

DAVID TALBERT

Resurrecting Langston

(*The lights come up on two bands of CHRISTIANS entering from either side, marching in time to the music, as the NARRATOR sits to one side.*)
(*SONG: "MEETIN' HERE TONIGHT"*)
SINGERS THERE'S A MEETIN' HERE TONIGHT,
MEETIN' HERE TONIGHT,
MEETIN' ON THE OLD CAMPGROUND.
NARRATOR And so the star of Bethlehem became a symbol. The manger became a church. The three kings became Princes of the Church. Wise men became its ministers. The heavenly hosts became the singers of God's praises all over the world—for almost two thousand years ago now in the Bethlehem of Judea, Christ was born—born to preach to the elders in the temple—to pass the miracle of the loaves and fishes—to turn water into wine—to heal the sick and raise the dead—to cause the lame to walk and the blind to see. He was crucified, dead, and was buried, and on the third day arose from the dead, ascended into heaven and sitteth at the right hand of God, the Father—who gave His only begotten Son that man might have eternal life. Now, today, here in this place, nineteen centuries removed from Bethlehem—in a land far across the sea from Judea—we sing His songs and glorify His name. This church where you see us gathered—this gospel church where His word is spread—is but an extension of His manger. Those gathered here are His worshippers who have come tonight to make—as the Bible says—a joyful noise unto the Lord.
—Langston Hughes, *Black Nativity*[1]

The second act of Langston Hughes's 1961 musical *Black Nativity: A Gospel Song-Play for a Variable Cast* begins with this sequence of performance events. If effectively realized onstage, this opening act not only reorients spectators back into the sanctified world of the musical, after a possible intermission, but also successfully conjures an African American church environment, perhaps most associated with African American Baptist and Pentecostal denominations. The lyrics in the singers'/choir's song "Meetin' Here Tonight" frame the event and aurally, if not also performatively, signal to live audiences of the musical that they are no longer simply attending a play; rather, they are and have been in a sanctified space of worship and praise. The narrator's monologue joins in this effort as it guides the audience through an aesthetic conjuring: the stage becomes an altar, the performers become biblical practitioners, and spectators become assembled congregants. Hughes's *Black Nativity*, a musical brimming with biblical text and imagery, becomes a praise event—"in a land far across the sea from Judea"—that celebrates the birth of Jesus Christ, as it didactically preaches to the sinners and the saved in its auditorium.

I read *Black Nativity* as the most sanctified wing of Hughes's gospel musical triad— *Simply Heavenly: A Comedy* (1957), *Black Nativity: A Gospel Song-Play for a Variable Cast* (1961), and *Tambourines to Glory: A Comedy* (1963)—and, in this vein, I position it as the aesthetic and ideological core of Hughes's gospel musical productions. Literally set within an environment of worship, *Black Nativity* is less of a dramatic narrative and more of a dramatic staging of popularly represented African American church ideologies, aesthetics, and practices. Although, as I have discussed, Hughes departs from a sanctified environment in his next musical *Tambourines to Glory*, it is the faith-based core of *Black Nativity* that this chapter will unpack, as it is repackaged and transferred to *Tambourines to Glory* and then resurrected in the late-twentieth-century work of circuit playwright David Talbert.

In Hughes's creative transition from *Black Nativity* to *Tambourines to Glory*, metaphors become grounded realities, and everyday contexts foreground heightened text. Examples of this include, Hughes's substitution of universal characters in *Black Nativity*—such as Woman, Man, Singers, Narrator, Old Woman, Four Shepherds, and Elder—for specific and named African American characters, such as Laura Wright Reed, Essie Belle Johnson, and Big-Eyed Buddy Lomax. Settings and contexts also illuminate how the central aesthetic environment of *Black Nativity* is transplanted into the real and lived spaces of Harlem, New York. Whereas *Black Nativity*'s audiences experienced *church* through textual and aesthetic invocations, the settings in *Tambourines to Glory* are literally set in a diegetic storefront church and temple, among other neighborhood places, that are rife with immoral secular issues. Popular culture is also deployed differently across the musicals. In *Black Nativity*, Hughes relies on an audience's ability to identify, connect, and be moved by established and circulated iconicity and textual references from the Bible as well as positive representations of African American worship practices. Differently so, in *Tambourines to Glory*, secular and popularized gospel music are packaged alongside gospel originals in a musical that contains positive and negative cultural references and images that were circulated in Black popular culture at that time. The characters and content of *Tambourines to Glory* would have been far removed from the mainstream representation of African American church and life and, as the harsh reviews reflected, alienating to racial outsiders and embarrassing to higher-class gatekeepers of African American culture. Looking through these lenses, I connect Hughes's *Tambourines to Glory* to the work of twentieth-century circuit playwright David Talbert in order to capture repetitions, consistencies, innovations, and departures. As I have written elsewhere, "Joseph Roach reminds us, 'performances so often carry within them the memory of otherwise forgotten substitutions—those that were rejected and, even more invisibly, those that have succeeded.'"[2] Along this vein, I am interested in drawing a nuanced line between the musicals of Hughes and those of Talbert in order to excavate, identify, and trace nuances in the faith-based theatrical aesthetics that lie at the core of Chitlin Circuit theatre. Always and already, I am particularly attuned to the ways that contemporary aesthetic choices in the circuit illuminate how Black artistry, minority spectatorship, and Black theatrical pleasure in Chitlin Circuit theatre are conditioned by historical precedents and innovatively pursued and realized by its practitioners.

Inspirational Theatre and "Romantic Inspirationals," According to Talbert

David E. Talbert's achievements and distinctions in the arena of contemporary circuit theatre set him apart in the field as an accomplished and established elder among his peers. His career on the circuit spans 25 years and began well before African American audiences became familiar with the names Je'Caryous Johnson, Gary Guidry, or Tyler Perry. A graduate of Morgan State University and an accelerated film program at New York University,[3] Talbert, who some refer to as the "original Tyler Perry,"[4] has developed a patented contemporary circuit product with a loyal and US-wide fanbase by rendering dramatic presentations of African American relationships in the established framework of circuit musicals.

A typical Talbert production centers on the love relationship of two middle-class, heterosexual African Americans and their day-to-day experiences in their home, work, and/or neighborhood environment. Plays are usually set in modern and urban settings in major US cities. The surrounding characters represent a range of age, gender, and economic means. Although Talbert's plays tend to be serious in nature, in all cases, there are one or more characters who periodically inject the narratives with comedic relief. Although religion is a necessary component of contemporary circuit productions, in most cases, Talbert's characters do not come across as overtly religious. Generally, his characters demonstrate their spirituality through casual professions of faith, morals, and Christian values; however, exceptions to this model do occur and sometimes depend on whether a church interior is used as an actual setting. While his productions use gospel songs, they proportionally tend to incorporate more secular music than sacred or religiously oriented music. In addition, Talbert stands out as the only circuit playwright of the four in this project who expands his presentation of secular music to include jazz. Talbert uses jazz as an additional sensory layer in his shows. His musicals are made complete by the musical renderings of live musicians who provide the instrumentation for the show's multiple gospel and R&B numbers sung by various actors. The live band also underscores scenic action and dialogue with original jazz compositions. In fact, the use of music is so pervasive in Talbert's productions that the non-musical moments are used to emphasize important scenic action. Similar to his counterparts, his celebrity casting and character-specific costuming decisions are made intentionally, and the plays take place on functional and moving sets with integrated lighting designs.[5]

Talbert attributes his start in theatre to a California production of Shelly Garrett's *Beauty Shop* that made him think to himself, "Wow, people are laughing at this and I could do something. . . . I went home that night and started my first play."[6] A vision was born, and Talbert left the familiar terrain of disc jockeying on the radio, a job that he had done in Baltimore, Oakland, and San Francisco, for a career in writing for the stage.[7] Since then Talbert has written, directed, and produced numerous circuit productions. In the order of their national touring dates, some of his most recognizable musicals are *Tellin' it Like It Tiz* (1991–1993); *Lawd Ha' Mercy* (1993); *What Goes Around Comes Around* (1994); *He Say . . . She Say . . . But What Does God Say?* (1996); *A Fool and His Money* (1997); *Talk Show Live* (1998); *Mr. Right Now* (1999); *His Woman, His Wife* (2000); *The Fabric of A Man* (2000–2001); *Love Makes Things Happen* (2002); *Love on Lay Away* (2003); *Love In the Nick of Tyme* (2007); *What My Husband Doesn't Know* (2011); *Suddenly Single* (2012); and *Another Man Will* (2015). Many of his plays have received nominations and awards from the National Association for the Advancement of Colored People (NAACP) Image Awards committee in the categories of best play, best playwright, best supporting role, best wardrobe, best lead actor, and best director. His plays *The Fabric of a Man* and *Love in the Nick of Tyme* were also selected as the New York Literary Award's Best Play in their respective years of publication. As highlighted in Fern Gillespie's article, Talbert was also the 2008 recipient of the NAACP Trailblazer Award in honor of his body of work across theatre, film, television, and fiction-writing.[8]

In many respects, Talbert's varied personal, educational, and vocational experiences contribute to his diversity as an artist and heavily influence his work. In his interview with Chris Lee for the *Los Angeles Times*, the Washington, DC, native notes that he "was brought up in an immersive religious background—his great-grandmother was a Pentecostal preacher, his grandmother is a touring evangelist, his mother was a preacher and his father and brother are pastors."[9] Despite this deeply religious upbringing, Talbert says that

> he grounds his optimistic worldview with real-world experiences. . . . He has resisted putting any specific dogma into his plays, bestselling novels . . . and movie[s] in lieu of more general social messages. "I'm not a religious

guy," Talbert said. "There's a much bigger audience when you're not hitting them over the head with, 'You have to feel this way or feel that way to take part.' A lot of times, religion can be a way to keep people from coming together."[10]

This faith-based yet secular approach to his work is grounded by his bachelor of arts in marketing degree from Morgan State University[11] and his completion of an accelerated film program at New York University.[12] In 1997 and 2008, respectively, he wrote and directed two screenplays that share similar themes with his stage work: *A Woman Like That* and *First Sunday*. In recent years, he has continued to work in the medium of film as a writer, producer, and director of the films *Baggage Claim* (2013) and *Almost Christmas* (2016). He has also directed films for Netflix, such as *El Camino Christmas* (2017) and *Jingle Jangle*, which is expected to be released in 2020. Talbert's television resume includes his stint as a sitcom writer for the UPN network, his role as a producer of the nationally televised musical television special *Jamie Foxx's Unpredictable: A Musical Journey* (2006), and his involvement as coproducer and star of his own television reality series *Stage Black* (2007)[13] that aired on the TV One network. He has written and published three novels: *Baggage Claim* (2003), *Love Don't Live Here No More* (2006)—coauthored with hip hop musical artist Snoop Dogg—and *Love on the Dotted Line* (2005). To date, Talbert remains the only circuit playwright to publish and make available a collection of some of his performance texts in the 2001 book *The Collected Plays of The People's Playwright, Volume 1*.[14]

While the overall form and content of Talbert's theatre allow his musicals to fit neatly under the umbrella of contemporary Chitlin Circuit theatre, I aim to make recognizable how every aspect of Talbert's musicals—including writing, directing, music, and acting—are executed in adherence to the playwright's cultivated aesthetic philosophy, which he labels *inspirational theatre*. I am also keenly interested in how the playwright incorporates faith-based ideologies into contemporary circuit narratives. A third major avenue of inquiry tracks how Talbert transforms uninhibited circuit spectators who freely respond to onstage presentations into controlled character-like participants whose dialogue, responses, and actions are largely predetermined by the writer-director-producer. I begin with a look at the playwright's perspective on his work.

In March 2007, I interviewed Talbert for a feature article that was later published in Chicago's weekly entertainment magazine *Time Out Chicago*.[15] During our conversation, he revealed that he began writing "because of a broken heart":

[A]ffairs of the heart really got me into writing and so I guess that's what will sustain me. Those are the most interesting things in our community . . . how we get along as man and woman, you know. It's really the foundation of everything. Once we can . . . if we can ever fix that, everything else can kind of flow from that.[16]

I later asked him to tell me about his formula for writing and developing his plays, to which he responded with the following:

> Well, I think anyone who you can credit for something I don't really think they had a formula. I think what they did was put their heart and soul into their work. You know, I love love. I love love. You know my wife [Lyn Talbert] tells me, you know, that I live with the Easter Bunny and the Toothfairy and my mother used to always say, well you know, "you live in this make-believe world, but one of these days you're gonna have to, you know, deal with reality." And I believe in fairytales. I believe in that. So, I'm not writing to try to cater to an audience. I'm writing what is really from my heart and my soul and that's what helps it resonate with the audience. Because I always say that you can't touch people unless you're first touched yourself, so I'm affected and touched by [my] material first which helps other people to be touched when they get a chance to experience it.[17]

These perspectives were a part of Talbert's way of doing, shaping, and making African American theatre long before my interview with him. As he stated in the director's commentary recorded on the 2005 DVD release of the play *Fabric of A Man*, he continues to "get lost in these romantic musicals because . . . there is not enough opportunity for us to really see ourselves in love."[18]

To be clear, Talbert is the only circuit playwright I have found who discusses his particular brand of theatre in ways that clearly distinguish it from other types of theatre existing outside of the circuit. For Talbert, his plays, along with those authored by other circuit producers, belong to a category of theatre he classifies as inspirational theatre.[19] Politically, Talbert's designation is an active and conscious attempt by the playwright to move this type of theatre away from the stigmatized associations embedded in the word *chitlin* and the entertainment category Chitlin Circuit that I historicized in the previous chapter. Talbert's act of relabeling desires to advance the artistic merit of not only his productions but also the original and unique work produced by other circuit playwrights. Moreover, the use of the word *inspirational* encourages us to understand this theatre's connection to religion. I expand on this religious connection in this and other chapters of the book, with an eye toward the ways that circuit productions share many of its objectives and desired spiritual outcomes for its participants/spectators with real African American church services and gatherings. By this, I mean that in ways similar to how we might understand a hypothetical church pastor hoping that congregants leave church uplifted and recommitted to their faith as a result of communal teaching and worship, the term *inspirational theatre* calls attention to the fact that Talbert and his counterparts aim for audiences to leave their productions moved, motivated, and with their faith restored. Cementing this point even further, Talbert uses the church concept of ministering to explain the collaborative process in inspirational theatre:

> It's important that everybody in the production of inspirational plays [understand that] you're all a part of the *ministry*, the business, the performance. Everybody has to be in the moment, you know, everybody has to be there.[20]

After this statement, Talbert stretches the contours of circuit theatre even further by bracketing his specific style of inspirational theatre into a category he calls romantic inspirationals. Talbert's subcategory speaks to the playwright's desire to heal, foster, and promote successful African American love relationships through dramatic narratives that are enveloped in Christian values.

Similar to the other circuit artists examined in this project, Talbert consistently sells DVD recordings of his musicals in major retail outlets and platforms, such as Amazon, Walmart, and Target. Over the years, recorded circuit productions have become increasingly sophisticated in their editing and presentation. On each DVD, one live performance is recorded in its entirety. Instead of recording a performance by using a single longshot from one stationary camera, many circuit performances are now recorded by using multiple cameras stationed at different angles in the theatre. Many of Talbert's DVDs contain sophisticated video images and uniquely offer bonus features to in-home audiences in the form of director's commentary. In what follows, I use Talbert's statements, mined from the recorded director's commentaries found on the respective DVD recordings of his musicals *The Fabric of A Man, He Say . . . She Say . . . But What Does God Say?*, and *Love on Lay Away*, to assemble Talbert's tenets for *inspirational theatre* and reveal the interior dimensions of his *romantic inspirationals*.

In 1996, *He Say . . . She Say . . . But What Does God Say?* appeared on national circuit stages. The musical presents a layered story of contemporary African American life set in 1990s Detroit, Michigan. The play's action takes place in three alternating locations: the interior of a church, the interior of a nightclub, and the dark alley shared by the church and the nightclub. Its long roster of characters is divided by their each having an affiliation with either the church or the nightclub. One side is composed of the congregants of the True Vine Church, their deacon, and their new pastor. The opposing side consists of head gangster and owner of the neighboring nightclub Satin Jones, his two henchmen Demetrius and Forty, and his girlfriend Alexandria. During the production run, Talbert presented these characters in a two-hour play with four interwoven plotlines. The first plotline focuses on the congregants of the True Vine Church, who are in search of a new pastor to replace their former one, who was gunned down in an alley by Demetrius during the play's opening scene. The congregation eventually hires the young and well-liked Pastor Jackson, who spends the remainder of the play trying to revitalize the church and raise enough money to save it from being closed. The second plotline is driven by the generational power conflict between Satin Jones and his younger protégé Demetrius.[21] Meanwhile, the third and fourth plotlines focus on the evolution of the play's two romantic relationships: the new relationship between Pastor Jackson and church member Michelle and the old relationship between Satin Jones and Alexandria.[22] As these plotlines unfold, Talbert uses the latter couple as a foil to the faith-oriented and emerging relationship between Pastor Jackson and Michelle. In true Talbert fashion, as the play progresses, these respective relationships begin to look more alike than dissimilar. The audiences witness religiously bound love and commitment blossom in both couples. In the final scene, Satin Jones and Alexandria stand alongside Pastor Jackson and Michelle before the production's live audience and the fictional onstage church congregation and pledge their commitments to God and each other.

Talbert's musical *The Fabric of A Man* toured US circuit stages in 2000 and 2001. Set on Fulton Street in Brooklyn, New York, the musical presents a story about an aspiring designer and clothing boutique owner, Dominique Majors, and her failing relationship with her longtime boyfriend, stockbroker Blair Godfrey. At the opening of the play, Blair tries to convince Dominique to sell her boutique and take on the full-time job of being his caretaker and wife. Dominique soon becomes torn between pursuing success in the fashion industry and keeping her relationship with Blair. She quickly comes to the realization that their relationship will not work unless she gives up her aspirations. On a routine visit to the dry cleaners she meets Joshua King, the owner's nephew and a tailor who also has visions of having his own clothing line. What begins as a friendly encounter between likeminded individuals soon develops into mutual flirtation. Dominique finds herself faced with yet another choice: does she remain with her misogynistic, money-oriented, and controlling boyfriend, or does she pursue a relationship with the humble, churchgoing, ambitious, and supportive Joshua? The twists and turns that lead to her ultimate decision are peppered with stirring gospel and R&B ballads; morality and faith-based advice from her father, the pastor; and a secondary plotline that involves the burgeoning and comedically framed relationship between Joshua's uncle, "Uncle Ray," and a frequent neighborhood customer and churchgoer, Ernestine. By the end of the play, two new and sanctified romances are formed between Dominique and Joshua and between Ernestine and Uncle Ray, respectively.

The last musical is Talbert's 2003 *Love on Lay Away*. For this narrative, Talbert takes inspiration from the popular African American television series of the mid 1980s *227* (1985–1990). Incorporating a guest appearance by *227* star Marla Gibbs at the start of the 2005 production, which was filmed for DVD release, Talbert suggestively positions the action of the play in Washington, DC, where the iconic setting of Gibbs's long-running sitcom took place. Like *227*, Talbert situates the characters of *Love on Lay Away* in a single apartment building. Scenes take place either in tenants' apartments or on the front sidewalk and steps of the building. The crux of the story surrounds the long-term relationship of 20- to 30-somethings Monique and Anthony. Although this couple had been living together for years, Monique feels like it is time for Anthony to ask for her hand in marriage. Anthony, however, feels that their relationship is fine in its current state and for the majority of the play continues to maintain his belief that marriage is unnecessary because they are already committed to each other. Talbert juxtaposes the relationship woes of this middle-class African American professional couple against the respective comedy-infused relationship portrayals of Epiphany and Reggie, and Ms. Willanetta and Renzo. Epiphany and Reggie represent working-class 20-year-olds who are attracted to each other but who have been unable to actually start dating because of Epiphany's fear of starting a relationship with a man who is not the father of her six-year-old son. Ms. Willanetta is characterized as an older churchgoing neighbor who has been ignoring the advances of Renzo, her persistent suitor, for years because he does not share her interest in church or religion. As expected, all three couples are able to reconcile their differences by the play's end and all are committed to new moral-abiding relationships that adhere to traditional Christian values.

The DVD commentaries of each of the aforementioned plays are filled with Talbert's thoughts on the aesthetic and performance fundamentals of inspirational theatre and Talbert's specific areas of foci in romantic inspirationals. I have divided his tenets into four categories that respectively detail how one should write, direct, incorporate music, and act in circuit musicals, according to Talbert.

A recurring rule for Talbert is that writers of inspirational theatre should "focus on the written word":[23]

> So often in the inspirational plays you don't get a chance to really let dialogue breathe and characters really develop because a lot of times we feel we gotta have so much stuff going. We gotta have so many songs and so many characters. . . . But really if you build strong characters and you cast talented actors and you structure your story well, you can let it breathe and the audience won't feel like they are missing out on anything which is important to know. For directors and playwrights coming up, you don't have to have a bunch of stuff going on onstage all the time. That is not what Inspirational Theatre is.[24]

He expresses similar sentiments during a comedic point in the plot of *Love on Lay Away*:

> One of the biggest lies of Inspirational Theatre is that you have to be doing cartwheels onstage and people have to be doing a bunch of ghetto schtick and all this stuff, in order for an audience to enjoy the production. . . . [H]ere you have two people just sitting on a stoop and it's some of the biggest laughter in the production. Because the characters have been established,

the actors are staying true to the character and the arcs are beginning to happen, and the audience has gotten a chance to know the characters. . . . I say this over and over again, there's no better gimmick than a good story, with good characters, and good actors, and good writing, good set, good music.[25]

Talbert also persuades playwrights to develop strong and in-depth characters:

An audience wants to go on a journey, and a journey with these characters has a beginning, a middle, and an end. And you make an audience feel like they've gotten a full, [like] they've gotten . . . more than their money is worth when you allow them to go on that journey. Now you can't go on it for them. Let them go on that journey. And you let them go on that journey by following the characters and the characters' development and the characters' arc.[26]

When directing, Talbert adheres to the advice given to him by his directing mentor Paul Roach: "Allow yourself to be moved and touched by the material. . . . If you are touched, then the audience will be touched."[27] It is also important for Talbert that playwrights and directors remember to layer the theatrical elements in productions: "The mood of the music is married to the mood of the theme which is important to make it as full of an experience as possible."[28] He also urges directors to keep in mind the perspective of the audience when directing actors, especially during emotional moments:

Moments onstage are so important. As a director it is important that you allow the actors to live in an emotional moment so the audience can get a chance to digest it, so that everything doesn't have to all happen at the same time. So that you let a scene breathe, I'm big on that.[29]

Similar to many directors, Talbert encourages directors of inspirational theatre to create a family environment during rehearsals:

I like to create an atmosphere when I'm directing. . . . [W]e are all in here together to try to figure out [how] to, you know, create this magic and, you know, nobody is greater or lesser than the other person and it creates a kind of family atmosphere. . . . Everybody's coming in there with one mind and a singular intention to get the best, you know, out of the production.[30]

Talbert also has fixed ideas about the purpose of music and how it should be incorporated into inspirational plays. It can be said that his romantic inspirationals benefit from the close attention that he pays to the lyrics, timing, and rationale of and behind the music. His productions boast large eight- and nine-piece orchestras that privilege the use of intentional underscoring during dramatic moments, particularly during non-musical plot points that help to "set the mood."[31] Included among the roster of musical collaborators Talbert has worked with over the years is songwriter Brent Jones, who Talbert says "writes songs like [I] write dialogue," and musical director Robbie Lewis, a graduate of the Berklee College of Music. Talbert compels artists of inspirational theatre to recognize that "songs in musical theatre are not stand-alones, they are extensions. You are never stopping the story. You are still keeping the dialogue going."[32] Additionally, he insists that the transitions between the "song and dialogue should be seamless."[33] Thus, we should understand that for Talbert the music of his romantic inspirationals, specifically, and inspirational theatre, generally, is as purposeful and has as much significance and intentionality as a musical score presented in film, dance, or other types of theatrical productions.

Lastly, Talbert's principles on acting in his romantic inspirationals outline the practices that the playwright and director hopes will become prevalent in all inspirational theatre productions. First, Talbert advises directors to incorporate different levels of performance into their productions. He warns that actors should not present their characters in ways that can be read as always "loud," "comic," or of "high intensity."[34] In a related point, he insists that actors incorporate silence into their dramatic moments: "A lot of times with plays, directors or actors are afraid to let moments breathe and . . . let there just be silence, but there's a lot of power in silence."[35] It is also important for Talbert that his actors connect and sing to the other actor(s) onstage as opposed to singing straight to the audience. The latter is a recurring practice done by many "gospel actors," which the playwright says results in unsatisfying outcomes.[36] Instead, he finds that audiences appear to be more engaged and interested in a developing plot when they are granted access to the story as if they were "a fly on the wall,"[37] eavesdropping on private moments. Similarly, he stresses that actors should never break character even during comedic moments.

> Actors feel as if they have to laugh at something in order for the audience to laugh at it, but when you stay true to the moment. . . . you live in there. [This actor] knows the audience is going crazy but he stays in character which makes the audience, again who wants to be a fly on the wall, enjoy the moment even more. . . . A lot of actors, they just want to start laughing or they want to break character and all that stuff, but unless that is part of that character and what that character does, then it's a distraction to the story line. But you know if that's the way the character has been built then so be it. But when you're telling a straight story and it's a straight play, you don't want to do that onstage because then you cheat the audience from the moment and you cheat the other performer from their moment as well.[38]

Thus, Talbert's actors do not play to the audience. Instead, they "keep the action and the drama onstage."[39] He instructs his cast to "be in the scene," to "be in the moment," and not to "fall into the trap"[40] of becoming what he calls a "prostitute for laughter."[41] He also encourages his actors to execute "fourth walling" during the singing of songs. In this method, his actors are allowed to use the downstage area when singing, but they are instructed to not make eye contact with audience members while doing so. Instead, they are trained to always look at the invisible fourth wall—the wall behind the audience—when singing, except during those previously rehearsed moments in which they are given permission by him, as director, to actually look at the audience. Taken together, Talbert's musings on acting express how important it is for him that his actors and those of other inspirational theatre productions "stay in the moment during performances" and "carry [these] moments over into transitions and scene actions."[42]

The import of Talbert's tenets for inspirational theatre lies in, as compiled here, their representing the only manifesto in existence that intricately details the mechanics and objectives behind these productions. I read Talbert's model of circuit theatre as one that conditions spectatorship in his theatrical events by purposefully aiming to incite audience engagement through the direct and sophisticated development of a production's writing, directing, music, and acting components. As a result, Talbert's productions present African American audiences with a polished and neatly packaged production that has been structurally formed for their entertainment.

Theatre historians and critics may find themselves propelled to compare Talbert's formulaic approach to his productions with other existing and historical forms of structured theatre-making, mainly Eugène Scribe's well-made play. However, as many contemporary scholars have noted,

> the search for a formula that will explain the structure of the well-made play is doomed to failure. There is no general structure that is common to all such plays. One can, however, describe common practices and tendencies in order to understand better the meaning of that term as it applies to Scribe.[43]

Yet with Scribe's work noted as being the singular formula that "has had so extraordinary an influence on the social drama of Europe and American since the middle of the nineteenth century,"[44] it is perhaps expected that Talbert's work, like the work of much of American drama that focuses on social narratives, bears resemblance to some aspects of Scribe's content and/or form. As Christopher Innes has written,

> [Scribe's] structural principles for introducing and developing interlinked dramatic situations, with a dénouement that leads into the next situation, until all strands of the plot are neatly resolved in the conclusion, created

an impression of logical coherence. Theatrically effective, this structuring rapidly became codified.[45]

Furthering this point, Carlson notes that

> The influence of Scribe on subsequent drama can hardly be overestimated. The realistic dramatists of the later nineteenth century—most notably Ibsen—drew upon his technique of careful construction and preparation of effects, and through their example the well-made play became and still remains the traditional model of play construction.[46]

While Scribe's emphasis on conflict, obstacles, romance, secrets, a steady development of plot action, successful dénouements (plot resolutions), and a general "concern for pleasing his audience"[47] may broadly align with the content of many Talbert productions, most of the content, plot components, and character presentations found in Talbert's productions are noticeably removed from those of Scribe. As examples, Talbert's productions are not presented in a neatly framed conflict between a hero and "his adversary."[48] While conflict and mild suspense can be found in a Talbert play, unlike Scribe, Talbert's dramas are not built on suspense and the resolution of that suspense through what Stephen S. Stanton describes as a "series of complications and crises, with each act closing on a climactic curtain."[49] Additionally, Talbert's productions do not rely on their unpredictability—another common feature in Scribe's work. Expanding on this last point, Cardwell writes that for Scribe,

> much of the art of the well-made play lies in the preparation of its elements in such a way that the audience will not be able to put them together before the right moment, but will quickly realize the logic of the solution once it is presented to them.[50]

Differently constituted, Talbert's productions and the work of other circuit practitioners thrive on predictability. Audiences arrive at these productions with a measured horizon of expectations that practitioners in turn manipulate for heightened entertainment. Included in this predictability is an awareness that—surprising content aside—audiences are already cognizant of how a given plot will resolve at the onset of every production. Nonetheless, I do find Scribe's general philosophy surrounding the purpose and appeal of his type of theatre—the comedic and romantic melodrama—to be distinctively aligned with common perceptions about why contemporary circuit audiences attend these musicals in droves. Carlson provides the following Scribe statement regarding the appeal of his work for spectators, taken from an 1836 speech presented at the Académe Française:

> Spectators go to the theatre "not for instruction or improvement but for diversion and distraction, and that which diverts them most is not truth but

fiction. To see again what you have before your eyes daily will not please you, but that which is not available to you in everyday life—the extraordinary and the romantic."[51]

Similarly, circuit musicals such as Talbert's use fiction as a means of entertainment and escape for its audiences. While audience instruction and motivation may occur, I have found that by a performance's end, these outcomes are generally unexpected byproducts for spectators who are going to the theatre mainly to be entertained and arguably distracted from their everyday lives by a good story, live entertainment, and good music.

Putting Scribe aside and considering Talbert's productions on their own terms reveals how Talbert's tenets guide us toward an understanding of the multiple parts of the whole in circuit theatre. Along these lines, then, a successful circuit production, gospel theatre production, gospel musical production, urban theatre production, and inspirational or romantic inspirational theatre production—regardless of its moniker—must conscientiously put said parts into motion and always execute them with its audience in mind. This perspective pushes beyond a general conception of these audiences as simply lively and vocal by default and instead moves toward an appreciation of the fact that, for Talbert, these audiences, like other theatre audiences, must be cultivated, navigated, and escorted through the process of engaging with live performance. Talbert's acknowledgment of this process is clearly demonstrated in the writing, crafting, and directing of his theatre and can be seen in the purposeful development of his characters, the intentional training of his actors, and the cohesive and audience-centered theatre-making that he and his collaborators undertake. Moreover, Talbert's musings provide sharp evidence that spectating during his theatrical events is not only an active process but one that he believes must be heavy-handedly guided by both playwright and director. Accordingly, in Talbert's theatre, African American reception processes are earnestly and thoughtfully developed in the live theatrical event.

David and Langston: Melding Faith and Experience into African American Musicals

I insert Talbert's musicals into a long lineage of African American musical artistry and innovation that begins with Hughes's 1961 production of *Simply Heavenly* and revitalizes itself in the beauty shop and barbershop musicals of the 1980s. As noted in Chapter Two, gospel music and religious themes continued to be prevalent in African American–authored dramas and musicals during and beyond the late 1950s and early 1960s context of *Simply Heavenly*, *Black Nativity*, and *Tambourines to Glory*. Including Hughes's *Jericho-Jim Crow* (1964) and James Weldon Johnson's *Trumpets of the Lord* (1969)—a musical adaptation of Johnson's 1927 book of poetry, *God's Trombones: Seven Negro Sermons in Verse*[52]—the 1960s and the 1970s witnessed an increase in aesthetic experimentation in gospel musical theatrical fare in terms of character, form, dramatic content, presentation, and featured adaptations.[53]

Vinnette Carroll's gospel musical innovations in the 1976 musical *Your Arms Too Short to Box with God*, stand out in this history. As Burdine recalls, the musical, which was produced through the collaborative efforts of Carroll, Alex Bradford, and Micki Grant, "united a pair of seemingly incompatible philosophies . . . a profound faith in Christianity, and uncompromising black pride."[54] The performance history discussion of *Black Nativity* was discussed in Chapter Two, as was both Carroll's and Bradford's respective work on Hughes's landmark production, as director and composer. *Your Arms Too Short to Box with God* featured original gospel songs, "a decidedly non-traditional story line," and a theatrical reimagining of Jesus as an unspeaking male African American dancer.[55] Performers, notably, "wore standard church choir robes in the earlier scenes of the play, but changed later to garments that combined 'a Biblical look with dashikis.'" Critic Clive Barnes framed the musical as "the Christ story from Palm Sunday, through the Passion in the Garden, the Betrayal, the Trial, to the Crucifixion and the Resurrection."[56] The plot of *Your Arms Too Short to Box with God* made efforts to detail Christ's nativity and immortal resurrection in the context of a religious event, which appears to be reflective of *Black Nativity*'s ceremonial display.

After the success of *Your Arms Too Short to Box with God*, gospel musicals continued to be produced throughout the 1980s and the early 1990s. With increased interest in the music came more variety and experimentation on the stage. Included on the roster of productions that broke new ground was Stephen Lemberg's 1980 Off-Broadway production of *Jazzbo Brown*, described as "a revamping of *The Jazz Singer*,"[57] and the 1983 award-winning Bob Telson and Lee Breuer's avant-garde spin on Sophocles's trilogy *Oedipus Rex*. In the Telson-Breuer adaptation, African American actor Morgan Freeman led an entirely African American cast, composed of a professional gospel choir and well-known gospel singers, through an interactive theatrical presentation of morality, loss, and redemption that is perhaps best described in the words of D'Aponte: a "marriage of Black Pentecostal ritual and Greek myth."[58] Soon after, the 1986 Broadway season featured a musical adaptation of James Baldwin's play *The Amen Corner*, which was developed by the producers of the musical *Purlie*, an adaptation of Ossie Davis's drama *Purlie Victorious*. Unfortunately, the Baldwin musical that shared the same name of the original drama closed after a few short weeks after opening to weak reviews.[59] The 1980s and 1990s also witnessed other noteworthy "low-brow comedies" and gospel musicals like Ken Wydro and Vy Higgensen's 1983 production *Mama, I Want to Sing*, Ron Milner's 1987 *Don't Get God Started*, and long-running productions of Shelly Garett's *Beauty Shop* and *Barber Shop* musicals[60] and Adrian Williamson's *My Grandmother Prayed for Me* (1996).[61] I insert Talbert's musicals into the lineage of Black artistry and African American musical theatre-making by turning the focus toward the historical connections Talbert's musicals share with Hughes's penultimate "urban-folk-Harlem-*genre*- melodrama"[62] *Tambourines to Glory*.

Nowhere is the connection between the past and the present of gospel musicals and the long-standing desire to cultivate Black pleasure in African American musical contexts seen more clearly than in a comparative look at Hughes's *Tambourines to Glory* and Talbert's *He Say . . . She Say . . . But What Does God Say?* As has been previously mentioned, *He Say . . . She Say . . . But What Does God Say?* toured nationally in 1996 and was later restaged and recorded before a live theatre audience in Los Angeles, California, during one weekend in 2004. It is one of three previously staged plays selected by Talbert to be remounted and made available for purchase on DVD in 2005.[63] According to Talbert, the entire remount of *He Say . . . She Say . . . But What Does God Say?* was rehearsed in ten days. This updated version benefited from the addition of new scenic design elements, some new musical arrangements, and some revised stage directions. Additionally, although most of the original cast members were available for the remount, new actors were found to fill three roles. The popular gospel singer and choir director Kirk Franklin was replaced by D. J. Rogers Jr., a singer and award-winning R&B songwriter. The actor David Mann, who is discussed later in this project as a recurring Tyler Perry actor, was replaced by the comedian Rodney "Red" Grant. Finally, the role played by Bern Nadette Stanis, the actor popularly known for her role as the sister character Thelma Evans in the 1970s sitcom *Good Times*, was filled by film actor NaBushe Wright.[64]

Despite being separated by a time span of more than 30 years, Hughes's *Tambourines to Glory* and Talbert's *He Say . . . She Say . . . But What Does God Say?* share striking commonalities that are not overtly evident in other musicals in the historical trajectory of African American gospel musicals after 1963. For starters, where Hughes's production can be credited for holding up a microscope to a 1960s Harlem that is ravaged by poverty, crime, drugs, and desperation, Talbert's production provides an introspective look into a 1990s Detroit that is plagued by similar social and economic maladies. Both narratives contain characters that represent the two sides of a divided community. Broadly summarized, side one of each community is composed of characters who are interested in engendering social, economic, and spiritual uplift. Side two is composed of characters who recklessly wreak havoc and harm the social well-being of each community's inhabitants. Central to both musicals is an African American storefront church that serves as the crossroads in which each side is forced to contend with the beliefs and activities of the other. Additionally, both musicals contain a bar or nightclub that serves as the lair for the unsanctified and/or evil villains of the narratives.

When audiences first encounter Essie, one of the main protagonists of *Tambourines to Glory*, she is sitting on her suitcase outside of her former apartment building in Harlem. Essie has finally been evicted after being unable to pay rent for the third month in a row. Her friend and neighbor Laura soon comes around the corner and suggests that Essie move in with her temporarily. A drunk Laura then tries to brighten Essie's spirit by encouraging her to take charge of her future and her financial means. In her surprisingly clear-headed stupor, Laura comes up with the idea for them to start their own church and reap the monetary benefits of doing the Lord's work.

LAURA You never do nothing but just set, like you're setting now—throwed out of your place, yet setting looking peaceful. Me, I'd be raising hell.

ESSIE About all I can do, Laura, is ask the Lord to take my hand.

LAURA Why don't you do that then? Get holy, sanctify yourself—since we're setting out here on the curb discussing ways and means. The Lord is no respecter of persons—if He takes the pimp's hand and makes a bishop out of him. You know Bishop Longjohn right over there on Lenox Avenue? That saint had three whores on the block ten years ago. He's got a better racket now—the gospel! And a rock and roll band in front of the pulpit.

ESSIE Religion don't have to be a racket, Laura. Do it? Maybe he's converted?

LAURA All the money he takes in every Sunday would convert me. Say, I got an idea! Why don't you and me start a church?

ESSIE What denomination?

LAURA Our *own*—then we won't be beholding to nobody else. You know my grandpa was a jackleg preacher, so I can rock a church as good as anybody.

ESSIE Did you ever preach?

LAURA No, but I've got the nerve to try. Let's start a church. Huh?

ESSIE Where?

LAURA On the street where the Bishop started his—outdoors—rent free—on the corner.

ESSIE You mean down here on the gutter where I am.

LAURA On the curb—*above* the gutter. We'll save them lower down than us.

ESSIE Who could that be?

LAURA The ones that do what you can't do—drink without getting sick. Gamble away their rent. Cheat the Welfare Department—more'n I do. Lay with each other without getting disgusted—no matter how many unwanted kids they produce. Blow gauge, support the dope trade. Hustle. Them's the ones we'll set out to convert.

ESSIE With what?

LAURA The Lord Jesus—He comes free. Just look up at the Lord above and the squares will think God is staring you dead in the face. Dig? We'll make money's mammy![65]

As the conversation continues, Laura uses examples of other lucrative religious undertakings in the neighborhood to convince Essie that starting their own church is a good idea. Laura even shows off her impromptu preaching skills by mimicking the heightened tone and religious fervor that would get people in the seats to hear her message.

LAURA (*She mounts a pile of furniture imagining herself as a preacher.*) I'll tell them Lennox Avenue sinners: You all better come to Jesus! The atom bomb's about to destroy this world and you ain't ready. Get ready! Get ready! Lord above, I am lost I have strayed from the cross And I cry, Yes, I cry, save me now!

ESSIE Lord hear my plea And from sin set me free. Fill my heart with righteousness right now!

BOTH Lord above, you I seek And I pray, humble, meek, That you'll help me on my way. Lord above, let your light Be my guide through the night. Hear, oh, hear me, Lord as I pray.

LAURA Step right up, join us, all you hellions of sin! Join our gospel band and live in grace. (*Descends from pile of furniture*) Essie, broke as we are, we *better* start a church.[66]

The conversation in this first snapshot from *Tambourines to Glory* marks the beginning of the Reed Sisters' corner church, which by Act 1 Scene 7 has been moved into an old theatre under a new name: Tambourine Temple. As Soyica Diggs Colbert notes in her analysis of Black religiosity in Hughes's musical, dialogue such as this sets the tone for Hughes's dichotomous representation of the interiority of Black Harlem churches and African American religious practices.[67] Tambourine Temple becomes the mixed meeting place not only for Harlemites seeking salvation but also for those in search of financial wealth and easy prey.

At first glance, there are definite similarities found in the ways both Hughes and Talbert present divergent romantic relationships whose longevity is determined by the level or amount of religious faith that each couple possesses by the end of the respective plots. I argue that starting here with Hughes and continuing in the work of Talbert, Johnson, Guidry, Perry, and other circuit playwrights not considered in this project, this outlook on and treatment of African American relationships has become a standard depiction found in most circuit plays. As I have previously mentioned in my synopsis of *He Say . . . She Say . . . But What Does God Say?* in Talbert's case, he has juxtaposed the criminal-soaked relationship between Satin Jones and Alexandria against the God-inspired and sanctified courtship between Pastor Jackson and Michelle. In *Tambourines to Glory*—similar to *He Say . . . She Say . . . But What Does God Say?*—the presentation of divergent romantic relationships is unraveled in the developing plot.

In Hughes's play, the driving tension of the plot is experienced by Essie, who has to contend with the scheming nature of Laura. Although both women initially get into business together to "make [their] fortune saving souls," Essie has a change of heart early on and quickly realigns her intentions. She decides to build a righteous church in which she can actually save the disadvantaged and maligned of Harlem. Laura's desires, however, remain unchanged, and she succumbs easily to the "Devil"-like influence of her new boyfriend, Big-Eyed Buddy Lomax, who encourages her to swindle the congregation by using money-making ploys and false prophecies.[68] Lomax's character brings the interiority of contemporary Harlem street life centerstage. He revels in the vices of the fast nightlife and easy money: alcohol, promiscuity, and deception. His attempts at dominating the church and its congregants soon become intertwined with the propelling arc of the plot. Amid all of this, Laura and Buddy's relationship is juxtaposed with the new and innocent relationship developing between Essie's devout daughter Marietta, who has just arrived from the South, and C.J., a college student and musician in the church. Near the play's end, Laura's jealousy over Buddy and his other women leads to an intense argument between the two. When Buddy becomes physically violent toward her, Laura uses Essie's knife to stab and kill Buddy before he can do her further harm. Essie's false arrest compels Laura to confess in an attempt to save her friend and cleanse her sins. Essie's freedom and Laura's conviction and eventual release incite a change in the women and the entire congregation of Tambourine Temple that cements the group's faith in worship and fervent service to God. Perhaps as a testament to real love and ardent faith, although Laura and Buddy's relationship is over, Marietta and C.J.'s relationship remains intact. Emphatically, Hughes's urban morality tale showcased the church as the literal and symbolic stage on which the righteous battle between good and evil was fought in this Black community.

Sprinkled throughout all of Buddy's scenes and layered into most of the context of other scenes are numerous signs and symbols of presumably real Harlem life that I suggest were purposely used by Hughes to engage and connect with his African American spectators. In fact, Hughes's use of Black music genres, Black popular culture, and African American comedy foreshadowed how these elements are now used by Talbert and his peers. As I have mentioned in earlier discussions, a dominant characteristic of circuit plays is the use of identifiable music that would be familiar to an African American audience and the presentation of new, play-specific music. Not only did Hughes's script include gospel music that would have been familiar to an African American audience at the time—in the songs "Upon this Rock," "Home to God," and others—he also presented new, play-specific music, as was showcased in the original production song "Tambourines to Glory!" Moreover, similar to how Talbert and other circuit playwrights purposefully infuse familiar experiences and elements that are meant to be reflective of inner city life and/or a contemporary African American experience, Hughes's play would have been capable of engaging with its audience through its inclusion of jazz, popular iconic Black images, and presumably authentic representations of Harlem's real night life, as was presented in Buddy's scenes that took place in The Roamer Club. It is possible to surmise, then, that his African American audiences would have been attracted to—and his white audiences confused by or less interested in—presentations such as this one appearing in the opening moment of Act 1 Scene 5, in which the set description reads:

> *The interior of a storefront church with, behind the rostrum, a large mural of the Garden of Eden in which a brownskin Adam strongly resembles Joe Louis and Eve looks just like a chocolate Sarah Vaughn. Only the Devil is white.*[69]

In this visual commentary on Black Christianity, Hughes used the iconic visages of boxer Joe Louis and the attractive singer Sarah Vaughn to not only connote African American beauty but also advance a particular African American take on religion.

In an equally determined manner, Hughes injects humor effortlessly throughout the narrative. Perhaps, the best examples of his brand of comedy is found in the characters Chicken-Crow-for-Day and Birdie Lee, both of whom are former wayward souls who join the church in hopes of redemption. Their shining moments in the production take place when both are so moved by the spirit that they stand up and give testimonials about their conversions:

> CHICKEN-CROW-FOR-DAY Oh, I am here to tell you tonight, since I started to live right, it is my determination to keep on—on the path to glory. In my sinful days, before I found this church, I were a dyed-in-the-wool sinner, yes, dyed-in-the-wool, sniffling after women, tailing after sin, gambling on green tables. Saratoga, Trenton, New Orleans—let 'em roll! Santa Anita, Tanaforan, Belmont, Miami, I never read nothing but the racing forms. In New York, the numbers columns in the *Daily News*, and crime in the comic books. Now I've seen the light! Sister Essie and Sister Laura brought me to the faith. They done snatched me off the ship of iniquity in which I rid down the river of sin through the awfullest of storms, through gales of evil, hurricanes of passion purple as devil's ink, green as gall.[70]

He continues to testify and Birdie soon becomes overwhelmed with emotion and interrupts.

> BIRDIE Set down? I can't set down—too happy to set down—got to stand—got to talk for Jesus—testify this evening in His name. I got to tell you where I come from—*underneath* the gutter. On the street, I heard Sister Laura preaching, Sister Essie praying, I said I got to take up the Cross and come back to the fold. Yes, they preached and they prayed and sung me into the hands of God! I said goodbye to sin—and I wove my hand. (*She waves her hand.*) Yes, I wove my hand to the devil—and said goodbye. That's why tonight, brothers and sisters, *I'm* gonna testify! (*Gradually her speaking rhythm merges into song as she returns to her drums and begins to play and sing.*)[71]

If we think in terms of theatrical reception, characters like Chicken-Crow-for-Day and Birdie Lee had the potential to elicit humor from an early-1960s Harlem or New York City–based African American audience for several reasons. The colorful names of Hughes's characters were part of a long-standing, albeit controversial, tradition of African American humor. As Mel Watkins scholar of African American humor and comedy explains, Hughes's writing was similar to that of Zora Neale Hurston[72] in how both authors "concentrated on fictional characters drawn almost exclusively from the ranks of ordinary black folks."[73] Although, Watkins considered Hughes's brand of comedy to be "sophisticated,"[74] his humor was inspired by his interest in African American folk culture in that it was influenced by the predominance of these stereotyped Black figures in the surrounding media. Watkins provides additional historical context:

> Radio, the era's new media, also echoed that distorted vision as it reprised slavery caricatures of blacks, unleashing a rash of minstrel-style shows in which whites portrayed dimwitted black characters with outlandish names like Sugarfoot, Sassafrass, Moonshine and Sawdust, Watermelon and Canta-loupe, Buck and Wheat, and Anesthetic and Cerebellum. . . . These popular, mass-media comic stereotypes influenced all Americans—even the Afri-can American performers who worked the black theater circuit. For one thing, most club and theater owners on the TOBA circuit were white, and they often demanded comedy that reflected their own expectations. And, as the numskull folktales illustrate, black audiences were certainly not above laughing at themselves or, at least, at other inept Negroes—unlike many whites they didn't assume that *all* black folks looked or acted alike.[75]

In consideration of this history, Chicken-Crow-for-Day and Birdie Lee should be considered representative of how Hughes chose to once again reclaim stereo-typed and comedic Black caricatures, as he had done with his Jesse B. Semple character years earlier. Hughes's execution is not without its complexities, iro-nies, and representational issues. Chicken-Crow-for-Day and Birdie Lee represent struggling Black Harlemites who trade in their temptations and street vices for fellowship and salvation. While these are positive attributes, their characters are enveloped in parody, mimicry, and representational humor founded in stereotypes. Both characters imitate standard worshiping practices and physicalities commonly found within Black Baptist and Pentecostal church environments, such as testi-fying and catching the spirit, but their portrayals are presented in the extreme. Importantly, the geographic location of the Northeast, coupled with the varied socioeconomic realities of African Americans in New York City during the 1960s run of *Tambourines to Glory*, opens the possibility for Chicken-Crow-for-Day and Birdie Lee to elicit laughter from African American spectators in the theatre in response to their discordant presentation of American Southern dialects and deeply ingrained Southern cultural retentions.

Although I have not been able to locate examples of the auditorium environ-ment during the production run of *Tambourines to Glory*, I believe that it is safe to presume that Hughes's musical would have been able to trigger verbal and physical reactions from its African American spectators on the basis of the form, content, and modes of presentation in the play. I will go a step further by propos-ing that any identification by the African American spectators with *Tambourines to Glory* would have been encouraged by how they were able to relate aspects of the narrative back to their own lives—particularly in Hughes's depictions of the Black church and Harlem street life. Thus, in Hughes's desire to create a Black theatre that would resonate with Black audiences, he decisively played on the horizons of expectations that he thought African American audiences would bring into a 1963 culturally specific theatrical event.

Comparatively—and with regard to Talbert's live viewing audience and/or the in-home viewers of his 2005 DVD production of *He Say . . . She Say . . . But What Does God Say?*—I also suggest that he played on what he believed to be the experiences and held knowledge of his African American spectators. In *He Say . . . She Say . . . But What Does God Say?* Talbert not only presents fictional representations of the interior dimensions of a storefront church but also offers lifelike caricatures of church congregants and mimetic reenactments of worship and praise traditions. Moreover, in the setting of Satin Jones's nightclub and the scenes that take place on the street outside of the church and the club, Talbert presents lifelike reenactments of the palpable inner city crime and violence that has ravaged actual streets of Detroit and other urban locales across the country. Thus, when his spectators witness the following opening scene from the start of the production—presented here as snapshot number three—a clear tone is set, and audiences know that they are about to enter a world in which they will witness a familiar battle between church members and street criminals in a devastated community.

(*At the start of the play drug dealers Demetrius and his sidekick Forty Ounce are standing on a dark street in front of the building that houses the storefront church "True Vine Church" on the right and Satin Jones's nightclub on the left. Demetrius is dressed in a dark suit and hat and Forty Ounce is dressed in jeans and a sweatshirt with a hood. Demetrius and Forty Ounce are seen counting money as the dialogue begins.*)

FORTY OUNCE *says the following lines humorously and with high-energy to Demetrius.* This is what is going on man! I'm telling you man! You crazy!

DEMETRIUS *laughs.* I got five more to drop, we go back, we re-up. We come back and do it again.

FORTY OUNCE I got two more. I got two more.

DEMETRIUS That's cool.

FORTY OUNCE *sees an approaching drug addict and taps Demetrius on the shoulder.*

DEMETRIUS See I ain't got time for this. (*Walks a few steps away and continues to count his money.*)

SLIM THE DRUG ADDICT Hey D! Hey D what's up baby! I need a hit D come on man. I need a hit D. (*He walks towards Demetrius and Forty Ounce who are standing centerstage and stops when he is standing between them. Demetrius stands to his right and Forty Ounce is standing to his left.*)

DEMETRIUS You need a hit Slim?

SLIM I need a hit man!

DEMETRIUS You need a hit?

SLIM I need a hit!

DEMETRIUS Hit him Forty.

FORTY OUNCE *hits Slim from behind with a blow to his shoulder. Audience laughter is heard.*

DEMETRIUS Now you've been hit.

SLIM Come on D! I need a hit man, bad!

DEMETRIUS Where my money at Slim? (*Slim begins searching his tattered pockets frantically.*) Where my money at?

SLIM You know my mother ain't got paid this week, man.

DEMETRIUS You waitin' on your momma to get paid?

SLIM Come on D! (*Scratches his head frantically.*) Come on D!

DEMETRIUS Boy that crack is something else ain't it Forty?

FORTY OUNCE Man, look at that man shaking. This man is shaking!

SLIM, *increasingly desperate and near panic.* Come on D! Come on!

DEMETRIUS Look here Slim. (*Shouts.*) Look at me! I'm gone give it to you this time. (*Shouts.*) You hear me? But the next time I see you Slim, you got to have me my money. (*Shouts.*) Do you hear me?!

SLIM I hear you man! You know I'm good for it baby! I'm a have it. Come on baby! Come on!

DEMETRIUS *reaches into his pants pocket and pulls out a packet.* Here man. (*He hands the packet to Slim who grabs it with excitement and leans towards Demetrius as if to hug him.*) Don't you put your hands on me.

SLIM *excitedly retreats back towards the way he entered.* Yo D, you a good man, man! God! God bless ya! (*He runs offstage.*)

PASTOR CLEOPHUS E. GREENFIELD, III *Unbeknownst to Demetrius and Forty Ounce, Pastor Greenfield has just witnessed the last few minutes of Demetrius's exchange with Slim as he exited his church.* Young man! You cannot sell drugs in front of the church!

DEMETRIUS Here he go man.

PASTOR If you don't have respect for yourself, at least have respect for the House of the Lord!

DEMETRIUS *laughs along with Forty Ounce.* Old man let me tell you something. I sell drugs anywhere and to anybody. I'll sell drugs to your mama.

FORTY OUNCE You need to back off before you get yourself shot man.

PASTOR *approaches Demetrius and Forty Ounce fearlessly.* Son your weapons don't scare me. See, God has got my back.

DEMETRIUS *approaches the Pastor who is now standing between himself and Forty Ounce.* Look to me like old Forty's got your back. Let me ask you something preacher man. Why you bothering us huh? Ain't nobody messing with you. You got your thing over there, we got ours over here. You know what? One day you gone mess around and you gone say the wrong thing and it's gone be too late.

PASTOR Get thee behind me Satan.

DEMETRIUS What you call me?

PASTOR I said get thee behind me Satan!

DEMETRIUS *reaches behind his jacket to the small of his back and pulls out a gun.* I tell you what, you get behind this huh?! (*Demetrius shoots the Pastor who falls backwards on the ground. Demetrius laughs and the Pastor lays lifeless.*) See there Forty, the good Lord giveth and Demetrius take it away. (*He reaches into the Pastor's coat and removes his wallet and gives it to Forty Ounce who searches for money*.) I guess this just been one of them days huh? (*Demetrius laughs at his own joke.*) Let's roll Forty. (*Approaching sirens are heard.*) Oh yeah! Just one of them days baby! (*Demetrius and Forty Ounce quickly exit stage left in the same direction that Slim exited earlier.*)[76]

A second example of Talbert's melding of faith and urban experiences comes in the final confrontation scene between Satin Jones and Demetrius. Earlier in the plot, Satin Jones kicked Demetrius out of his crew when he discovered that Demetrius and his henchmen broke into the church while a meeting was in session. Demetrius threatened the new pastor and his congregants and warned them that if they did not abandon their lease earlier than planned and sign the building over to Satin, more harm would come to them. To prove his point, Demetrius beat up the young pastor, Jackson, in front of his defenseless and terrified church members. The next day, Satin learns about Demetrius's actions and becomes furious that Demetrius went outside of his orders and did not leave the church and its members alone. Enraged, he ends his 15-year friendship with Demetrius and tells him that he never wants to see or work with him again. After Demetrius's banishment, things begin to fall into place for Satin. He dreamed of owning the entire block, and he just had to wait a few more days for the lease to run out on the True Vine Church. He knew that there was no way that the church members would be able to come up with all of the money needed to buy the property from the city before the upcoming deadline.

Despite his elation, at the start of this snapshot, Satin finds himself alone in his club. As he sits sipping a quiet drink of victory, Demetrius and Alexandria are seen sneaking into the club and approaching Satin from the back with their guns aimed at his head. They announce their presence by making it clear that they have broken into the club with intentions of taking it over and forcing Satin into an early retirement. In an instant, Satin finds himself betrayed by his girlfriend and facing the barrel of a gun, along with an unarmed Forty Ounce who had aimlessly wandered into the club, unaware of Demetrius's and Alexandria's presence or plan. Soon a knocking at the door is heard, and in walks Pastor Jackson, who has also unknowingly walked into to this generational battle over turf, power, and machismo between two gangsters. Demetrius eventually orders Satin to his knees and after a series of taunts and insults eventually shoots him when Satin attempts to take his gun away from him. A distraught Alexandria turns on Demetrius after he shoots Satin and shoots Demetrius herself. Demetrius is now dead, and an injured Satin lies horizontally on the stage floor with his body facing the audience as he writhes in pain. A distraught Alexandria and Forty Ounce leave the room to call an ambulance, and Satin is left with Pastor Jackson. In the following redemption scene, Pastor Jackson pleads with Satin to ask God for help during his time of need and to let God into his life to change whatever remains of his future.

PASTOR JACKSON Satin? It's Pastor Jackson. It's gonna be alright.

SATIN Pastor Jackson.

PASTOR It's gon be alright . . . just . . . just hang on in there.

SATIN Let me die.

PASTOR You not gon die Satin.

SATIN Oh no . . . no . . . let me die. Let me just die.

PASTOR Oh Jesus . . . you not gon die.

SATIN No . . . no pity for me just let me die with dignity Pastor, let me just die.

PASTOR You not gonna die. Shhh . . . just . . . just be still, be still.

SATIN *writhes with increased pain and begins weeping.* I . . . can't . . . I can't . . . I . . . can't . . . breathe.

PASTOR It's gonna be alright. Sometimes God have to knock you down in order for him to get your attention. I been there. I was knocked down. He had to get my attention. I used to be out there in the streets just like you. But God's got a purpose for your life. You been out there selling drugs and poison to the kids, driving these fancy cars and wearing fancy clothes and . . . Oh Jesus! You gotta know this, these kids look up to you. But if you just call on Jesus's name. If you give your life to Jesus, he can save you Satin. He will use you. I'm not trying to tell you what I've heard Satin. I'm trying to tell you what I know.

SATIN I don't know . . . my God . . . all I know is this gangster life, this being in the streets.

PASTOR Well maybe it's time you get to know him Satin. Your time could be short, but I'm telling you if you make the choice and the decision right now God will save you Satin. You're already dead. If you don't make the choice to live your life more abundantly, you're already dead Satin. Just call on his name.

SATIN *Inaudible. Tries to speak and writhes in more pain.*

PASTOR Call on his name. His name is Jesus. Call him from the bottom of your heart. Come on Satin.

SATIN *speaks in quiet anguish.* Jesus.

PASTOR Yes! Come on Satin! (*Begins weeping.*) That's what I'm talking about! Call his name Satin! Call his name Satin!

SATIN Jesus.

PASTOR Yes! Thank you Jesus!

SATIN Jesus!

PASTOR *continues to weep.* Yes! Oh Jesus! Oh Jesus! Thank you Jesus! That's what I said! He'll deliver you! He'll save your soul Satin! I'm trying to tell you! Call him! (*His lines are overlapped with Satin's below lines.*)

SATIN, *visibly moved now and is also weeping profusely. He begins to smile as he continues to say the name Jesus over and over again.* Jesus! . . . Jesus! . . . Jesus! . . . Jesus! (*Stage lights slowly fade to black and loud audience applause is heard.*)[77]

Although this fourth snapshot does not present a mimetic representation of common African American experience by any means, Talbert's scene does successfully play on existing culturally specific and faith-based knowledge about the power of faith and redemption during times of need and struggle. Talbert's audiences become witnesses to Pastor Jackson's ministering, which moves Satin away from his criminal past and helps him to crossover into a life of deliverance and hope. As Grace Sims Holt notes in her article "Stylin' Outta the Black Pulpit," African Americans have historically used religion and the salvation found inside church walls as a means to cope with a variety of social, economic, and personal circumstances.

> [B]lacks, denied access to other forms of institutional development, took the white man's religion and from within the black church developed routines and variations of form, substance, and ritual to satisfy black psychological needs.
>
> A primary function of the church was to nourish and maintain the souls of black folk by equating them with the essence of humanness. Religion was molded into an adaptive mode of resistance to the dehumanizing oppression, degradation and suffering of slavery. The black church developed as an institution which counteracted such forces by promoting self-worth and dignity, a viable identity, and by providing help in overcoming fear. It did this by using the power of the Holy Spirit to transform black suffering and equate it with the suffering Jesus. The religious aspect was always correlated with the common denominator of oppression. By enumerating perversions of the Christian ethic by white society in an emotional manner, the preacher hoped to alleviate the inhumane conditions under which blacks labored.
>
> Similarity of problems (e.g., poverty, travail) was tied to release and redemption by the Lord. A slave seeking release from an overseer's whip could call on the Lord to help him and give him relief. The religious form of hallucination provided the basis of hope that allowed him to get through another week, when emotional release could again be provided.[78]

Transferring Holt's discussion to Talbert's circuit production, then, Pastor Jackson attempted to use the curative qualities of African American religious faith to heal Satin Jones in his time of need. In Holt's terms, Satin experienced a "hallucination" at the hands of Pastor Jackson that enabled Satin to turn his life around after his life was spared despite his being shot. At the end of the play, it is no surprise, then, that it is Satin who saves the church by donating the needed money. He turns his back on the streets and ends his lifelong criminal career. He and Alexandria, who has also been changed by this experience, become new and saved members of True Vine Church.

Although these particular works of Hughes and Talbert are separated by almost five decades, I highlight how both playwrights blend common archetypes of African American life into packaged musical productions that entertain, elucidate, and provide moral instruction. Both plays bring experiences concerning religion, faith, and the dangers of street life, which are respective of the time and locale of each playwright, to the forefront of African American theatre. On one hand, the similarities across the two plays are uncanny. On the other hand, I find that these commonalities are made justifiable by the parallel efforts undertaken by both playwrights. Hughes and Talbert aimed to re-create Black experiences onstage for Black audiences by developing plays that highlighted their cultural specificity through the use of African American musical forms and practices surrounding religion and faith and recognizable Black representations of humor and popular culture. These methods proved successful for Hughes in the 1960s and again for Talbert at the start of the twenty-first century. Moreover, with regard to Talbert's circuit theatre audiences, my discussion in this section aimed at proving the effectiveness of his productions in their ability to condition Black spectatorship. I suggest that Talbert's theatre engages with African American spectators via theatrical productions that directly play on his audience's presumed horizons of expectations through the use of culturally specific storylines, strategic modes of African American cultural representation, and African American vernacular–based performance content. Yet Talbert's strategies of audience engagement do not end here. In the final section of this chapter, I introduce a unique quality of Talbert's theatre-making that involves the playwright likening his spectators to characters in his plays. In what follows, I reveal how this particular technique adds another dimension to his theatrical events during live performances.

African American Audience as Character in David Talbert's Inspirational Theatre

> I love the audience. The audience to me is always another character that adds to the whole experience, especially [in] Black theatre. Black Theatre is Black theatre because of the audience and I love the talk-back.
>
> —David E. Talbert[79]

In the brief stretch of time before David E. Talbert's comment here, the DVD viewer of his play *The Fabric of A Man* watches, along with the in-theatre spectator and an unseen Talbert, to a point in the play when the male lead, Joshua, makes a direct and sexually suggestive statement toward the object of his affection, Dominique:

JOSHUA But, you know . . . where I am going . . . you can come with me.
DOMINIQUE Well, that depends on where you're going.

JOSHUA I'm going to church.

DOMINIQUE Is that some new hip hop club downtown?

JOSHUA No. Church.

DOMINIQUE Church? Church?

JOSHUA No, my church church. See we get our worship on. Folks be shouting and dancing and singing down the aisles. And besides, tonight there's a fashion show and a fundraiser. You can check out some of my designs and help out the building fund at the same time.

DOMINIQUE Hmmmm!

JOSHUA Why are you looking at me like that? You look like you just saw a ghost.

DOMINIQUE Ahhh . . . tims[80] . . . kangol[81] . . . church? I don't know, somehow those things just don't add up for me you know. You just don't look like the church type.

JOSHUA That's because it's not about what's out here, it's about what's up here *(he points to his head)* and in here *(he points to his heart)*. So you down or what?

DOMINIQUE Alright . . . yeah, sure.

JOSHUA Perfect. Well I'll pick you up in your boutique in about an hour. I just need to take a quick shower.

DOMINIQUE Okay, yeah. You may want to do that because the funk was burning my nostril hairs! *(Audience laughs. Dominique appears to be drawn towards Joshua instead of the door.)*

JOSHUA One hour and ah the front door is that way that is unless you plan on getting wet. *(Joshua seductively refers to the fact that he is about to take a shower.)*[82]

As this last sentence is spoken, the audible swoon of the female spectators in the theatre is heard on the DVD. One woman's voice in particular is heard yelling an extended "yeah!" accompanied by the laughter of other audience members. Talbert is then heard erupting with laughter on the overlaid voiceover in response to this sequence of events. It is in this brief comedic recess that we hear Talbert share his thoughts on the African American audiences who attend his theatrical events.

Unsurprisingly perhaps, I have discovered that Talbert's perspective on his attending African American spectators as a collective character during live productions extends well beyond this particular moment in *The Fabric of a Man* play and is carried over into all aspects of his theatre-making. From my earlier discussion of Talbert's tenets for his inspirational theatre and romantic inspirationals—as he terms them—we know that Talbert does not take the development of his theatre lightly. Instead, the writer-director-producer considers all angles and possibilities in order to enhance his final product. His consideration of his audience during the writing, staging, and rehearsal processes and their reception of tightly packaged productions should then come as no surprise. Yet what is surprising is the control that he maintains over his audience in the arena of circuit theatre. As I have previously discussed, circuit environments are known for having active audiences who defy the conventions of traditional theatregoing by verbally addressing performers and physically reacting to unfolding performances. For many circuit playwrights, including those in this project, these types of reactions are welcome additions that in most cases serve as acknowledgments of performances well done. However, during my attendance at Talbert's April 2007 productions of *Love in the Nick of Tyme* at Chicago's Arie Crown Theater, I realized that the auditorium environments of Talbert's theatrical events were remarkably different from those that I had observed while watching the theatre produced by his peers.

During the Chicago production run of *Love in the Nick of Tyme*, I attended five shows, interacted with audience members, and took detailed notes of the stage performances from different seat locations in the Arie Crown's cavernous auditorium that seats 4,239 people.[83] As part of my methodology for this project, I also studied the spectators in the auditorium and attempted to monitor simultaneously those who were seated near me and those who were far away from me. At all of the productions, I attempted to get a sense of an audience's level of engagement and how, if at all, their reception might have been triggered by particular onstage content or actions. At the end of the *Love in the Nick of Tyme* production run and after careful evaluation of other Talbert productions that took place outside of my designated period of field research, a better understanding of Talbert's consideration of his audience began to emerge.[84] In what follows, I revisit my evaluations of those 2007 Chicago productions of *Love In the Nick of Tyme* and consider them alongside my evaluation of the recorded performance made available by Talbert on his *Love In the Nick of Tyme* DVD released in December 2009. As stated in the opening pages of this chapter, my objective in this discussion is to point out the dedicated ways that Talbert transforms circuit audiences from uninhibited viewers who are accustomed to freely responding to onstage presentations into controlled character-like participants whose dialogue, responses, and actions are largely predetermined by Talbert, the writer-director-producer.

The storyline of *Love in the Nick of Tyme* takes place in an unspecific neighborhood on the southside of Chicago. The main area of Talbert's set displayed the interior of a hair salon that was co-owned by Tyme Prentice and her on-again, off-again boyfriend of 17 years, jazz musician Marcelles Wynter. The salon was filled with recognizable furniture, including work stations for the stylists, a waiting area for clients, and a receptionist's desk. A large rear window of the salon provided a view of the sidewalk outside of the salon. This outside space had been designed as a working segment of the set, and throughout the production, audiences were able to see characters and hear their dialogue as they passed by the salon's window. A third area of the set periodically appeared in the downstage left corner of the stage. This area had been designed to look like the outside doorway of a jazz club, and the locale was highlighted by the large posters of upcoming performances that flanked the door frame. All of the unfolding drama in the *Love in the Nick of Tyme*'s plot took place on this functional single-level set.

In this play, Talbert focused on his female protagonist Tyme and her fleeting relationship with Marcelles, the father of her 17-year-old son. Although Marcelles refused to commit to her and was often out of town playing music and ignoring her phone calls, Tyme continued to hold onto their relationship because of the love-filled times in their past and the fact that he was the one who helped her finance the initial renting of her salon. When audiences encounter Tyme at the start of the play, Marcelles is back in town, and Tyme is trying her best to ignore his advances. She finally confronts him and urges him to take his name off the lease so that she can move on with her life. Marcelles refuses to let go of her so easily, and the remainder of the play is partly about Marcelles trying to keep Tyme in his web of women. Another portion of the plot covers Tyme's developing relationship with the attractive yet humble UPS delivery man, Harvey, whose personality is the polar opposite of Marcelles's self-centered and cocky demeanor. Throughout the play, Tyme finds herself torn between both men, but near the play's end, she discovers that Marcelles has been secretly seeing one of her employees and that he is soon to be the father of this woman's unborn child. By the last scene, Tyme has pushed Marcelles out of her life for good, and luckily Harvey has been waiting in the wings for a happy reconciliation.

Notably, *Love in the Nick of Tyme* represents Talbert's slight departure from the established circuit formula. Gospel music was absent from the entire play, and while spirituality and humor were infused in small doses, they did not have a large presence in the production. Instead, R&B ballads appeared throughout, and Talbert's trademark use of jazz underscoring was heard underneath most of the dialogue and scenic action. In so doing, Talbert presented an urban play about middle-class African Americans in which religion and/or religious behavior was not the focus. These changes aside, however, the production, like others on the circuit, still boasted a roster of familiar African American celebrities made famous by their film, television, and music careers. The role of Marcelles was played by Morris Chestnut, who has appeared in numerous films in which he played a young and attractive heartthrob. The popular R&B singer Avant was also cast in the production, along with Trenyce Cobbins, a former finalist on *American Idol*, and Ella English, an established actor popularly known for her work on the network television sitcom *The Jamie Foxx Show* and HBO's *Curb Your Enthusiasm*. Talbert also cast his wife, Lyn Talbert, as one of the salon's stylists. These slight changes and mainstays aside, according to my ethnographic sojourns to Talbert's productions, his musicals appeared to operate in ways that were similar to the plays produced by his peers until I began to focus on the behavior of his audiences during live performances.

One of the unique features of this production was Talbert's use of a narrative voice to frame the important plot action. During moments of narration, the stage lights would darken on the salon area of the stage, and an older African American male character who introduced himself at the start of the production as a jazz musician would appear outside of the jazz club's doorway and directly address the audience. Played by actor and spoken-word artist C.O.C.O. Brown, who is known for his signature deep voice, this character always wore a tailored dark suit and a matching fedora. What I discovered during live performances was that these moments of narration were scripted instances in which the fourth wall was broken between actor and spectator. However, unlike in other circuit productions where audiences would use moments of direct address to freely engage with characters, during Talbert's *Love in the Nick of Tyme* production, audiences did not verbally or physically respond to Brown's dialogue, because he was supplying them with important plot information. In C.O.C.O. Brown's character delivery, Talbert had created a dynamic in which an onstage actor spoke to assembled spectators as if they were another character onstage—instead of an audience member. This role-playing enabled spectators to "participate" in the production as inside information holders who alternated between being Brown's silent confidants and flies on the wall. Brown's direct addresses positioned spectators as familiar friends to whom he was telling an old story about some people he knew in his past, and as a result, their role as silent eavesdroppers was effectively rendered during the plot's main actions. This controlled audience environment was set in place by Brown's introduction at the start of the play, as reconstructed in this snapshot:

(*Marking the start of the play, the onstage clapping of a small unseen crowd is heard. The dimly lit outside entrance of the 312 jazz club is revealed and unidentified characters are seen exiting the doorway and walking offstage, stage-right. The deep male voice of an unseen actor is heard thanking the unseen club attendees for their applause.*)

BROWN Oh too kind. Too kind. One show on Friday, two on Saturday, eight if you're grown, eleven if you're grown and up to no good! Alright then, aww thank you man! Yeahhhh . . . hmm . . . hmm . . . yeah. (*Brown appears in the doorway. He exits the club entrance, walks downstage and approaches the audience. Once in position he lights a cigarette.*) Huh, they seem to love me in here! Hah! Southside of Chicago's own! Yeah, been playing here now, bout thirty years. The pay is good. The pay is good, but the people ohhhh . . . the people are even bettah!

UNIDENTIFIED MALE JAZZ CLUB PATRON (*Approaches Brown from behind.*) Yeah . . . that was a good show tonight man, a good show! Yes sir!

BROWN Thank you man! One show on Friday, two on Saturday, eight if you're grown and eleven if you're grown and up to no good! (*The Patron simultaneously says Brown's patented line with him and offers him a handshake as he exits the stage.*) Take care man, Alright.

PATRON Alright man. Take Care. Peace.

BROWN *directly addresses the audience.* Yeah, I seen a lot of things. You can't help but to when you've been in one place as much as I have, see. People tipping in people tipping out. People falling in people falling out—of love that is. Oh I got stories! One in particular happened not too far from this jazz club in a salon called the "Nick of Tyme." I wouldn't have believed it myself if I hadn't seen it with my own eyes you see. It all started on one fall night when something set off that salon's alarm. Yeah, I remember that. I remember just like it was yesterday. (*Stage lights begin to dim on him.*) Hmmm . . . hmmm . . . it was . . . aww yeah . . . ha ha ha. . . (*Brown's voice trails away as he walks offstage in darkness and lights come up on the salon.*)[85]

The next time the audience encounters Brown is at the end of that first scene. At the start of this particular snapshot of Brown's narration, the stage lights darkened on the salon, and he once again appears in front of the doorway of the 312 jazz club, cigarette in hand.

BROWN Time, the most precious commodity on the planet. A lot of folk think it's money but oh they print that up every day. Now you show me somebody that's printing up more time and I'll show you a unicorn and a three dollar bill. (*Takes a puff on his cigarette and talks about Tyme.*) Which is why I guess she decided it was time to stop wasting it given the relationship she had with the man that she had it with, could you blame her? I don't think nobody could. So what happened next was ah (*stage lights begin to dim*) . . . yeah . . . uh huh (*Brown exits stage in darkness*) . . . ha..ha..ha . . . (*Lights rise over the salon area marking the beginning of the next scene.*)

In the ensuing scenes, Harvey invites Tyme to a concert. Although she turned him down at first, she still accepted his telephone number. After some reflection, she decides to take him up on his offer and gives him a call. As the stage lights dim on her conversation, Brown appears again, this time with a flask in his hand. His direct address to the audience is captured in the following snapshot.

BROWN She might not have wanted to call it a date, but ohhh it was a date alright! (*Audience laughter is heard.*) They say all a fire needs is a spark and a flame. A steady wind and it'll stay lit for a lifetime. Pretty soon, they (*referring to Tyme and Harvey*) were all over the town, doing the type of nothing that seemed to add up to a whole lot of somethings, if you know what I mean. I guess the best way to get over an old love is with a new love, either that or a good drink. (*Brown takes a swig from his flask and the audience laughs.*) The tricky part is realizing that the old love is the old love. Now that's the tricky part it gets me every time. So what happened next in the story . . . (*Stage lights darken on Brown*). Yeah . . . hmmm..hmmm (*He exits stage in darkness*).

As the play proceeded, Brown continued to appear at the end of every scene, dropping kernels of wisdom and providing segues into the next portion of the story. By the end of the play, his closing observations, reconstructed here in this final snapshot, left the audience with a surprising revelation.

BROWN *appears onstage. The lights are still dimly lit over the salon area. Harvey and Tyme have reconciled and are frozen in motion just as they were about to kiss. As Brown speaks, Marcelles is seen looking inside of the salon through the street window. There* is something magical about kissing that woman. It's like time stands still. (*Audience laughter is heard.*) The reason that I know so well is because I used to kiss her too! (*Audience laughs.*) You see, my name is Marcelles (*audience reacts loudly with surprise*) and that was me thirty years ago and the only thing that I ever played better than that horn was myself (*Audience claps in approval. Tyme and Harvey remain frozen. The young Marcelles played by Morris Chestnut slowly enters the salon from outside and watches the frozen couple as he places the documents that remove him from the lease on Tyme's salon chair. As Chestnut's character stops and stares at the couple, Brown continues his monologue and ends his now familiar saying with a slight twist*) Well if you're ever on the Southside of Chicago, come and check me out. One show on Friday, two on Saturday, eight if you're grown and eleven if you're grown and all alone. (*Lights fade to black marking the end of the scene and loud audience applause is heard.*)

Although I also recall a few instances during the Chicago run of *Love in the Nick of Tyme* when Talbert's jazz underscoring also signaled to the audience that they should react to an important upcoming moment, I found Brown's direct audience addresses in this production to be a new twist to Talbert's mode of theatre-making. By the time of this 2007 production, underscoring had become a Talbert staple on the circuit, but what he had not mastered until this point was how to manipulate circuit audiences into being active yet predominantly silent spectators. Through the use of narration, however, he was remarkably able to achieve an engaged yet controlled circuit audience who exhibited many of the theatregoing behaviors experienced in traditional regional theatre houses across the country. I argue that his character-like treatment of the spectators, while not historically uncommon in theatrical events of traditional plays or musicals, was still a rare approach to theatre-making in the circuit.[86] Resultantly, spectators in Talbert's theatrical events unknowingly experienced a play in which their dialogue, responses, and actions were largely predetermined by the production's mastermind.

Reflections

In retrospect, the audible audience responses on the DVD recording of the San Diego, California, production were extremely similar to what I witnessed during my experience at the play's Chicago run. Although, my memory cannot accurately compare the nuances contained in the verbal responses of those live performances with the subtle differences that may have been present in the San Diego production, I can attest to the fact that both audience groups were similarly active or non-active during the same moments in the play. Moreover, this final aspect of Talbert's theatre-making completes the triad of factors that effectively enable this writer-director-producer to profoundly condition African American spectatorship.

Notes

1 Langston Hughes, "Black Nativity," in *The Collected Works of Langston Hughes*, ed. Leslie Catherine Sanders, vol. 6 (Columbia and London: University of Missouri Press, 2004), 371–72.

2 Shaw, "Insert [Chitlin Circuit] Here," 68; Joseph Roach, *Cities of the Dead: Circum-Atlantic Performance* (New York: Columbia University Press, 1996), 5.

3 David E. Talbert's official website, "About David," www.davidetalbert.com/about, accessed July 18, 2019.

4 Steven Zeitchik, "Fox Searchlight Tweaks Its Urban Efforts," *Los Angeles Times*, Entertainment, June 3, 2010, 1, http://latimesblogs.latimes.com/movies/2010/06/fox-searchlight-david-talbert-tyler-perry-urban-movies.html, accessed June 5, 2010.

5 I mention the set construction and lighting design here to call attention to the high production value of Talbert's theatre in spite of the fact that contemporary Chitlin Circuit theatre, on a whole, is assumed to be of poor theatrical quality.

6 Fern Gillespie, "Urban Theater's David E. Talbert Honored by NAACP," *The Crisis* 115, no. 3 (Summer 2008): 40.

7 Please see Gillespie, "Urban Theater's David E. Talbert Honored by NAACP," 40–41, and Chris Lee, "He's Still Writing His Own Story," *Los Angeles Times*, Article Collections, December 30, 2007, http://articles.latimes.com/2007/dec/30/entertainment/ca-talbert30, accessed June 6, 2010, for comments regarding Talbert's former employment as a radio disc jockey.

8 Gillespie, "Urban Theater's David E. Talbert Honored by NAACP": 40–41.

9 Lee, "He's Still Writing His Own Story," 3.

10 Lee, "He's Still Writing His Own Story," 3.

11 Lee, "He's Still Writing His Own Story," 3.

12 David E. Talbert's official website, "About David."

13 Ten contestants on the reality series received acting and musical training while they competed for a chance to be cast in a Talbert production.

14 David E. Talbert, *The Collected Plays of the People's Playwright*, vol. 1 (Woodland Hill, CA: David Talbert Presents, 2001).

15 Rashida Z. Shaw McMahon, "Gospel, According to David," Theater, *Time Out Chicago*, 111 (2007): 141.

16 Telephone conversation with David E. Talbert during an interview for *Time Out Chicago*, Wednesday, March 28, 2007 (6:17 p.m.).

17 Telephone conversation with David E. Talbert during an interview for *Time Out Chicago*, Wednesday, March 28, 2007 (6:17 p.m.).

18 It may be the case that, here, Talbert is also expressing his dissatisfaction with dominant American media representations that continue to feature heterosexual African American relationships that are primarily based on sex rather than love and commitment. Quote taken from David E. Talbert, "Bonus Features: Behind the Scenes Commentary with David E. Talbert (Writer/Producer)," in *The Fabric of a Man: The Musical Stageplay*, DVD, dir. David E. Talbert (Thousand Oaks, CA: UrbanWorks Entertainment, LLC, 2005).

19 David E. Talbert, "Bonus Features: Feature Commentary with Writer/Director David E. Talbert and Musical Director Robbie Lewis," in *He Say . . . She Say . . . but What Does God Say? The Musical Stageplay*, DVD, dir. David E. Talbert (Thousand Oaks, CA: UrbanWorks Entertainment, LLC, 2005). I first heard Talbert use the term *Inspirational Theatre* while I was watching the director's commentary of this play during my research.

20 Talbert, "Bonus Features: Feature Commentary with Writer/Director David E. Talbert and Musical Director Robbie Lewis."

21 When audiences first encounter Satin, they soon realize that he has been keeping track of the church's financial problems and is first in line to purchase the property in sixty

days when it goes into foreclosure. His plan is to have the entire block under his control. Unbeknownst to him, the violent-tempered Demetrius has gone outside of his orders and threatened the church members to pack up and leave before the deadline; otherwise, they will all face the penalty of death by his gun. Satin soon discovers what Demetrius has done, and this triggers a verbal and physical conflict between the two men that plays itself out throughout the course of the play.

22 In the Pastor Jackson and Michelle pairing, the audience witnesses a relationship that begins as a light and playful courtship but by the play's end has developed into a partnership that melds romance with strong faith and a shared commitment to put God first in their lives. On the contrary, Satin and Alexandria's relationship occurring right next door could not be more different. This high-strung duo has spent the past 15 years of their lives reaping the benefits of Detroit's drug game, yet when Satin admits to Alexandria that he is getting tired of this life, the couple soon realizes that they are growing in different directions. At first, Alexandria tries to convince Satin that there is no other life for them and urges him to reconsider, but after Satin confesses that his mind is made up, Alexandria begins to seek alternatives that would help her to remain in the drug world and support herself, which includes going into dealings with Demetrius.

23 Talbert, "Bonus Features: Behind the Scenes Commentary with David E. Talbert (Writer/Producer)."

24 Talbert, "Bonus Features: Behind the Scenes Commentary with David E. Talbert (Writer/Producer)."

25 David E. Talbert, "Bonus Features: Feature Commentary with Writer/Director David E. Talbert," in *Love on Lay Away*, DVD, dir. David E. Talbert (Thousand Oaks, CA: UrbanWorks Entertainment, LLC, 2005).

26 Talbert, "Bonus Features: Feature Commentary with Writer/Director David E. Talbert."

27 Talbert, "Bonus Features: Feature Commentary with Writer/Director David E. Talbert."

28 Talbert, "Bonus Features: Feature Commentary with Writer/Director David E. Talbert and Musical Director Robbie Lewis."

29 Talbert, "Bonus Features: Behind the Scenes Commentary with David E. Talbert (Writer/Producer)."

30 Talbert, "Bonus Features: Feature Commentary with Writer/Director David E. Talbert."

31 Talbert, "Bonus Features: Behind the Scenes Commentary with David E. Talbert (Writer/Producer)."

32 Talbert, "Bonus Features: Feature Commentary with Writer/Director David E. Talbert and Musical Director Robbie Lewis."

33 Talbert, "Bonus Features: Behind the Scenes Commentary with David E. Talbert (Writer/Producer)."

34 Talbert, "Bonus Features: Feature Commentary with Writer/Director David E. Talbert."

35 Talbert, "Bonus Features: Feature Commentary with Writer/Director David E. Talbert and Musical Director Robbie Lewis."

36 Talbert, "Bonus Features: Behind the Scenes Commentary with David E. Talbert (Writer/Producer)."

37 Talbert, "Bonus Features: Behind the Scenes Commentary with David E. Talbert (Writer/Producer)."

38 Talbert, "Bonus Features: Feature Commentary with Writer/Director David E. Talbert."

39 Talbert, "Bonus Features: Behind the Scenes Commentary with David E. Talbert (Writer/Producer)."

40 Talbert, "Bonus Features: Behind the Scenes Commentary with David E. Talbert (Writer/Producer)."

41 Talbert, "Bonus Features: Feature Commentary with Writer/Director David E. Talbert and Musical Director Robbie Lewis."

42 Talbert, "Bonus Features: Feature Commentary with Writer/Director David E. Talbert and Musical Director Robbie Lewis."

43 Douglas Cardwell, "The Well-Made Play of Eugène Scribe," *The French Review* 56, no. 6 (May 1983): 877.

44 Stephen S. Stanton, "Scribe's 'Bertrand Et Raton': A Well-Made Play," *The Tulane Drama Review* 2, no. 1 (November 1957): 59.

45 Christopher Innes, "Introduction," in *A Sourcebook on Naturalist Theatre*, ed. Christopher Innes (London and New York: Routledge, 2000), 7.

46 Marvin Carlson, *Theories of Theatre: A Historical and Critical Survey from the Greeks to the Present* (Ithaca, NY and London: Cornell University Press, 1984), 216.

47 Cardwell, "The Well-Made Play of Eugène Scribe," 881.

48 Stanton, "Scribe's 'Bertrand Et Raton'," 59.

49 Tice L. Miller, "Well-Made Play," in *The Cambridge Guide to World Theatre*, ed. Martin Banham (Cambridge: Cambridge University Press, 1988), 1064.

50 Cardwell, "The Well-Made Play of Eugène Scribe," 881.

51 Carlson, *Theories of Theatre*, 216.

52 James Weldon Johnson, *God's Trombone's: Seven Negro Sermons in Verse* (New York: Penguin Books, 1927).

53 The transformation of Ossie Davis's 1961 comedic drama from *Purlie Victorious* into the 1970 Broadway musical *Purlie* and the creation of the 1978 Broadway musical *Raisin* are of note here for the expansion of the gospel and religious content in the adaptations. In the case of *Purlie*, the comedic aspect of Davis's original endured, and the musical adapters remained cognizant of the fact that Davis's title character, Purlie, was a "new-fangled preacher man" trying to start his own church. With an African American church and religion already a part of the original plotline, the creators—Ossie Davis, Peter Udell, Gary Geld, and Philip Rose—ensured that gospel music figured largely in the production. Meanwhile, *Raisin*'s creative team—Robert Nemirroff, Charlotte Zaltzberg, Judd Woldin, and Robert Brittain—chose to showcase the exterior and the interior world of the Youngers by incorporating dance-inflected street scenes and church scenes that were infused with gospel music and large choir production numbers. For "new-fangled preacher man" reference, please see Ossie Davs, Peter Udell, Gary Geld, and Philip Rose, *Purlie: A Musical Based on the Play "Purlie Victorious"* (New York, NY: Samuel French, Inc., 1971), 15. In Act 1 Scene 1 of the musical, Purlie sings a song about himself titled "New-Fangled Preacher Man."

54 Burdine, "The Gospel Musical and Its Place in the Black American Theatre," 194.

55 Burdine, "The Gospel Musical and Its Place in the Black American Theatre," 194.

56 Burdine, "The Gospel Musical and Its Place in the Black American Theatre," 194.

57 Burdine, "The Gospel Musical and Its Place in the Black American Theatre," 195.

58 D'Aponte, "*The Gospel at Colonus* (and Other Black Morality Plays)," 101.

59 Burdine, "The Gospel Musical and Its Place in Black American Theatre," 197.

60 Notably, Shelly Garrett passed away in 2018. The producer and playwright was often referred to as "the godfather" of urban theater. Please see Fisher Jack, "Shelly Garett 'The Godfather of Urban Theater' Has Died," *Black America Web.com*, https://black-americaweb.com/2018/05/04/shelly-garrett-the-godfather-of-urban-theater-has-died/, accessed July 21, 2018.

61 Burdine, "The Gospel Musical and Its Place in Black American Theatre," 200.

62 Rampersad, *The Life of Langston Hughes*, 255.

63 *The Fabric of a Man* and *Love on Lay Away* are also included in this box set collection titled *The Soul Theatre Series*, distributed and produced with the help of UrbanWorks Entertainment, LLC.

64 The remaining original cast members were Clifton Powell, Tommy Ford, Thomas Miles, Maurice Wilkinson, Julie Dickens, Cassie Davis, and Orlando Wright.

65 Langston Hughes, "Tambourines to Glory," in *The Collected Works of Langston Hughes*, ed. Leslie Catherine Sanders, vol. 6 (Columbia and London: University of Missouri Press, 2004), 286.

66 Hughes, "Tambourines to Glory," 287.

67 Colbert, *The African American Theatrical Body*, 124.

68 Buddy introduces himself in the prologue of the play as the Devil.

69 Hughes, "Tambourines to Glory," 299.

70 This dialogue takes place in Act 1 Scene 7.

71 This dialogue also takes place in Act 1 Scene 7.

72 As many theatre historians have revealed, the literary objectives of Hughes and Hurston were so similar that they began crafting a play titled *Mule Bone* in 1930. Unfortunately, *Mule Bone* was never completed, due to interpersonal conflicts. For more information, see Langston Hughes and Zora Neale Hurston, *Mule Bone: A Comedy of Negro Life: And the Complete Story of the Mule Bone Controversy*, ed. George Houston Bass and Henry Louis Gates, Jr. (New York: HarperPerennial, 1991).

73 Mel Watkins, *On the Real Side: Laughing, Lying, and Signifying—The Underground Tradition of African-American Humor That Transformed American Culture, from Slavery to Richard Pryor* (New York: Simon & Schuster, 1994), 420.

74 Mel Watkins, *African American Humor: The Best Black Comedy from Slavery to Today* (Chicago: Lawrence Hill Books, 2002), 111–12.

75 Watkins, *African American Humor*, 112.

76 This transcription is based on the DVD recording of this production. Please see David E. Talbert, *He Say . . . She Say . . . but What Does God Say?: The Musical Stageplay*, DVD (Thousand Oaks, CA: UrbanWorks Entertainment, LLC, 2005).

77 Talbert, *He Say . . . She Say . . . but What Does God Say?*

78 Grace Sims Holt, "Stylin' Outta the Black Pulpit," in *Signifyin(g), Sanctifyin', & Slam Dunking: A Reader in African American Expressive Culture*, ed. Gena Dagel Caponi (Amherst, MA: University of Massachusetts Press, 1999), 332.

79 Talbert, "Bonus Features: Behind the Scenes Commentary with David E. Talbert (Writer/Producer)."

80 Tims is an abbreviated name for casual men's boots produced by the footwear company Timberland that are popularly worn by African American men in urban areas in the United States, including Brooklyn, New York, where this play is set.

81 A kangol hat is a beret-style knit hat that can be worn by men or women usually during the winter months. The hats are sold and distributed by the Kangol Headwear USA and Kangol Headwear Europe. Although they are popularly worn by some African American men, they should not be considered indicative of African American culture or American urban wear.

82 "Let's Get a Bite to Eat," in *The Fabric of a Man: The Musical Stageplay*, DVD, dir. David E. Talbert (Thousand Oaks, CA: UrbanWorks Entertainment, LLC, 2005). This dialogue and blocking are taken from the recorded production of this play as cited. Although Talbert has published some of his scripts, I noticed differences between the published play text of *The Fabric of a Man* and the live production as recorded on the DVD. My analysis in this chapter is based on the recorded production. For the published play text, please see Talbert, *The Collected Plays of the People's Playwright*.

83 I discuss the Arie Crown Theater in greater detail in Chapter Six, "Tyler Perry: Minstrelsy Inverted," during my analysis of the theatrical events of Tyler Perry.

84 The 2007 production run of *Love in the Nick of Tyme* is the only Talbert play that I was able to attend live. Before 2007, his previous production run of *Love on Lay Away* appeared on circuit stages in 2003, a year before my acceptance into graduate school. To date, he has not produced many plays due to his developing film and television projects. However, I do not think that Talbert's hiatus from theatre is a sign that his

theatrical career has been put to rest. Similar to other circuit playwrights—including those focused on in this project—Talbert is dedicated to working across different performance mediums.

85   This transcription is based on the DVD recording of this production. Please see *Love in the Nick of Tyme*, DVD, dir. David E. Talbert (Recorded live at Spreckels Theatre, San Diego, CA: 260 Degrees Entertainment, LLC, 2009).

86   Consider the discussions in the following articles as representative examples of how playwrights and directors have attempted to control and/or position audience reception during performances. For a recent discussion of Brecht's alienation effect that focuses on his ideas concerning audience reception, please see Herbert Blau, "The Thin, Thin Crust and the Colophon of Doubt: The Audience in Brecht," *New Literary History* 21, no. 1 (Autumn 1989): 175–97. For a targeted discussion of the relationship between Shakespeare's character Kent and the audience of *King Lear*, see Robert Egan, "Kent and the Audience: The Character as Spectator," *Shakespeare Quarterly* 32, no. 2 (Summer 1981): 146–54. Additionally, for a discussion relating to audience participation and casting in environmental theatre productions, please see Natalie Crohn Schmitt, "Casting the Audience," *TDR* 37, no. 4 (Winter 1993): 143–56.

5

JOHNSON AND GUIDRY

Vaudeville 2.0

SIMPLE I tell you, something's always happening to a colored man! Stormy weather! Boyd, I been caught in some kind of rifle ever since I been black. All my life, if it ain't raining, its blowing. If it ain't sleeting, it's snowing. Man, you try to be good, and what happens? You just don't be good. You try to live right. What happens? You look back and find out you didn't live right. Even when you're working, and you try to save money, what happens? Can't do it. Your shoes is wore out. Or the dentist has got you. You try to save again. What happens? You drunk it up? Try to save another time. Some relative gets sick and needs it. What happens to money, Boyd? What happens?

BOYD Come on, man, snap out of it! Let's go down to Paddy's and gave a drink. At least we can sit up in the bar and get warm—and not think about what happens.

—Langston Hughes, *Simply Heavenly*[1]

JOYCE Free! Jess, you're free! Like in *Uncle Tom's Cabin*!

SIMPLE Yes, baby, I'm free. That's the paper.

—Langston Hughes, *Simply Heavenly*[2]

In August of 2005, *Black Enterprise* magazine introduced the entrepreneurial duo of Je'Caryous Johnson and Gary Guidry to a world of business and economically minded African American readers in a one-page feature that opened with the following paragraphs:

> Fed up with the lack of quality parts available to black actors in Hollywood, self-described "starving actor" and Houston native Je'Caryous Johnson left Tinseltown behind and instead decided to create an outlet for African Americans to acquire good roles. Along with his uncle, Gary Guidry, who left a stable job as a senior accountant for an oil and gas company, the two

tapped into their creative passions to start I'm Ready Productions Inc., a now 7-year-old theater, film, and music production company that specializes in adapting black novels into stage plays and films.

From its days as a fledgling operation, I'm Ready Productions has built its reputation around quality performances and turned itself into a multimillion-dollar enterprise that tours the country.[3]

To readers who may have been unaware of available financial opportunities in the world of African American theatre and to whom Je'Caryous Johnson and Gary Guidry were almost unknowns, Michelle K. Massie's piece formally heralded this team as thriving movers and shakers in the Chitlin Circuit theatrical market. Visually, the article's main photograph presented the image of two young clean-cut professional men standing inside of a vast and unidentified theatre auditorium wearing business suits and wide smiles. Guidry is positioned on the left side of the photograph's frame, and Johnson stands close behind him, near center. In the background, crimson-red seats and an aisle descend toward an expansive proscenium stage. The article's title, "Finding a Niche in Black Theater: Producers Specialize in Adapting Black Novels into Stage Plays," is emblazoned over the lower left corner of the snapshot and is positioned underneath a caption that encapsulates the thrust of the piece: "Making It."

In the spread, Massie narrates the launching and eventual commercial failure of Johnson and Guidry's first theatrical production. As the story goes, back in 2000, the pair produced a small-scale national tour of the play *Heaven's Child: The Legacy of Emmett Till*. Although the authorship of the play goes unmentioned in the piece, the play itself is touted as a dramatic narration of the life and tragic murder of Emmett Till, the 14-year-old African American teenager whose death received national attention in 1955, after he was beaten and lynched for allegedly whistling at a white woman while visiting family members in Money, Mississippi. To finance the tour, Johnson and Guidry strung together $400,000 from their own personal accounts and the savings and 401K accounts of supportive family members. Unfortunately, what began as a well-financed theatrical venture in Houston, Texas, eventually closed in the red by the time the production graced its final stage in Chicago, Illinois. The entire *Heaven's Child* tour was able to generate only $60,000 in total box office receipts, a far cry from the profits that Guidry and Johnson had hoped to see.[4]

However, Johnson and Guidry's first foray into commercial theatre was not a complete failure. Ticket sales were indeed low, yet perhaps as luck or fate would have it, the number of people who saw the show paled in importance to how those who saw the show felt when they left the theatre. Their audiences, composed of consumers from the local Black communities and representatives from various Black radio stations and Black press outlets such as the *Chicago Defender* praised their efforts and offered positive reviews. In fact, by the tour's end, the Johnson–Guidry team had managed to attract investors interested in future projects. As Massie's article implied, the impact of receiving the positive feedback and interest of discerning African American spectators at this critical juncture in their careers overwhelmingly enabled the theatre-making of Johnson and Guidry to continue. In time, the financial numbers began to match the enthusiasm of their audiences. By the publication of Massie's article, I'm Ready Productions had grown into a stable production company that consisted of 32 employees and boasted revenues of $6.5 million. Their 2005 financial projections predicted that the company would see an $8.5 million increase that would bring them to a grand total of $15 million by year end.[5] As Massie's title tellingly stated, Johnson and Guidry had indeed found their "niche."[6]

With marked innovation and a desire to set their work apart from the rest, Houston natives Je'Caryous Johnson and Gary Guidry decided to leave behind historically topical African American theatre fare, like *Heaven's Child*, and instead put their own twist on the circuit theatre formula. By the time they entered the scene, contemporary circuit routes were already filled with plays written and produced by Talbert, Perry, and a pool of hopeful unknowns. Their unique contribution to the genre of Chitlin Circuit theatre came in the form of full-length African American musical dramas that contained narrative plotlines and characters that had been adapted from popular and African American novels. In 2002 and 2003, two years after the closing of *Heaven's Child*, they consecutively staged two novels authored by Baisden: *Men Cry in the Dark* (2002) and *The Maintenance Man* (2003). In 2004, they created another revenue success with their adaptation of Eric Jerome Dickey's novel *Friends and Lovers*.[7] By 2008, *The New York Times* was including Johnson and Guidry among a short list of "the circuit's big producers" that boasted only two other names: David Talbert and Tyler Perry.[8] Their roster of plays continued to include popular novel adaptations, such as their reworking of Eric Jerome Dickey's book *Cheaters*, and it eventually expanded to include productions that Johnson and Guidry wrote themselves. Advertisements for these latter productions boasted originally conceived storylines, catchy titles, and star-studded casts, as was evident during the production runs of their hits: *3 Ways to Get a Husband*; *Casino: The Comedy Stage Play*; *Cheaper to Keep Her*; *Love Overboard*; *Men, Money, and Gold Diggers*; and *Whatever She Wants*.

This chapter presents a nuanced investigation into the form and content of Johnson and Guidry's unique theatrical models alongside analyses of the performance and reception practices found in their theatrical events. In one vein, my discussion here is specifically dedicated to understanding how the Johnson–Guidry model infuses secular African American novels with religious and/or sacred content and then (re)presents these same narratives within a theatrical and performance frame. In another vein, I consider how these resultant theatrical productions are representative of the kind of theatre commonly found on circuit stages and yet is markedly different from the theatrical fare presented by their peers. All of this is undertaken through an analysis of how comedy, popular culture, religion, and vernacular practices are referred to and/or used in productions.

My driving argument in this chapter is that African American spectatorship in Johnson–Guidry theatrical events is conditioned by the following factors working in tandem with each other during productions: an audience's familiarity with the original literary text used in the theatrical adaptation; the inclusion of religious material in ways that align the novel's narrative arc with mandatory religious content and mimetically re-create an African American religious experience onstage that is recognizable to audiences; and, the insertion of vaudeville-like, variety show–styled performance acts that intentionally interrupt and manipulate the plot to offer audiences more varied forms of entertainment with the hopes of increasing their level of engagement.

Secular to Sacred: Turning Black American Popular Fiction into Theatrical "Chitlins"

In the realm of theatre and performance, literary texts have historically and consistently found their way onto theatre stages via theatrical and/or performance-based adaptations. Included among a long list of novel-to-stage adaptations are the numerous transformations of Mary Shelley's 1818 novel *Frankenstein; or, The Modern Prometheus*, Harriet Beecher Stowe's 1852 novel *Uncle Tom's Cabin; or, Life Among the Lowly*, and even various adaptations of Franz Kafka's writing, such as Steven Berkoff's 1969 dramatic rendering of Kafka's 1915 book *The Metamorphosis* into a play of the same name. African American theatre has also benefited from collaborations that have united reader-oriented texts and dramatic performances. Here I am reminded of Langston Hughes's previously discussed 1957 musical *Simply Heavenly*, adapted from his fictional stories of Jesse B. Semple. This chapter's opening epigraphs, taken from the text of *Simply Heavenly*, signal the pervasiveness of popular culture in Hughes's musicals with representative references to both *Uncle Tom's Cabin* and the popular 1930s song "Stormy Weather" that also shares its name with the similarly popular, African American cast Hollywood film musical of 1943.[9] George C. Wolfe in his 1991 musical *Spunk* presented an adaptation of three short stories originally penned by Zora Neale Hurston: *Sweat, Story in Harlem Slang*, and *The Gilded Six-Bits*. Respectively, in 1999 and 2000, Suzan-Lori Parks premiered her adaptations of Nathaniel Hawthorne's 1850 novel *The Scarlett Letter*, in dramas titled *In the Blood* and *Fucking A*. In 2005, Chicago playwright Lydia Diamond brought Toni Morrison's 1970 novel *The Bluest Eye* to the stage in a production of the same name, and a few years later, in 2008, she dramatized Harriet Jacobs's 1861 novel *Incidents in the Life of a Slave Girl* into *Harriet Jacobs: A Play*. Examples such as these illuminate a proven tradition of literary adaptation in American theatre. However, before the advent of the Chitlin Circuit theatre market, popular African American novels were never selected as the go-to material for theatrical and/or performance projects. In walk Johnson and Guidry.

In a realm of theatre where popular culture is used not only as a means of drawing audiences to the theatre but also as a mechanism that triggers social, cultural, and ideological identifications, Johnson and Guidry's decision to adapt this particular brand of African American novel to the contemporary circuit stage becomes apparent once we understand the growing rate at which African American readers have been consuming these texts and the types of stories that are attracting them. Susanne B. Deitzel explains, in her article "The African American Novel and Popular Culture," the driving popularity behind these books:

> The market for African American popular fiction experienced an upsurge in the 1990s when the number of hardcover books and paperback originals by black authors rose tremendously, giving rise to a new subgenre of African American popular fiction that some have called "sister-girl" and "brotherman" novels. These sometimes steamy novels cover the ups, downs, and sexual politics of romantic relationship[s] from either a female or male perspective.[10]

Dietzel provides further context for these books by explaining that although "African American popular or commercial fiction is too large a field to be condensed into a simple formula," the stories in subgenres like the *sister-girl* and *brotherman* novels are part and parcel of this larger category.

> [T]hey can be called black novels of manners that have picked up on Terry McMillan's focus on chronicling the social and love lives of black petty bourgeoisie. Characters are almost exclusively members of a suburban middle class with college educations who have overcome, or never even faced racial discrimination and/or economically disadvantaged backgrounds. They have succeeded in a capitalist society; they may live in predominantly black worlds, but they are not very different from the worlds white characters inhabit in similar novels aimed at white readers. . . . Not surprisingly, much emphasis is placed on those material possessions that constitute or mark a new class: education, careers, lineages, houses, taste, and cars just to name a few. Most important, though, is how characters relate to each other in these new social circumstances; women and men, parents and children, gays and straights, all struggle to figure out where one belongs and what blackness means in the twenty-first century.[11]

Deitzel contextualizes the popularity of these texts by pointing out how changing class dynamics in the American economic structure granted African American readers greater purchasing power that in turn influenced publishing houses to supply books to meet the needs of an ever-growing demand.

> During the 1980s and 1990s growing class distinctions in the black community increased the number of middle- and middle-upper [*sic*] class black Americans and subsequently produced a greater market of black readers.

For example, a 1994 study showed that "African Americans spend more than $175 million per year on books" and that book purchases in the black community rose by 26 percent between 1988 and 1991.... [D]emographic changes and increased demand did not go unnoticed by the mainstream publishing industry. Beginning in the early 1990s, publishers began to look at blacks as customers and consumers whose demands deserve attention and started recruiting black writers who could write in those genres.[12]

If we take these factors into consideration, it becomes clear that a union between popular African American novels and African American theatre becomes not only an economically feasible choice but also one that is culturally and con-temporaneously motivated. Thus, Johnson and Guidry's decision to adapt this particular brand of African American fictional writing stands as a bold testament to their economically and culturally savvy business acumen and, as I will demon-strate, their innovative creativity. As I will discuss in the pages that follow, Johnson–Guidry plays simultaneously maintain the foundational elements of the larger African American popular fiction genre and adhere to the characteristics of the smaller *sister-girl* and *brotherman* subgenre as defined by Dietzel. Moreover, the theatre of Johnson and Guidry succeeds in incorporating the accepted aesthetic and performance conventions of Chitlin Circuit theatre.

Yet to transplant these stories into an already-established circuit frame, John-son and Guidry had to contend with the secular nature of these literary texts to transform them into religiously grounded dramas that feature sacred plotlines of contemporary African American life. Gerald L. Davis, in his book *I got the word in me and I can sing it, you know: A Study of the Performed African-American Sermon*, devotes considerable attention to a category of African American cultural perfor-mance that intentionally incorporates and reveals its secular and sacred dimen-sions as a means of connecting, instructing, uplifting, and/or healing its African American audience. In Davis's study, I find three aspects of his investigation into the "performed African American sermon"[13] to be particularly helpful in the con-text of this chapter. The first is his theoretical claim that there are three "active components in the maintenance of performance standards and forms for African-American materials." These components are "the performer," "the audience," and "tradition."[14] While the terms *performance* and *audience* carry the definitions that we in theatre and performance studies are familiar with, his definition of tradition is identified as the "characteristic customary, habitual, and dynamic employment of folk ideas in a performance context."[15] In what follows, I will examine this relationship between the audience, the performer, and tradition in the context of Johnson and Guidry's theatrical events; yet Davis's concept of folk ideas will be expanded to include popular culture, vernacular, and religiously codified African American materials. Second, Davis argues that "[s]o consistently are the patterns of agreements evidenced in performance that those who participate in any given performance—audience and performer—can be considered to participate in an aesthetic community."[16] For Davis, "[t]he aesthetic community concept assumes the existence of an established cultural community having the capacity to identify the forms and types of its cultural products."[17] Davis's aesthetic perspective falls in line with my view of circuit audiences as being members of a unique and specific group of African American spectators who share particular cultural, racial, and gendered experiences and are familiar with the assembled popular culture, vernacular, and religious references in the plays in ways that outsiders are not. Yet Davis's interest primarily lies in determining how both the African American performer and their African American audience take part in this community during the performance in ways that reveal and shape the performance's aesthetic. Here I am interested in applying Davis's concept to Johnson and Guidry's work and expanding his perspective to include a consideration of the performer, the audience, *and* the playwright. Lastly, I am equally interested in Davis's exploration of the "sacred/secular tension"[18] that in his case manifests in performances of the African American sermon but that in the case of this chapter reveals itself in the African American–conceived, African American–performed, and African American–received theatrical events of Johnson and Guidry.

The African American Sermon Tradition as Performed on the Circuit Stage

I begin my examination of Johnson and Guidry's productions with a speculative look at their 2003 touring stage play *The Maintenance Man*, adapted from Baisden's book of the same name. Of the many novels that this playwriting team transformed into circuit plays, I find that their adaptation of Baisden's *The Maintenance Man* singularly exemplifies their literary-to-theatrical adaptive techniques as well as the secular-to-sacred transformations undertaken by the duo to adhere to established circuit standards.[19] Different from the analysis presented in the previous chapter of David E. Talbert's play *Love in the Nick of Tyme*, my analysis in this section is a historical case study because my review of the production took place before the beginning of my ethnographic research. As one of the two plays that helped to solidify Johnson and Guidry's elevated position on the circuit scene, *The Maintenance Man* serves as an important case study for the following discussion not only because it is the first production in which their developed technique of secular-to-sacred transformation was fully realized but also because it is the production that laid the standard from which all of their subsequent sacred-to-secular theatrical adaptations followed. Thus, the analysis in this section will reconstruct the theatrical event as presented in the live video recording distributed and made available for purchase by Johnson and Guidry in 2002 and compare its content to the particulars of Baisden's novel.

Baisden's *The Maintenance Man* arrived in bookstores and bookstands across the country in 1999 on the heels of his first novel, *Never Satisfied: How and Why Men Cheat*, published in 1995. *Never Satisfied*'s content was part fiction and part research. Baisden claimed to have interviewed over "1000 unfaithful men" and then compiled their stories into a book that "reveals everyone's part in the cheating game. The tolerant wife or girlfriend, the despicable other woman, and of course the conniving cheater":[20]

> I wrote this book out of pure frustration out of years of listening to hundreds of angry women and out of touch psychologists attempting, unsuccessfully, to uncover the truth about why men cheat. In my opinion, only a man who has played the games can thoroughly break down the hows and whys of infidelity. . . . Besides, today's woman is bored to death with futile arguments and scientific theories. She wants to hear the absolute truth, no matter how painful. Well, this book tells it all. The stories are the most raw, revealing, and comical you will ever read. Never before has such a realistic examination been put together.[21]

For Baisden, this book was an articulation of everything that he was hearing, doing, seeing, and, most of all, talking about in his everyday life. The brief author's bio included on the book's Amazon.com webpage notes that at the time of publication, Baisden was employed by the Chicago Transit Authority as a train driver. Although Baisden tried the conventional publication routes, Amazon.com states that his work was rejected by the "large New York publishing companies" for not being "marketable." Baisden, in turn, decided to publish his book himself with the help of family, friends, and the sale of personal items. Accordingly, "[w]ithin eight months, he [had] sold more than 50,000 books and was on *Essence* and *Emerge* magazines' best seller lists."[22] By the time his third book *The Maintenance Man* was published, Baisden was doing guest appearances across the country on radio and television and at book fairs and conventions.[23] By 2003, he was offered a chance to be the afternoon host on New York City's popular R&B station 98.7 KISS FM, where his popularity soared.[24] Today, he hosts his own nationally syndicated radio show that airs in cities across the Eastern seaboard and as far west as Illinois and Arizona and as far south as Florida, Louisiana, and Texas.[25]

The Maintenance Man's plot, as developed by Baisden, revolves around the character Malcolm Terrell. Malcolm is described as a six-foot, three-inches tall, attractive, and physically fit African American bachelor from Chicago who earns his living by temporarily renting his body and his time to women at expensive rates. As Malcolm explains in the prologue of Baisden's book, this is a negative trait that he picked up during his childhood from watching his father cheat on his mother with different neighborhood women. Baisden begins the story of *The Maintenance Man* by positioning Malcolm at his father's funeral. Malcolm's father was shot twice in the head by the jealous husband of the woman next door whom he was secretly seeing. Although the cheating wife survived a gunshot wound to her chest, Malcolm's father was unable to survive his injuries. Standing in front of his father's grave, Malcolm finally has a heart-to-heart with him:

> I'm making this confession because my prayers went unanswered. Not only have I become you, I've become worse than you. I'm a gigolo. Now, don't start your preaching. I'm not some cheap prostitute hanging out on street corners. My job is escorting rich women out to business functions and social events. I've already earned twenty thousand dollars. Not bad for a twenty-five-year-old rookie. I lied to you and Mama because I didn't want you to know that I dropped out of music school. I thought about calling home for help with tuition but my pride wouldn't allow it.
>
> So, I decided to make it the best way I knew how, and that meant playing women. Everything I needed to know I learned from watching you: how to walk, talk, dress, and how to use sex to control women. By the time I was fifteen, I was charging my classmates fifty dollars each to escort them to prom.[26]

This opening scene is the first encounter that readers have with Malcolm, and it directs the trajectory of the plot through Malcolm's manipulation of women. The plot twist occurs when Malcolm unsuspectingly meets Antoinette Grayson, a professional dancer and choreographer, at a United Negro College Fund fundraiser while escorting one of his repeat clients, Helen, a wealthy, married Atlanta socialite. Eventually, Malcolm's genuine attraction and interest in Antoinette leads him to pursue a real relationship with her—the first of its kind for him. Yet his decision to not tell her the truth about his occupation and his past leads to conflict in their relationship when the truth is revealed by Antoinette's jealous exboyfriend. Malcolm finds himself caught in a struggle between his traumatic past, his corrupt present, and the honest and loving future that he would like to have with Antoinette if he could only tell her the truth.

Considering Dietzel's assessment of "African American popular or commercial fiction,"[27] *The Maintenance Man* falls squarely within her parameters for the genre and the smaller subgenre of "sister-girl"[28] and "brotherman"[29] novels. Written from the male perspective, *The Maintenance Man* features middle-class and upper-middle-class African American characters living comfortably and spending their time in major American cities like Atlanta, Chicago, Los Angeles, New Orleans, and New York. Baisden packs his pages with references to good living and upscale possessions. The lives of his characters are filled with frequent traveling, fine dining, fancy cars, expensive designer clothing, and an appreciation for the fine arts. His characters are well educated, and many are at the top of their chosen field. The music school from which Malcolm dropped out is none other than New York City's Julliard School. Antoinette teaches dance but also performs professionally across the United States and Europe. Helen is depicted as a married

Atlanta socialite who rubs shoulders with celebrities and politicians. Malcolm's best friend, Simon, owns his own club, Club Obsession, and Melvin, Malcolm's father figure in the novel, is also the owner of his own club, Melvin's Jazz Club. Lavish lifestyles notwithstanding, the characters also live in a world that is cultured and intertwined with African American social and charitable events that champion the legacy of African American history makers such as W.E. B. Du Bois, Malcolm X, Martin Luther King Jr, and Sojourner Truth. By the time the novel concludes, not only have Antoinette and Malcolm reconciled their differences, but Malcolm has also been willed the deed to Melvin's club after Melvin's passing. This turn of events enables Malcolm to continue to play his music, which he confesses is his true passion, and leave the sex worker lifestyle behind without a fear of losing money because he is now the owner of a profitable business.

Johnson and Guidry's theatrical adaptation keeps most of the main plot content and character depictions yet removes some of the story's minor characters and settings. For example, circuit audiences are not introduced to Malcolm's mother in Chicago, nor do they see any hint of Club Obsession and the smaller characters who occupied that world. Instead, Simon and Melvin are seen together working and entertaining at Melvin's Jazz Club even though the play references the fact that Simon owns his own club. The relationship between Malcolm and Antoinette remains a focal point, as does the relationship between Simon and his fiancée Cynthia. In the novel, Cynthia attends the Essence Music Festival in New Orleans with her friend Debra. Cynthia, who has been feeling neglected by Simon's long hours at the club, is easily distracted by the male attention she receives in New Orleans, especially from Reverend James Young. James introduces himself to Cynthia as a "marriage and substance abuse counselor" in Atlanta, where they are both from.[30] Near the end of her trip, an intoxicated Cynthia winds up in bed with Reverend James, sparking the beginning of an affair that continues once the two return to Atlanta. Simon, who has become suspicious of Cynthia's actions, hires a private investigator and discovers the affair between Cynthia and Reverend James, who is also the preacher at the First United Baptist Church. Simon soon gets revenge for himself and for the other men whose women have been sleeping with Reverend James by publicly humiliating the preacher in front of his congregation. On the morning of a special ceremony honoring an important Civil Rights leader, Simon breaks into the projector room of the church and airs the recorded footage of Cynthia and the preacher engaging in sexual intercourse before an audience filled with regular church attendees and the local media stations there to broadcast the event. A shocked and embarrassed Cynthia realizes that her relationship with Simon is over and her career as a television news anchor is now in jeopardy. Despite this public revenge act, after the dust settles and Simon learns that Cynthia is pregnant, he decides to take responsibility for his absence in their relationship and proposes to her again, and she accepts. By the end of the novel, Simon decides to raise Cynthia's unborn child even if he may not be the father.

I would like to examine Johnson and Guidry's different adaptation of this Simon and Cynthia plotline in order to chart what I referred to earlier as their literary-to-theatrical adaptive techniques and their secular-to-sacred transformations of Baisden's text. In Johnson and Guidry's version, the story takes place in six settings: Melvin's Jazz Club, Antoinette's apartment, Simon's apartment, the inside of a New Orleans hotel room, a sidewalk outside of an apartment building, and the interior of a church. In line with Chitlin Circuit theatre casting practices, the production contains three familiar African American celebrities, along with a few hopeful unknowns. Malcolm is played by Darius McCrary, an African American actor who is popularly known from his role as Eddie Winslow in the television sitcom *Family Matters* that aired in the late 1980s through the 1990s. The role of Malcolm's father figure Melvin is played by African American actor Billy Dee Williams. Although the depth and range of Williams's acting resume is too lengthy to enumerate in successful detail here, his career began with the 1959 film *The Last Angry Man*. Since then, Williams has worked on numerous film and television projects. Some circuit audiences may have remembered Williams from his starring roles with Diana Ross in the films *Lady Sings the Blues* (1972) and *Mahogany* (1975). Others may have been familiar with his roles in two *Star Wars* films released in the 1980s (*Star Wars Episode V: The Empire Strikes Back* and *Star Wars Episode VI: Return of the Jedi*), and still others may have recognized him from his many television appearances, which include reoccurring roles on the soap operas *Dynasty*, *Guiding Light*, and *General Hospital*. Finishing the list of popular African American celebrities is Arnez J., a comedian and former host of *Comic View*, a long-running comedy showcase on the Black Entertainment Television (BET) network. On the DVD case, Baisden's novel is given credit and the executive producers are listed as Johnson and Guidry. The story is listed as being created by Johnson and Guidry, while the play script is listed as being written by Johnson and a lesser-known Dana Hali. Guidry and two others, Nikki Ross and D. Edgecombe, are credited with developing the music. The co–musical directors are listed as D. Edgecombe and Marcus Bryant. Je'Caryous Johnson is listed as the director.

The moments in question occur in the second half of the production in a scene comically titled "Pimpin' Woods Baptist Church." Here the word *pimpin'* is used to liken the fictive character of Reverend James to those real men— colloquially referred to as pimps—who control the financial earnings of female sex workers and commonly flaunt their wealth via expensive clothing, cars, and an always-present flock of devoted women. Although Cynthia's character is not presented as a sex worker and we do not have evidence of the Reverend's controlling her finances or her actions, the scene title is meant to play on the deceptive nature of the man behind the pulpit. Through Baisden's original storyline and the ensuing Johnson and Guidry adaptation, readers and/or spectators know that it is through this church and James's self-presentation as a preacher that he has been able to secure the trust of his parishioners and others whom he encounters in his everyday life. Thus, the irony of the title lies in that this place of worship is being led by a man who is using the pulpit to gain wealth and seduce women. The credit for the name Pimpin' Woods Baptist Church, however, must be given to Johnson and Guidry. In Baisden's novel, James is the pastor of the realistically named First United Baptist Church. Yet because Johnson and Guidry were working in a theatrical medium that partly relies on the utility of comedic devices and the appeal of popular culture references, they deftly used the church's name not only to highlight these particular aesthetic conventions but also to engage with their audience on a sensory level.

As the scene begins, James (played by actor Darrell Blair) stands behind the pulpit dressed in a white suit with thin black checkered lines and a black tie tucked into a black vest with white buttons. The subject of his sermon is ironically about the temptations of the flesh. For the purposes of the secular-to-sacred adaptation discussion that I have embarked on in this section, I have set my analysis of James's performance in this scene, including its techniques of dialogic audience engagement, aside and will return to it in the next section of this chapter. For now, however, what stands out about this confrontation scene between the deceitful preacher and the jilted husband is its marked difference due to its enhanced sacred, and arguably, comedic dimensions. As previously mentioned, in Baisden's novel, the confrontation occurred in front of the church's congregation. However, in the Johnson and Guidry adaptation, the production's real audience stands in for the fictive "Pimpin' Woods" congregation. Using the masterful and albeit popularized qualities that Davis discusses in his book, I demonstrate how Johnson and Guidry streamline and condense the well-known African American sermon into the context of their play. A sermon was not part of Baisden's narration; instead readers were provided with details about the church's environment, its attendees, and the unfolding actions of the characters in the plot. In the Johnson–Guidry version, however, the context of the church and the fact that James is indeed a pastor is capitalized on and what was a five-page chapter in a 305-page book was transformed into a theatrical scene that ran approximately ten minutes on the circuit stage.

I transcribe the performance of the "Pimpin' Woods Church" scene after this paragraph. This transcription is based on the recording of the production found on *The Maintenance Man* DVD,[31] and I have included notations of actor blocking and audible audience reactions where appropriate.

REVEREND JAMES *stands behind a pulpit and says most of the following lines in a lyrical manner that emphasizes the last word or the last syllable of the last word of each line. The last word of each sentence and each pause is pronounced further by the punctuating notes coming from a church organ being played by an unseen musician playing in the auditorium's pit.* Now come on church clap those hands! (*James moves from behind the pulpit and comes down centerstage where he remains for the rest of this monologue.*) How many know (*pause*) that the flesh can get out of control! Am I right about it? Can I get an amen? Sometimes (*pause*) when you're by yourself (*pause*) late in the midnight hour (*pause*) that flesh (pause) comes tippin' in (*pause*) and it tells you . . . (*James sings the following lines from the popular Al Green song "Tired of Being Alone"*) I'm so tired of being alone. I'm so tired of being alone. (*Stops singing.*) Hah! That's why (*pause*) you gotta watch out for that ole flesh. Cause that ole flesh (*pause*) will cause you to get in trouble! That ole flesh will cause you to have a oops (*pause*) in your life. I'm talking about a O (*pause*) for opportunity. I'm talking about a P! People I can't talk about that one right now! I'm talking about a S (*pause*) for that sinny-sinsin! I heard, oh I heard (*pause*) a songwriter said (*pause; James begins to quote the chorus of an R&B song made popular in 2002 by the African American singer Tweet entitled "Oops (Oh My)"*) "Oops! (*pause) There goes my shirt (*pause*) over my head. My myyy! Oops (*pause*) there goes my pants down to my feet." Say yeah! Say yeah! Look at your neighbor! Look at your neighbor and say neighbor! (*Audience is heard replying "neighbor!"*) Oops! (*Audience is heard saying "oops!"*) I did it again! (*Laughter is heard within the audience.*) Whoo! Yes sir! (*The call and response continues between James and the audience.*) Now look at your other neighbor (*pause*) and say neighbor! (*Audience is heard replying "neighbor!"*) Oh let me hear you say neighbor! (*Audience replies: "neighbor!"*) Oh neighbor! (*Audience replies: "oh neighbor!"*) Me too! Hah hah! Yeah! Yeah! (*The organ provides the background music as James begins to dance and move across the stage as if he has been caught by the spirit as depicted in his movement which incorporates fast-paced foot-stomping, quick foot-work, and short jumps.*) Whoo! Yes sir! (*After this climactic performance note, there is a tone shift in James's oratorical style. He no longer speaks in a lyrical manner and instead delivers the following lines very solemnly.*) The doors of the church are now open. There may be somebody sitting in here right now. You done had a oops (*pause*) in your life. You done had trouble (*pause*) with the flesh. But that's alright (*pause*), I'm gone give you an opportunity right now (*pause*) to just come on down (*pause*) and show the Lord your heart. Is there anybody (*pause*) anywhere (*pause*) who wants to testify?

SIMON *enters from stage left.* I do. I do Reverend.

REVEREND JAMES. Whoo! Yes sir! Come on down brother! Come on down brother and show the Lord your heart.

SIMON *walks closer to James who is standing centerstage in front of his pulpit. By the end of these lines he is standing squarely in front of James, inches away from his face.* That don't even matter right now. What matters is my heart is broken. My soul is heavy and my way is lost.

REVEREND JAMES *places his left hand on Simon's shoulder and backs away from him. He begins to speak using a lyrical voice again.* Well son, there's no heart that Jesus can't mend. There's no soul, God can't lighten. (*James turns to address his real and fictional audience.*) Brothers and sisters, how many know that there's no lost sheep (*pause*) that the Holy Ghost can't find! Am I right about it? Ahhh yeahh!

SIMON I don't know Reverend.

REVEREND JAMES Go 'head and testify.

SIMON See I had a light in my life.

REVEREND JAMES Yes!

SIMON I had a good woman.

REVEREND JAMES Hm hmm! Go on let Him use you brother! Yes sir! Whoo! Let Him use you! Yeah!! Yes sir, let him use you!

SIMON *gets angrier.* But a man dimmed that light with lust and infidelity.

REVEREND JAMES *forgets his lyrical preacher voice.* Say what?! (*The audience is heard erupting in laughter. High notes from the organ are played to punctuate the moment. With the delivery of the following lines, James transitions back into his lyrical preacher voice, yet this time he delivers his lines more aggressively.*) Lust! (*Turns and faces the audience.*) The deadliest of deadly sins! Now church (*pause*), I need somebody to help me tonight! Somebody tell me (*pause*) what kind of man? What kind of low-down dirty dog? What kind of snake crawling in the grass (*pause*) would come between a good man (*pause*) and the light of his life?

SIMON *pulls a gun from behind his back and aims it at James.* You!

REVEREND JAMES *staggers.* Oh Lord have mercy! (*Begins to fall on his knees.*)

SIMON What's wrong Reverend? You don't look so good? You don't get in nothing [*sic*] by messing with people's women.

REVEREND JAMES Brother, brother, brother, you don't want to do this brother.

SIMON You don't know what I want to do!

REVEREND JAMES I know you don't want to go to hell do you? 'Cause that's what's gon' happen if you pull that trigger man. I don't know you or your woman. I don't know you or your woman.

SIMON Cynthia Reed. New Orleans. Ring a bell? (*Simon fires a shot in the air that causes James to jump.*) You better tell me something!

REVEREND JAMES Okay, okay. Look, look, look, look, look brother. I was in New Orleans man, I was just counseling this young woman and didn't nothing happen I swear. I swear didn't nothing happen man.

SIMON Nothing happened?

REVEREND JAMES No!

SIMON Well in about eight months, you gon' have to take a DNA (*Simon wipes tears from his eyes*) and we gon' find out if nothing happened.

REVEREND JAMES Did you say a DNA? (*Audience is heard laughing.*) You know what brother, you must have me mistaken. Brother, you upset, you confused, you crazy.

SIMON Crazy?! I'm the craziest niggah you ever gon' meet. (*With these lines, Simon aims his gun closer to James's face.*)

REVEREND JAMES I didn't say crazy, I said praise him! (*Audience erupts into laughter.*)

SIMON *mockingly laughs at James.* You scared, ain't you?! . . . You something else. (*He laughs and walks over to the pulpit.*) This is the pulpit, huh, where you preach the truth from huh? (*Simon says the following lines in a more serious tone.*) Where

you sell thou shall not steal, commit adultery, fornication, infidelity. You
know what, I think Reverend there's too much violence in the world today.

REVEREND JAMES, *hopeful.* You're right brother.

SIMON I think too many good people being used by brothers just like you. You
knew this day was gettin' ready to happen for a long time. Wait a minute.
(*Simon pauses for a few beats.*) I got a sixth sense. I'm about to see dead people!
(*Simon lunges at James who falls on the ground. Simon keeps the gun inches away
from James's face as he stands over him.*)

REVEREND JAMES *says the following lines while lying in a fetal position on the stage. He
lies horizontally across the stage with his face towards the audience.* Alright alright
man. Alright, alright, alright. I did it! I did it! I did it, man! But I was only up
in it for about four, maybe five minutes at the most man! That's all! (*Audience
laughter is heard.*)

SIMON Well, guess that counts as an oops, don't it brother? (*Simon points the gun at
James's head but he is visibly struggling.*) Look at me!

REVEREND JAMES, *still on the ground, begs for mercy in a high shrieking voice.* Oh Lord
I need you! Somebody call 911. Help me. Help me, help me Lord Jesus, oh
help me please! Come on down right now Lord!

SIMON *looks up at the ceiling for a few beats and appears to have a change of heart.* Shut up.

REVEREND JAMES Ok, ok, ok.

SIMON Ain't nobody gon' kill you.

REVEREND JAMES Ok, ok, ok.

SIMON What you're going through is gon' be between you and your God. There's
too many good ministers doing the work of the Lord. Brothers like you, you
ain't even worth it! (*Simon backs away from James and walks offstage in the direction he came on—stage left. The audience bursts into loud applause. The lights fade
and the scene ends.*)

This Pimpin' Woods' Baptist Church scene, as I have transcribed it, provides us
with four major plot actions: (1) Reverend James's sermon, (2) Simon's moment
of testimony, (3) Simon's confrontation with the reverend, and (4) Simon's decision to leave the reverend alive. For the purposes of a discussion centered on
Johnson and Guidry's secular-to-sacred adaptation techniques, I focus solely on
the content of the first plot action: Reverend James's sermon. This action begins
the scene and ends with Simon's entry.

According to Davis's observations, the content of many African American sermons is built around a particular theme. These sermons are commonly divided
into multiple "formulaic units" that logically and progressively unfold throughout
the sermon's delivery and are connected to each other by "thematic bridges."
Davis describes this structure as one in which

> independent narrative units [are] held together through the use of theme-
> related bridges. . . . [T]he thematic-bridge mechanism is a category of

> formula that has the specialized function of bridging the sermon's inde-
> pendent units through restatements of the sermon's theme . . . by provid-
> ing temporary closure for the preceding formula and entry into the next
> formula.

Additionally, "each formulaic unit can be considered as having an 'independent'
existence within the environment of the performed sermon," and significantly, a
necessary component in each formulaic unit is the use or demonstration of what
he calls a "required sacred/secular polarity, or tension."[32]

I argue that although Reverend James's fictional sermon lacks much of the
complexity, verbal dexterity, and theological acumen of many real African American sermons that have been and continue to be delivered by African American
preachers, Johnson and Guidry's theatrical version offers recognizable signifiers
to their African American audience that play on the already-established and historical tradition of African American preaching styles and the contexts of various largely Christian and specifically African American Baptist and Pentecostal
worship environments. The end result is twofold. First, African American spectators are able to identify with Reverend James's performance through either their
own personal/culturally specific experience and/or their familiarity with other
real and/or fictive representations of African American preachers and worshiping
contexts made available on American popular culture mediums such as television,
film, and literature. Second, Johnson and Guidry achieve their goal of adapting a
secular literary text within a Chitlin Circuit theatre framework that demands the
infusion of sacred and religious content. In performance, the success or accuracy
of the sacred/religious content is in direct correlation with the audience's level of
engagement on any given night. Allowing the performance event as documented
on the DVD to stand in as historical evidence of the performance and the theatrical event at large, the audible and engaged audience response indicates that these
goals of Reverend James's sermon were achieved on the night of the recording
and presumably during subsequent performances.

Reverend James's sermon, contained in the first plot action, begins when he
captures his congregation's attention by asking them to clap their hands. In the
context of a theatrical performance, James's succinct opening can be understood
as a mimetic representation of the "lining up" that is done in real church settings.

> The use of the phrase "lining up" should not be taken to mean that African-
> American congregations can be browbeaten into predictable response pat-
> terns by a black-robed preacher-general. Rather, the term is intended to
> identify that portion of a congregation's energies that are voluntarily yielded
> to the preacher for the duration of the sermon. It is the preacher's task
> and duty to charge the preaching environment with dynamic energies and
> in so doing induce the congregation to focus oral and aural mechanisms
> on the content and structure of the sermon performance. Preacher and

congregation are locked into an aesthetic environment dependent on the continual transmission of messages between the units of the performing community for the successful realization of the performance.[33]

Once the "lining up" of the live circuit audience has been accomplished, Reverend James introduces the theme of his sermon with his next line: "How many of you know that the flesh can get out of control?" This question frames the overarching focus of his sermon around the theme of resisting lust and temptation. Proving this point, his sermon is filled with cautions for his congregation such as when he warns them about flesh: "That's why you gotta watch out for that ole flesh. Cause that ole flesh will cause you to get in trouble!"

Strikingly, James's sermon brims with African American popular culture references and African American slang and vernacular wordplay. As noted in the transcription, James seamlessly breaks into song at an early point in the sermon, singing the lines of Al Greene's song "Tired of Being Alone." Here I suggest that Johnson and Guidry hope that this song will resonate with an assembled crowd of African American spectators on the basis of the song's widespread popularity with African American music listeners since its original release date in the 1970s.[34] Similar intentions can be seen in their strategic use of song lyrics from Tweet's "Oops (Oh My)," written by Missy Elliot. This song, which can be described as an R&B ballad sung over slow pulsating dance beats, was released in February 2002 on Tweet's first album, *Southern Hummingbird*. According to Billboard.com, in 2002, the single spent 27 weeks at the number one position on the R&B/Hip Hop Songs chart, 20 weeks as number seven on the Hot 100 chart, 18 weeks at the number five position on the Radio Songs chart, and nine weeks at the number 13 position on the Pop Songs chart.[35] Knowing that the DVD of *The Maintenance Man* was released in 2003 and that it documented a live production near to the DVD's release date, Tweet's lyrics, infused in the sermon of Reverend James, had a strong possibility of resonating not only with the younger demographic of Johnson and Guidry's audience—those below the age of 35—but also with those spectators who would have been familiar with the song from urban radio stations and television music videos.

Additionally, by infusing secular material in the sacred context of an African American church sermon, Johnson and Guidry were also adhering to another familiar tradition of African American–performed sermons, one that Davis refers to as "the 'weighted secular factor' in African American preaching":

> The generalized sacred elements of a sermon's formulaic unit must always appear in the same morphological environment with specifically referenced secular elements. So careful is the preacher to include, specific contemporary secular elements in his sermon formulas that the structuring of this element in the preaching seems to claim a greater portion of the preacher's creative energies. In contrast, sacred referencing seems to be causal and is

obviously the result of a reasonably stable body of knowledge. . . . The demonstrated presence of this factor, and the process which generates it, in the sermons of African American preachers argues convincingly [that . . .]: the African-American preacher's principal mission is to speak to the contemporary needs of his congregation.[36]

Reassigning the context and the performer of Davis's statement, I extend his concept to contemporary African American circuit events and advance that once again Johnson and Guidry have theatrically restaged the content, tradition, performance, and aesthetic experience of Davis's performed African American sermons in ways that once again mimetically reproduce the actual and/or assumed-to-be-authentic African American cultural experiences that are in turn easily recognizable to contemporary African American circuit audiences.

In this section, I have paralleled a study of Reverend James's sermon alongside an awareness of Gerald Davis's theorizations on the performed African American sermon to demonstrate the ways that Johnson and Guidry have adhered to what I have advanced as the standard circuit form—African American musical theatre that melds religion, comedy, and the popular music forms of gospel and R&B music into contemporary narratives about urban African American life—in a manner that is uniquely their own. Like the other circuit writer-director-producers in this study, Johnson and Guidry present familiar and recognizable material in their theatrical narratives that condition audience attraction and engagement. Yet their circuit productions present a variation to the form by using popular secular African American novel texts that contain minimal religious content as their narrative foundation. Johnson and Guidry adapted these texts and, as is evident in this snapshot scene, capitalized on a brief church scene in the original novel by expanding it for the stage. Signifying on the historic and cultural tradition of African American preachers in performance of their sermons, the duo infused sacred or religious content into their otherwise secular production.

Traces of Vaudeville: Techniques and Performance Strategies of Johnson and Guidry

I now transition into the second half of my analysis, which focuses less on the secular-to-sacred adaptation and more on the production techniques, modes of representation, and performance strategies in Johnson and Guidry musicals. I became aware of the vaudeville-like components of Johnson and Guidry's work in 2007, during my live attendance of their production *3 Ways to Get A Husband* at Chicago's Arie Crown Theater. The play itself was about a woman who felt that her enlisted boyfriend was more interested in fighting in a war than being in a committed union with her. African American actor Leon, popular for his television and film roles, was cast in the role of her boyfriend and Billy Dee Williams, gospel singer Shirley Murdock, and a host of other recognizable celebrities rounded out the cast. As I sat in the dark auditorium with a notepad and binoculars, I was jolted in the second act by the sudden yet soundless lowering of a huge screen from the mouth of the proscenium's ceiling, mid production. A rapidly edited short film with a voiceover began to play that displayed mediatized images of what looked like the Vietnam War and the Persian Gulf War. Also projected were images of poor and impoverished Black people, and at one point, a clip from Dr. Martin Luther King's "I Have A Dream" speech was heard. The width of the large projector screen covered most of the stage; the onstage area behind the screen was in darkness; and none of the actors were visible. I sat there in amazement first at the fact that technology was being incorporated into a circuit play and second at the fact that I could find few connections between this film and the production at hand. Yes, Williams's character in the play was a Vietnam War veteran who in the context of the story had lost his mind and his sense of reality. Yet how did that relate to the snapshots of war-related current events in the film? Upon later consideration of all of the Johnson and Guidry texts that I reviewed for this project—including those that made it into the chapter and those that did not—I realized that all of their productions contain this strange, jarring, and heretofore undefined element. These circuit producers strategically insert an unattached performance element into their production with the intent of briefly interrupting the narrative flow and in so doing offering a respite from the plot. In what follows, I will align these unattached performance elements with the performance strategies and content of vaudeville theatre and will explain what Johnson and Guidry's productions, in particular, share with historic Black vaudeville performances. I also point out the positive and negative ramifications of such parallels.

In linking the performance aspects of today's circuit productions with that of vaudeville, I am most interested in instances when historians have been able to capture the sights and sounds of the performances. Theatre scholar Nadine George-Graves writes the following in her book *The Royalty of Negro Vaudeville: The Whitman Sisters and the Negotiation of Race, Gender, and Class in African American Theatre, 1900–1940*:

> Vaudeville combined variety acts that were carefully constructed along standard formulas but without connective plots. These familiar formulas provided rhythm, pace, and a sense of unity. A typical show offered a taste of many different styles in 8 to 14 turns consisting of musical numbers (especially solo and duo vocals), dance numbers, combination song and dance acts, comic routines, and sometimes magic acts, acrobatics, juggling and animal acts.

She continues:

> The overarching goal of vaudeville, with its smorgasbord of material, was to appeal to a wide variety of spectators. There was supposed to be something

for everyone; if one turn failed to entertain a person, the next would. Conspicuously absent from the artistic formulation of these objectives are the African American spectator and performer. . . . Black vaudevillians built upon these traditions to create entertainment that offered something for every black audience member. These performers had relatively steady and well-paid work and were given the freedom to create anything that would attract a paying audience. They also offered a different voice in the entertainment industry, making innovations in these styles and starting new traditions.[37]

According to George-Graves, a typical Whitman Sisters vaudeville show included "jubilee songs and coon shouts, cakewalks and breakdowns, comedians, midgets, crossdressers, beautiful dancing girls, pickaninnies, a jazz band, and after their invention in the 1920s, talkies."[38] On a given night, the lengthy list of acclaimed African American entertainers waiting in the wings included such names as jazz musician Count Basie, singer Ethel Waters, and the comedic husband and wife duo Jodie Edwards and Susie Edwards, popularly known as Butterbeans and Susie.[39] Speaking in general about the variety of vaudeville entertainment, white or Black, Richard Kislan writes: "[t]he vaudeville bill appeared to be a spontaneous sequence of assorted attractions, but skilled managers put together each program from a standard plan for the house or circuit."[40]

The information provided by Roach, George-Graves, and Kislan supports my claim that Johnson and Guidry strategically alter already-established presentation and performance forms in their brand of Chitlin Circuit theatre. In this case, strategic alteration is accomplished by including a seemingly random and/or separate segment of varied entertainment within the production in ways that I argue carry traces of early-twentieth-century vaudeville theatre. Keeping in mind George-Graves's statement about vaudeville's desire to appeal to a variety of people in the audience, I also suggest that Johnson and Guidry work in similar parameters and strive to present shows with content that have wide appeal. In so doing, they not only acknowledge that their African American audiences are not homogeneous assemblies but also realize that the members of this group do not possess homogenous tastes. Moreover, I find that Kislan's revelation that vaudeville programming was indeed structured and organized, despite common assumptions that they were simply acts performed in a random sequence with no intended purpose or import, parallels many current perceptions of Chitlin Circuit theatre that simplistically presume that all productions are the same and lack variation. In what follows, I analyze brief examples from the previously discussed 2002 production of *The Maintenance Man* and the 2003 production of *Men Cry in the Dark* to establish the vaudevillian lineage of their theatre-making and once again emphasize their use of unique and strategic innovations aimed at engaging with their attending audiences. Yet first, as a jumping off point, I return to the interactive and dialogic performance of Reverend James that was discussed in the previous section, as a moment of comparison and juxtapose it with the examples I will introduce later on.

Viewed on its own, Reverend James's theatricalized version of an African American sermon in the Pimpin' Woods Baptist Church scene should be understood as a moment in the production that was strategically intended to be dynamic, engaging, and dialogic. The actor playing Reverend James spoke directly to the audience as if he were addressing his church congregation and built on the free and fluid environment of circuit auditoria by funneling the audience's spontaneous and isolated feedback into a contained call-and-response formula that was reminiscent of many real African American church worship events. The fourth wall was broken during his sermon and as demonstrated by the audible volume of audience participants, Johnson and Guidry's culturally savvy audience not only knew how to play their assigned role but also had fun taking part in the production.

However, Reverend James's sermon, although new and different from Baisden's original text, was still in line with the plot and helped to move the narrative along. James's sermon provided additional information to the audience and enabled them to see this lust-filled preacher in his home environment—thereby adding dimension to his character. Additionally, as I stated earlier, although the style and format may vary from playwright to playwright and from production to production, religious content is a standard ingredient in circuit productions. Thus, although dialogic and interactive, I do not consider this scene to be participating in the historical tradition of vaudeville presentations, primarily because it fits neatly into the plot, the narrative, and the audience's expectations of circuit productions. However, a different moment occurred earlier in this production that I suggest acts as a varied form of entertainment that is reminiscent of the variety that appeared in a single vaudeville show.

Comedic Routines as Vaudeville-Inspired Variety Acts

Returning to Baisden's original protagonists Malcolm and Antoinette, in the novel and in the circuit adaptation, the two meet at a fundraising event for the United Negro College Fund (UNCF) being held at Melvin's jazz club. Malcolm is accompanying his date, the aforementioned Atlanta socialite Helen, and Antoinette has been escorted to the event by her fiancé, Eric, whose role is played by Je'Caryous Johnson. In the novel, Antoinette, the accomplished dancer, is one of the entertainment acts of the evening. Her solo dance performance captures all of Malcolm's attention. Their eventual meeting after her dance, both in the novel and in the play, marks the beginning of their mutual interest in each other. Yet as pivotal as this moment reads in Baisden's novel, on the Johnson–Guidry stage, Antoinette's dance is eclipsed by another disparate performance event that occurs just before her character appears onstage for the first time.

In an onstage moment that is slightly different from that in the original plot, Simon's character announces to those gathered that the show is about to begin and approaches the downstage center of the stage.[41] This action informs the attending audience that Simon is in fact the host of the event. This moment is also significant because Johnson and Guidry use it to smoothly transition *out of* the plot and narrative of both the play and the novel and *into* a comedy routine performed by the actor who plays Simon—Arnez J., the former host of BET's *Comic View*. The transition from play to comedy routine is seen in these lines at the top of the scene:[42]

SIMON *sits upstage on a bar stool that is adjacent to Cynthia. Stage left and right of the stage are flanked by small circle-top tables that are covered with table cloths. The onstage guests of the UNCF event—including Malcolm and Helen—are seated at these tables. The set design implies that the upcoming performance will be performed for these seated guests. Simon quickly drinks the remainder of his drink and says the following lines to Cynthia.* Baby, I got one more act to introduce then we gonna get on down to the club alright?

CYNTHIA *smiles.* Ok, you do that.

SIMON *walks downstage center and directly address the play's live audience.* How y'all doing Jacksonville? (*The wild applause of the audience is heard.*) Yes sah! How's everybody doing today? Thank y'all so very much for coming out tonight. Man, it's such a pleasure for me to be here and I think y'all know why. It's such an honor. Thank you so very much. Ah, I want to say this real quick, we need to—and the thing I was talking about—paying attention to our kids. We do need to start paying attention to them a lot more—(*Simon/Arnez J. begins to walk across the stage with an exaggerated limp as if one of his legs is significantly shorter than the other*)—because they are our future . . . We have to show them love, prosperity . . . (*as these lines are said his limp becomes more pronounced and the auditorium laughter becomes louder. Simon/Arnez J. uses this moment to transition into a joke about his handicapped younger brother through a physical and verbal comedic routine that sends the audience into raucous laughter.*)

During the next 10 minutes, Arnez J. continues to tell various stories about his disabled brother. Included among them is a story about Arnez's failed phone conversation with his brother after a dentist appointment that left Arnez's mouth numb. Arnez's ability to talk was so impaired that his brother thought he was speaking to a prank caller who was mocking his speech impediment. The comedian also recounted a story about his near altercation with a disabled man in a McDonald's parking lot that only ended when his disabled brother physically came to his defense. He also squeezed in two homophobic jokes about African American gay men whom he problematically portrayed as Southern and feminized. Finally, during the last minutes of his comic routine, in a segment he titled the "wardrobe check," Arnez took aim at the live audience by mocking their attire, their responses to his questions, and their overall presentations of self. The more spectators talked back, the more Arnez improvised and created individual jokes that targeted the responder. His routine slowly came to its end when the laughter subsided and the comedian seamlessly transitioned back into the reserved demeanor of his character Simon.

SIMON Let's go on and get this show started again. This next lady I'm about to bring up right now is going to be dancing to the song called "Destiny" and it will be sung by the beautiful Lady LaShay. She's going to be dancing in the tradition of Alvin Ailey. Y'all please give it up for the gorgeous (*audience clapping is heard*) there ya go! Give it up for the beautiful Lady LaShay and the gorgeous Ms. Antoinette Grayson. (*Antoinette twirls onto the stage while Simon walks upstage towards Cynthia and escorts her out of the club using a door that is positioned further upstage.*)[43]

I read this moment as a contemporary placement of a vaudeville-like variety act in the context of a circuit production. Again, different than the other playwrights in this study who use comedic characters in the narrative, Johnson and Guidry use Arnez to break away from the established circuit paradigm and in so doing offer their audience an additional form of entertainment. Simon the character becomes Arnez J., the man whom some of them may have intentionally paid their money to see based on his status as a well-known African American comedian. Thus, Johnson and Guidry use Arnez's well-known talent to, as Warren Burdine said quoting a line from a popular O'Jay song, "give the people what they want."[44]

My second brief example comes from the Johnson and Guidry novel-to-circuit play adaptation *Men Cry in the Dark*. Baisden's version of *Men Cry in the Dark* is about four successful African American men in their 20s who have been friends since childhood. Set mainly in Chicago, the 367-page novel charts the lives of Derrick, Mark, Tony, and Ben as they encounter individual dilemmas that challenge how they navigate their families, careers, and dating.[45] Like their production of *The Maintenance Man*, this Johnson–Guidry circuit adaptation keeps most of the foundational arc of the narrative and strategically inserts African American celebrity actors (such as Allen Payne and Richard Roundtree[46]), gospel and R&B music, religion, and popular culture references. Without delving too deeply into the layered twists and turns of Baisden's original plot, I highlight an onstage moment in Johnson and Guidry's adaptation that I will once again use as evidence of the vaudeville-like entertainment format uniquely advanced by the duo in their circuit plays.

As the story goes, in both Baisden's novel and the play, Derrick (played by Allen Payne) has invited his friends over to his apartment for a New Year's Eve Party. Derrick is a successful entrepreneur who resigned from a lucrative job at IBM in order to start his own publishing company. His national promotions for his magazine, *Happily Single*, landed him on a radio talk show in Atlanta, where he met Angela Williams after she called in and joined his on-air discussion about men and fidelity. Interests sparked soon after, and months later, Derrick was ready to introduce her to his friends and decided that a holiday party would be the perfect opportunity for everyone to come together. In attendance were Ben and his younger date, Nikki; Tony and his fiancée, Tracie; and Mark and his white girlfriend, Christie.

The moment in question takes place on a dimly lit stage in an area of the set that has been designed to look like a street outside of Derrick's apartment. The audience and viewers of the *Men Cry in the Dark* DVD watch as Ben and his less-polished date for the night, Nikki, make their way to the party. In both the novel and the play, Ben's friends are worried that she is with him for his money. Onstage, Ben is played by African American comedian Lavell Crawford, who, like Arnez J., has done numerous performances on BET's *Comic View*. Nikki is played by actor Heather Dolye. Although Lavell Crawford has a tall stature with significant weight, his character, Ben, dons a sparkling dark suit with a matching black hat. Heather has a short petite frame that is clothed in a short and tight-fitting black sequin dress, a short red jacket made of fake fur, red shoes, and matching red stockings. Her hairstyle features dyed hair that has been swept up into a tall loose ponytail with bangs that sweep across her face. She carries a small black handbag. It is clear from Nikki's style of dress and her stereotypically Southern accent and inner city vernacular manner of speech (distinguished by her slurred and slang-filled mode of speaking) that she is meant to represent someone with meager financial means and little education. This is compounded by her harsh attitude and a posture that often displays her hands on her hips and a rolling neck.

Although Ben and Nikki's arrival at the party is well within the context of Baisden's original novel, I read their six-minute scene as an interruption that showcases a comedic routine that shares commonalities with the vaudeville performances of Butterbean and Susie, albeit with a contemporary twist. Furthermore, like the comedic routine of Arnez J. in *The Maintenance Man*, Ben and Nikki's act, as transcribed after this paragraph in its entirety,[47] offers the audience a different entertainment medium without advancing the plot.

The stage lights rise and reveal Ben and Nikki standing centerstage. Nikki stands stage right and Ben stands stage left.

BEN *says to Nikki.* We already late, by the time we get there the food gone be picked over and it might be gone. If it be gone, I'll have a problem with you! (*Audience laughs.*)

NIKKI Food, food, food. Is that all you ever think about? Gimme a break, you been eating ever since you scooped me up. Shoot, I know there's got to be something else on your mind besides just eating and sex, okay! (*More audience laughs.*)

BEN Matter fact there is! I'd like to put something on your mind if you could hold a thought that long! Look here girl! *(Walks closer to Nikki.)*

NIKKI *raises her left hand—in the stop gesture with her index finger pointed—in protest of Ben's advancement on her.* Unnh-Unnhh! Unnh-Unnhh! Unnh-Unnhh! Don't "look here girl" me! Shoot, you better recognize I am all wo-man! *(Snaps her fingers.)* Don't you evah forget it. *(More laughs.)*

BEN Girl will you shut up and listen, you bout to set me off over here. Ever since you got in my Lexus you been running off at the mouth. Don't let me take you back to the hood! I'm Ike Turner, you Tina Turner. It's about to be some trouble up in here! *(Audience laughs.)*

NIKKI *appears unimpressed by Ben's attempt at taking charge, raises her left hand up in the stop gesture again.* Why don't you just save your drama for your M . . .

BEN *interrupts Nikki's sentence.* Nikki, don't you say it, don't you say it! You know I don't play that momma stuff. Girl, I got one right here for ya! *(Ben balls his upstage right hand into a fist and gestures towards Nikki.)* And I gotta spare one for you if you keep on acting the fool with me. *(He rolls his other hand into a fist. Audience laughter heard.)*

NIKKI *rolls her neck, puts her hand on her hip and says matter-of-factly.* Oh I know you ain't gon hit me. *(More laughs.)*

BEN *backs away from Nikki.* You right, you right. I ain't gon hit you, but I'll shake the shit out of you. *(Loud audience laughter is heard.)* And drink your ass like Slim Fast! *(More audience laughter.)*

NIKKI See there you go threatening me again. My psychic had told me something like that was gon happen and you know something you acting just like my ex.

BEN, *in a serious tone.* I told you a thousand times I don't want to hear nothing about your exes. Them clowns can't hold water to me. Half of them on crack, rest of them in prison giving that booty up to some cocky niggah straight outta the hood. *(Laughter heard. Ben points at Nikki.)* And speaking of being straight out of the hood. Let me tell you something sistah, you better be on your P's and your Q's when we get up in Derrick's penthouse 'cause my best friends and their ladies gon be up in there. Don't you be up there trying to sell them food stamps! *(More laughter.)*

NIKKI, *visibly mad.* Oh ok.

BEN 'Cause they're educated. They have lots of money. Don't you get up there and start embarrassing me, you got it?!

NIKKI What you mean embarrass you? Make you look bad. I mean, you must not know who you talking to. *(Nikki begins to dance as if she's in the middle of a party with fast music.)* Heyyyyy!! Shoot, you better recognize! Don't let this pretty face and this firm body fool you, ok! I's edu-ma-cated like erryyy-body else. *(Loud audience laughter.)*

BEN *makes a face in disbelief of Nikki's slurred speech and dance moves.*

NIKKI I mean, just cause I didn't go to college don't make me no dummy! I know how to act when I'm supposed to. Besides, a college degree don't do nothing but teach you how to mem-ber-ize big words. (*More laughter.*)

BEN See that's what I'm talking about! Mem-ber-ize! Your ass need a dictionary, that's what you need! You can say what you want to but if you get up there and embarrass me girl! I'm gon put something on you! So untwist that face and straighten up that back so we can go in here and do this New Year's Eve thing and turn some heads. Now let's go.

NIKKI No! See what I ought to do is turn around and make you take me back home if I'm such a em—barrassment to you. (*Laughter.*)

BEN Oh really!

NIKKI Really!

BEN You can go home if you want to, but I came here to eat with you or without you! Bye! (*Turns away from Nikki.*)

NIKKI Oh so you mean you just gon leave me out here in the skreets huh? (*Laughter.*)

BEN *nods his head.* There's a bus stop right across the street. That's where I met you at. That's where I'm gon leave you at. (*More laughter.*)

NIKKI *shakes her head.* Miss Cleo had told me! Sho did! A change was gon come!

BEN Clown that wasn't no Miss Cleo that was Sam Cooke! (*Laughter.*) Miss Cleo can't even get her accent right! One day she Irish one day she Jamaican, we don't know if she's selling weed or Lucky Charms! (*More laughter heard.*) But I can tell your future, you about to be on the bus if you don't stop messing with me!

NIKKI Man, stop acting a fool and let's go in here alright. Crazy, I know how to act.

BEN Oh you better know how to ACT. (*Audience laughter heard.*) I didn't get this suit out of lay-away for nothing. (*More laughter.*) Only reason I got this is cause Barry White got one just like it! (*More laughter.*) But you know, he a little bigger than me. You know I'm on that Slim Fast. (*Laughter.*) I'm slimming down you know, I only eat half the—half the dozen Krispy Kremes. You know baby, I'm looking good, I'm working out. (*Voice changes into a more seductive tone.*) But you are looking good though baby. Pretty hair on your head. You got Indian in your family? (*Ben reaches out and touches Nikki's hair and realizes that he has just pulled out a fake lock of hair. Loud laughter from audience.*)

NIKKI *has not seen this and says affirmatively.* Yeah, you know I got a little Indian . . . (*She turns and sees him holding her fake hair and her mouth drops open. She grabs the lock of hair out of his hand. Loud laughter from audience.*) You play— you play too much. You play too much.

BEN Oh my God! What kind of Indian are you? I heard of a Navajo, I ain't never heard of no Broke-a-hoe. (*Audience laughter.*) Ain't nothing else gon fall out is it?

NIKKI Oh so you got jokes now huh?

BEN No baby, you still looking good, you got on your fur and this looks nice . . . what is it squirrel? (*More laughter.*)

NIKKI Oh you like it?

BEN Yeah, I like it. I like it. I like it. (*Overlapping.*)

NIKKI I thought you was gon like it. (*Overlapping.*)

BEN You look good. We both look good. Put that arm right here. (*Nikki intertwines her left arm with his awaiting folded right arm.*) Shoot. We look like Easter Sunday morning.

NIKKI *laughs.*

BEN We could be on the church van.

NIKKI *laughs.*

BEN Yeah, but you know what baby? You look like a supermodel to me anyway.

NIKKI For real?!

BEN Yep, you look like Naomi Campbell.

NIKKI You so crazy!

BEN Why don't you go on and walk like Naomi Campbell for me baby. You know I like that.

NIKKI Alright. Move back, move back. (*Nikki gets in position and proceeds to do a party stroll walk across the stage that is in no way similar to Naomi Campbell's or any other model's walk. Loud laughter from the audience is heard.*)

BEN Hold up Boo. I think you must have misunderstood me. I said Naomi Campbell not Tevin Campbell. (*Audience laughs.*)

NIKKI, *feelings hurt.* And what's that supposed to mean? Look don't be trying to talk over my head 'cause I ain't ill-er-ate ok.

BEN *shakes his head.* You know Nikki baby, you sure would be dangerous if you had some brains. (*More laughter*)

NIKKI What?

BEN Nothing, I'm tired of arguing, just ring the doorbell. I'm hungry, got on this tight ass suit, I can't even breathe.

(*Stage lights fade to black as Ben and Nikki walk stage right and end up in place for the beginning of the next scene that opens with Nikki ringing Derrick's doorbell.*)

Ben and Nikki's act showcases a lively exchange between a young African American couple. The duo uses skilled wordplay, colorful costumes, and exaggerated physical gestures to poke fun at themselves and each other. Their routine is rife with stereotypes about African Americans and includes those that are featured in popular culture as well as those that African Americans commonly only reveal between and among themselves. The heavier and more educated Ben makes fun of his date's speech patterns; the father of her child, who is in prison; her lack of education; her taste in clothing; and her fake hair. Nikki teases Ben about his weight, his preoccupation with sex, and his elite view of the world that looks down on her status and lifestyle. The routine also reveals an uncomfortable power dynamic in which Ben controls the purse strings in the relationship and suggests that Nikki has been granted access to better people, places, and things only through him. Although Nikki stands her ground when Ben threatens violence if she does not "act right" in front of his friends, Ben only reduces his threat from hitting to shaking, an equally violent substitute that can still cause her bodily harm.[48] Later, when Ben mocks her ability to pronounce "big" words, Nikki demands to be taken home. Ben refuses at first and directs her toward the bus stop where they met, then suddenly has a change of heart and decides to shower her with affection and compliments laced with humor and mockery. There are two competing yet intertwining ways we can understand the performance and content of Ben and Nikki's routine. On the one hand, Johnson and Guidry's audience is presented with an emotionally charged and near-violent gender relationship, laden with class and sexuality implications, that thrives on mockery and belittling. On the other hand, we have a performance form that revisits turn-of-the-century African American comedic entertainment in ways that are dynamic yet archaic.

Reading Ben and Nikki's scene as a troubled representation of African American gender, class, and sexuality dynamics first, however, I am reminded of Collins's discussion on the changing face of contemporary representations of African Americans in a chapter titled "Get Your Freak On: Sex, Babies, and Images of Black Femininity":

> Because racial desegregation in the post-civil rights era needed new images of racial difference for a color-blind ideology, class-differentiated images of African American culture have become more prominent. In the 1980s and 1990s, historical images of Black people as poor and working-class Black became supplemented by and often contrasted with representations of Black respectability used to portray a growing Black middle class. Poor and working-class Black culture was routinely depicted as being "authentically" Black whereas middle- and upper-middle class Black culture was seen as less so. Poor and working-class Black characters were portrayed as the ones who walked, talked, and acted "Black," and their lack of assimilation of American values justified their incarceration in urban ghettos. In contrast, because middle- and upper-middle class African American characters lacked this authentic "Black" culture and were virtually indistinguishable from their White middle-class counterparts, assimilated, propertied Black people were shown as being ready for racial integration. This convergence of race and class also sparked changes in the treatment of gender and sexuality. Representations of poor and working-class authenticity and middle-class respectability increasingly came in gender-specific form.[49]

Following suit, Ben and Nikki's routine portrays an uneducated working-class African American woman juxtaposed against a portrayal of an educated middle-class African American male. Although differently constituted, Collins would argue that these Johnson and Guidry characters equally contribute to the reinsertion and recycling of damaging images of African Americans into popular culture.

Nikki's character falls neatly into what Collins calls "the controlling image of the 'bitch'" that has been "designed to defeminize and demonize" these African American women.[50] This African American woman is

> aggressive, loud, rude, and pushy. Increasingly applied to poor and/or working-class Black women, the representation "bitch" constitutes a reworking of the image of the mule of chattel slavery. Whereas the mule was simply stubborn (passive aggressive) and needed prodding and supervision, the bitch is confrontational and actively aggressive.[51]

Collins verifies that "[n]ot only do these images of sexualized Black bitches appear in global mass media, Black male artists, producers, and marketing executives participate in reproducing these images."[52] On top of Nikki's characterization as a Black bitch is her depiction as a "sexualized bitch":

> Black bitches are one thing. Black bitches that are fertile and become mothers are something else. In this regard, the term *bitch* references another meaning. Reminiscent of the associations of Africans with animals, the term *bitch* also refers to female dogs. Via this association, the term thus invokes a web of meaning that links unregulated sexuality with uncontrolled fertility.... In contrast to Black female bodies as animalistic, Black female bodies become machines built for endurance. The Black superwoman becomes a "sex machine" that in turn becomes a "baby machine." The thinking behind these images is that unregulated sexuality results in unplanned for, unwanted, and poorly raised children.[53]

While the audience does not receive concrete evidence that Nikki is in fact a "Bad Black Mother" in Collins terms,[54] we do know that she is in fact an unwed mother and that the father of her child is incarcerated. Moreover, Ben's desire of her "pretty face" and "firm body" despite her lack of education and a substantial income confirms that he is more interested in her sexually and less interested in her mentally as he repeatedly makes mention of during their routine.

Johnson and Guidry's problematic representation of Ben does not end here, unfortunately. Although Ben's character is written as a middle-class African American male who perceives himself to be Nikki's superior due to his class and education status, according to Collins's categories, his behavior and attitude toward her are more in line with the controlling images of working-class Black men. Collins asserts that "[t]he combination of physicality over intellectual ability, a lack of restraint associated with incomplete socialization, and a predilection for violence has long been associated with African American men."[55] She continues:

> Historical representations of Black men as beasts have spawned a ... set of images ... that center on Black male bodies, namely, Black men as inherently violent, hyper-heterosexual, and in need of discipline. ... Again, this

representation is more often applied to poor and working-class men than to their more affluent counterparts, but all Black men are under suspicion of criminal activity or breaking rules of some sort.[56]

Thus, although Ben pokes fun at his attire, his addiction to food, and his weight in ways that are not implicitly racial, gendered, or class-specific, his treatment of Nikki places him in a category of working-class Black male representation that is understood as being always already on the verge of a sexual, criminal, or societal infraction against the woman he loves and anyone else who crosses his path.

In a different vein, Ben and Nikki's act also harkens back to an earlier form of African American theatre, including vaudeville, that according to Krasner's work in *Resistance, Parody, and Double Consciousness in African American Theatre, 1895–1910* took place during a time in which

> African American theatre was just as cliché-ridden and just as limited by stereotyping as any other theatrical presentations. Black musical performers in particular were in the business of creating comedy, and comedy often demands self-effacement, burlesque, and clowning. Moreover, the business of black musical theatre was lucrative. The lure of financial rewards compelled many black performers to assume the mask of low comedy in order to appeal to white audiences eager to laugh at blacks.[57]

Upon the segregated vaudeville stages that sprung up in the 1910s, performers such as Butterbeans and Susie continued to employ the staples of African American comedic performances, but this time before Black audiences.

I return once again to the work of Watkins for information on the husband and wife performance team Butterbeans and Susie. Butterbeans and Susie are documented as being "one of the most enduring black stage acts."[58] The following example describes a typical Butterbeans and Susie's routine:

> Butterbeans appeared onstage in tight pants, a bowler hat, and oversized shoes that were in marked contrast to Susie's more stylish gowns. They usually began their act with a duet. Then, after she sang a blues tune, they might join in a cakewalk and begin the comic patter. Like Stringbeans and Susie May, their humor often revolved around marital relationships. One of their most popular routines—based on a song so ribald that it was spurned by Okeh records even though Columbia Records released Bessie Smith's version in 1933—was Susie's rendition of "I Want a Hot Dog for My Roll." Susie, in her usual flirtatious manner, belted out the lyrics: "I want a hot dog without bread you see. 'Cause I carry my bread with me. . . . I want it hot. I don't want it cold. I want it so it fit in my roll." And while dancing suggestively, Butterbeans would add such quips as, "My dog's never cold! Here's a dog that long and lean." The double-entendres continued as Susie

sang, "I sure will be disgusted, if I don't get my mustard. . . . Don't want no excuse, it's got to have a lot of juice."[59]

Watkins provides context:

> Despite the often racy material, their act was among the most beloved on the circuit. There was, ironically, something ingenuous and warm about it. The mock hostility and cutting quips aside, Susie was a plumpish disarmingly attractive woman who exuded charm, and Butterbeans, even when most truculent and loud, projected an aura of cheerfulness and affection. The humorous stage spats were inevitably seen as mock squabbles.[60]

Using the laughter and engagement that is documented on the *Men Cry in the Dark* DVD as evidence, I build on my reading of Ben and Nikki's routine by construing it as one that clearly contains damaging representations of African American relationships and yet, in similar ways to Watkins take on Butterbeans and Susie, is read by many of Johnson and Guidry spectators as simply humorous entertainment. Contributing to this alternative reading is that the main narrative arc of the play focuses on a complicated yet loving African American relationship between Derrick and Angela that is void of violent, abusive, demeaning, and/or hyper-sexualized behavior. I find it to be highly possible, then, that Johnson and Guidry's audiences were able to filter through the onslaught of representations in this production and actively separate the exaggerated humor from the lifelike dramatic components in ways that made sense and created meaning for them on an individual basis. Moreover, due to Johnson and Guidry's strategic and vaudeville-like approach to circuit theatre, which strives to engage with all facets of their audience, I also leave room for the possibility that some of the materials presented onstage could have been appealing to some and not others. It is highly plausible, for example, for their religiously inclined spectators to find Ben and Nikki's routine offensive yet indulge in Reverend James's sermon. Likewise, some fans of Ben and Nikki may have been unmoved by the religious overtones in the Pimpin' Woods Baptist Church scene. Of course, I also leave room for the possibility that both of these scenes may have had crossover appeal with attending spectators for various and individual reasons.

Reflections

While writing this chapter, I had the fortune of being invited to present on a panel for the 2010 Black Women's Playwright's Group Conference[61] alongside Johnson. What I found striking about his approach to creating theatre was the amount of time that he and his company spend trying to develop a personal relationship with each audience member who sees one of his plays. Similar to the other writer-director-producers in this project, I'm Ready Productions maintains a website and frequently distributes updates and messages to their fans via email. Messages are pre-written, and computer software ensures that each recipient will receive personalized greetings and birthday messages that are masked as being sent directly from the playwrights themselves. Johnson also spoke about his move away from popular African American novels toward plays that he personally writes and develops mainly because of the greater financial profit involved in the latter. Speaking to a room that was filled largely with playwrights, Johnson asserted that the key to a successful play was the successful incorporation of a playwright's personal experiences. He maintained that audiences are then able to relate to the personal in the fictional, and thus, the stories become more believable.

Johnson and Guidry's novel-to-circuit play adaptations invite us into the early stages of Chitlin Circuit theatre development and unpack foundational strategies and approaches toward audience development and engagement. Their circuit events create and consistently maintain an aesthetic community in which performers, audiences, traditions, and *playwrights* work in tandem to produce successful and long-running theatrical fare.

Here I am reminded of Davis's discussion of the "active components" of African American performances and performance events:

> It was stated earlier that there were two active components in the maintenance of performance standards and forms for African-American materials; the performer and the audience. There is, as well, a third component. That component is tradition, or *characteristic* customary, habitual, and dynamic employment of folk ideas in a performance context.
>
> The shared responsibility between the performer and his or her audience in the context of the performed narrative event is not casual and seems to follow well-defined sets of compacts. These compacts have historical implications even though most African-American narrative performers manifest what George Kent calls "isness," the power of contemporaneity in performance. So consistently are the patterns of agreements evidenced in performance that those who participate in any given performance—audience and performer—can be considered to participate in an aesthetic community. Elsewhere I have defined "aesthetic community" as "a group of people sharing the knowledge for the development and maintenance of a particular affecting mode or 'craft' and the articulating principles to which the affecting mode must adhere or oppose [in performance]. Both conditions, articulated in and evidenced in the mode itself, must be present."[62]

Johnson and Guidry enter into a flexible understanding of what Davis's notion of *tradition* can mean within contemporary circuit environments, by manipulating both traditional and recognizable facets of African American culture and African American performance practices and working across a spectrum of historical and contemporary representations. Their growing financial earnings and their increasing fanbase serve as evidence of not only the effectiveness of their theatre-making but also the successful components that they have developed in the circuit's shared aesthetic community.

Notes

1 Langston Hughes, "Simply Heavenly: A Comedy," in *The Collected Works of Langston Hughes*, ed. Leslie Catherine Sanders, vol. 6 (Columbia and London: University of Missouri Press, 2004), 233–34.

2 Hughes, "Simply Heavenly," 244.

3 Michelle K. Massie, "Finding a Niche in Black Theater: Producers Specialize in Adapting Black Novels into Stage Plays," *Black Enterprise* (New York) 36, no. 1 (August 2005): 48.

4 It is important to note that Massie's article does not provide information about the types of venues that hosted *Heaven's Child* while it was on tour. The article also does not provide information about other destination stops along the play's tour route between Houston, TX and Chicago, IL.

5 Massie, "Finding a Niche in Black Theater," 48.

6 Massie, "Finding a Niche in Black Theater," 48.

7 Massie, "Finding a Niche in Black Theater," 48.

8 Campbell Robertson, "The World of Black Theatre Becomes Even Bigger," The Arts/ Cultural Desk, *New York* Times, February 21, 2007, final late edition.

9 For more a production and performance history of *Stormy Weather*, please see Woll, *Black Musical Theatre*.

10 Susanne B. Dietzel, "The African American Novel and Popular Culture," in *Cambridge Companion to the African American Novel*, ed. Maryemma Graham (Cambridge: Cambridge University Press, 2004), 166.

11 Dietzel, "The African American Novel and Popular Culture," 167–68.

12 Dietzel, "The African American Novel and Popular Culture," 166.

13 Gerald L. Davis, *I Got the Word in Me and I Can Sing It, You Know: A Study of the Performed African-American Sermon* (Philadelphia: University of Pennsylvania Press, 1985), xv.

14 Davis, *I Got the Word in Me and I Can Sing It, You Know*, 30.

15 Davis, *I Got the Word in Me and I Can Sing It, You Know*, 30.

16 Davis, *I Got the Word in Me and I Can Sing It, You Know*, 30–31.

17 Davis, *I Got the Word in Me and I Can Sing It, You Know*, 31.

18 Davis, *I Got the Word in Me and I Can Sing It, You Know*, 33.

19 Here I elaborate on this point further. While it is true that the Johnson and Guidry's productions of *Men Cry in the Dark* and *Friends and Lovers* also contain secular narratives that have been infused with sacred and/or religious content, I find their methods to be more similar and less different to how other circuit playwrights in this study and beyond present religion on circuit stages. By this, I mean that although there is a marked difference that can be seen in some of the characters who have been directly taken from the original novels in terms of their now increased level of religious faith on the circuit stage, I find that these characters are demonstrating their faith through conventional methods that are commonly found across circuit stages—e.g., attending church, quoting scripture, singing gospel songs, and/or casually professing their spirituality and belief in God in their dialogue. For these reasons, I contend that these two other novel-to-stage circuit adaptations created and produced by Johnson and Guidry pale in comparison to the methods undertaken by the duo in their circuit production of *The Maintenance Man*.

20 Michael Baisden, "Back Book Cover," in *Never Satisfied: How and Why Men Cheat* (Katy, TX: Legacy Publishing, 1995).

21 Baisden, "Back Book Cover."

22 Amazon.com, "Michael Baisden *Never Satisfied: How & Why Men Cheat* (Paperback)," Editorial Reviews, www.amazon.com/Never-Satisfied-How-Why-Cheat/dp/0964367580/ref=sr_1_3?ie=UTF8&s=books&qid=1275660980&sr=1-3, accessed June 4, 2010.

23 Amazon.com, "Michael Baisden *Never Satisfied: How & Why Men Cheat* (Paperback)."

24 Michael Baisden's official website, "About Michael," www.michaelbaisden.com/biography, accessed June 4, 2010.

25 Michael Baisden's official website, "Stations," www.michaelbaisden.com/stations, accessed June 4, 2010.

26 Michael Baisden, *The Maintenance Man: A Novel* (New York: Simon & Schuster, Inc., 2003), 4–5.

27 Dietzel, "The African American Novel and Popular Culture," 166.

28 Dietzel, "The African American Novel and Popular Culture," 166.

29 Dietzel, "The African American Novel and Popular Culture," 166.

30 Baisden, *The Maintenance Man*, 78.

31 In order to watch the scene in its entirety, please see Je'Caryous Johnson and Gary Guidry, "Pimpin' Woods Church Scene," in *The Maintenance Man*, DVD, dir. Je'Caryous Johnson (Chatsworth, CA: I'm Ready Productions, Inc., 2002).

32 Davis, *I Got the Word in Me and I Can Sing It, You Know*, 56.

33 Davis, *I Got the Word in Me and I Can Sing It, You Know*, 17.

34 This song has not only been popular among African American listeners. In the December 2004 issue, *Rolling Stone* magazine listed the song as number 293 on its list of "500 Greatest Songs of All Times." For more information, please see Bill Crandall and other authors, "500 Greatest Songs of All Time," *Rolling Stone*, no. 963 (December 9, 2004): 65–163.

35 All of these chart lists are ranked weekly by Nielsen Broadcast Data Systems, and some gain additional information from Nielsen SoundScan. The Hot 100 and R&B/Hip Hop Songs lists chart the most popular songs across all genres, according to radio airplay, sales, and online streaming. The Radio Songs are based on radio airplay rankings across all genres. The Pop Songs chart is compiled from tracking the top 40 songs played across mainstream radio stations. For more information on ranking of Tweet's "Oops (Oh My)," please see Billboard.com, "Oops (Oh My)—Missy Elliot," Chart History, "www.billboard.com/#/song/tweet/oops-oh-my/3891627, accessed June 4, 2010. For information on Nielsen Broadcast Data Systems and Nielsen SoundScan, please see The Nielsen Company website, "Media Practice—Entertainment," http://en-us.nielsen.com/tab/industries/media/entertainment, accessed June 4, 2010.

36 Davis, *I Got the Word in Me and I Can Sing It, You Know*, 62.

37 George-Graves, *The Royalty of Negro Vaudeville*, 38–39.

38 George-Graves, *The Royalty of Negro Vaudeville*, 40.

39 For more information and a vivid description of one of these evenings, please see George-Graves, *The Royalty of Negro Vaudeville*, 39–49.

40 Richard Kislan, *The Musical: A Look at American Musical Theater* (Englewood Cliffs, NJ: Prentice-Hall, 1980), 43–44.

41 In Baisden's novel, the UNCF fundraiser event takes place inside a theater. Malcolm reads a program for the event that lists Antoinette's upcoming performance, and this signals to readers that he is about to watch Antoinette dance. For more details, please see Baisden, *The Maintenance Man*, 54–56.

42 The following scenic moment is transcribed from Je'Caryous Johnson and Gary Guidry, "Untitled Scene," in *Men Cry in the Dark*, DVD, dir. Je'Caryous Johnson (Chatsworth, CA: I'm Ready Productions, Inc., 2003).

43 Transcribed from Johnson and Guidry, "Untitled Scene."

44 Burdine, "The Gospel Musical and Its Place in the Black American Theatre," 202.

45 For more information, please see Michael Baisden, *Men Cry in the Dark: A Novel* (New York: Simon & Schuster, Inc., 2003).

46 In February of 2008, I interviewed Richard Roundtree about his role in a different Johnson and Guidry production entitled *Whatever She Wants*. To read the published interview, please see Rashida Z. Shaw McMahon, "Roundtree Hill," Theater, *Time Out Chicago*, 154, (2008): 119.

47 Laughter occurred throughout this entire comedy routine. When possible, I have attempted to make note of the especially loud bursts of laughter that were heard on the DVD. This scenic moment is transcribed from Johnson and Guidry, "Untitled Scene."

48 African American comedian Chris Rock delivered a comedic routine during the 1990s in which he delivered a joke about "shaking the shit" out of women as opposed to hitting them.

49 Collins, *Black Sexual Politics*, 122–23.

50 Collins, *Black Sexual Politics*, 123.

51 Collins, *Black Sexual Politics*, 123.

52 Collins, *Black Sexual Politics*, 128.

53 Collins, *Black Sexual Politics*, 130.

54 Collins, *Black Sexual Politics*, 131. Please see Collins's larger discussion regarding "Bad Black Mothers," in which she details how this representation expands the idea of Black women as bitches to include those who are perceived to be "abusive (extremely bitchy) and/or who neglect their children either in utero or afterward."

55 Collins, *Black Sexual Politics*, 152.

56 Collins, *Black Sexual Politics*, 158.

57 Krasner, *Resistance, Parody, and Double Consciousness in African American Theatre, 1895–1910*, 11.

58 Watkins, *On the Real Side*, 375.

59 Watkins, *On the Real Side*, 376.

60 Watkins, *On the Real Side*, 377.

61 Black Women Playwrights' Group Conference, "Linking Platforms: Theater & Digital Media in the 21st Century," Exploring Commercial Theater Panel, Doubletree Hotel, Skokie, IL, April 24, 2010.

62 Davis, *I Got the Word in Me and I Can Sing It, You Know*, 30–31.

6

TYLER PERRY

Minstrelsy Inverted

BODIDDLY What do you mean, passer?

MAMIE Chitterling passer—passing up chitterlings and pretending I don't like 'em when I do. I like watermelons and chitterlings both, and I don't care who knows it.

CHARACTER Just stereotypes, that's all. (*He shakes his head*)

MAMIE Man, get out of my face!

CHARACTER Stereotypes . . . stereotypes . . . stereo . . . (*He retreats muttering*)

MAMIE Why is it getting so colored folks can't do nothing no more without some other Negro calling you a stereotype. Stereotype, hah! If you like a little gin, you're a stereotype. You got to drink Scotch. If you wear a red dress, you're a stereotype. You got to wear beige or chartreuse. Lord have mercy, honey, do-don't like no blackeyed peas and rice! Then you're a down-home Negro for true—which I is—and proud of it! (*MAMIE glares around as if daring somebody to dispute here. Nobody does.*) I didn't come here to Harlem to get away from my people. I come here because there's more of 'em. I loves my race. I loves my people. Stereotype!

CHARACTER That's what I said, stereotypes!

MAMIE You better remove yourself from my presence, calling me a stereotype.

CHARACTER Tch-tch-tch! (*Clicking his tongue in disgust, the LITTLE MAN leaves the bar as MAMIE rises and threatens him with her purse. The PIANIST rushes over to congratulate her*)

PIANIST Gimme five, Miss Mamie, gimme five! (*They shake hands*).

—Langston Hughes, *Simply Heavenly*[1]

In 2009, the African American actor, writer, playwright, and director of stage and screen Tyler Perry was reveling in the success of another box office success with the release of his latest stage-to-screen film adaptation, *Madea Goes to*

Jail. Marking the confusion that this moment regenerated for critics, journalists, scholars, and even some artists of color, *Entertainment Weekly* published an article in their March 20 issue titled "How Do You Solve a Problem Like Madea?" The article's subheading pointed to the conflicting truths about Perry's work:

> His movies have grossed over $350 million, thanks mostly to his alter ego Madea. But is Tyler Perry reinforcing stereotypes? And even if he is, how do you weigh that against the good he is doing? Inside black America's secret culture war.[2]

In this chapter, I am interested in further complicating *a problem like Perry*. Different from the white-produced and controlled minstrel image of the late nineteenth century and early twentieth century, which depicted African Americans as dimwitted, buffoonish, and vulgar, among other negative characteristics,[3] Perry's contemporary African American images can be easily blamed for perpetuating some similar, yet contemporarily different, alleged African American traits. Undeniably, his productions have the propensity to circulate and/or reinforce notions that dangerously reduce African Americans to a non-exhaustive list of negatives such as loud talking, childlike, adulterous, greedy, abusive, violent, rude, delinquent, and sexually promiscuous. As cultural scholar and critic Nelson George reminds us, in the same *Entertainment Weekly* article, "[c]omedy and stereotypes go hand in hand."[4]

In what follows, I discuss the final case studies that were written, produced, and directed by the most popular writer-director-producer on the circuit, Tyler Perry. Although Perry's productions share many of the characteristics found in Johnson–Guidry and Talbert productions, my discussion here focuses on Perry's variation on the standard circuit form through his uniquely developed representational content and performance modes. Relying on snapshots taken from three of his productions, *I Can Do Bad All by Myself, Madea Goes to Jail*, and *The Marriage Counselor*, I analyze Perry's construction of African American spirituality, blackness, and femininity. The latter analysis refers to the writer-director-producer's own crossdressed performance as a Black grandmother named Madea. My interest lies in determining how meaning is produced, audience-performer interactions made, and African American cultural products infused in productions. I reapply my framing questions for this project and ask the following questions of each case study:

1. What are the horizons of expectations that audiences bring with them to the theatre?
2. How are dramaturgical and production techniques, such as modes of representation, choice of narrative content, and performance strategies, conditioned to elicit audience response and identification?
3. How do spectators ascertain a production's mimetic fidelity to life offstage?

In other words, how do these plays relate to a spectator's experiences?

My driving argument in this chapter is that Black spectatorship in Tyler Perry theatrical events is conditioned by three interrelated factors working in tandem. The first of these factors is an audience's encounter with production-specific materials and culturally specific African American content during their time inside of the theatre house's lobby (during pre-show, intermission, and post-show). Second, I take note of the dramaturgical and performative methods by which Perry presents mimetic representations of culturally and/or historically significant aspects of African American life onstage. Third, I consider an audience's introduction to innovative representations and performance strategies in an already-established Perry repertoire that serves to challenge their horizons of expectations and their assumed familiarity with his work. Although these factors can be thought of as occurring chronologically during a spectator's time in a Perry event, they should not be viewed as hierarchical or prioritized. Any one factor or combination of factors can impact a spectator at any given time during an event. As I demonstrate throughout the chapter, the successful result of their combined efforts is an audience that has claimed to engage with, identify with, and/or generate new meaning from their experience at a Perry event.

To prove this, I first provide detailed information about how two related yet distinct Perry–specific environments were created in the structurally distinct theatre houses of Chicago's Arie Crown Theater and Indianapolis's Murat Theatre. I then divide my examination of Perry's work and the Black spectatorial practices exhibited by his attending audiences into two types of case studies: the historical and the ethnographic. In the historical case studies, I reconstruct past performances and spectating experiences that took place before my field work began. My reconstruction relies on various collected materials, such as playbooks, advertisements, data collected in interviews, and information gathered by viewing videos of performances. In my ethnographic case studies, similar collected materials are considered alongside the data collected at my primary ethnographic field site, Chicago's Arie Crown Theater, and at my secondary ethnographic field site, Indianapolis' Murat Theatre. In all cases, my findings are supplemented with information derived from post-show interviews with audience members.

The Complexities of Perry's Reception

Since 1998, Perry has consistently produced plays on the contemporary Chitlin Circuit. Noteworthy mentions in his long roster of productions include *I Know I've Been Changed* (1998); *Woman Thou Art Loosed!* (1999 collaboration with African American pastor T. D. Jakes); *Behind Closed Doors* (2000 adaptation of pastor T. D. Jakes's novel of the same name); *I Can Do Bad All By Myself* (2000); *Diary of a Mad Black Woman* (2001); *Madea's Family Reunion* (2002); *Madea's Class Reunion* (2003); *Meet the Browns* (2004); *Why Did I Get Married?* (2004); *Madea Goes to Jail* (2005); *What's Done in the Dark* (2006); and *The Marriage Counselor* (2008). Film adaptations have been made of many of the storylines that originated as theatrical productions, such as *Diary of a Mad Black Woman*,[5] *Madea's Family Reunion*, *Meet the Browns*, *Why Did I Get Married?*, and *Madea Goes to Jail*. Perry continues to receive accolades for his film work that include being the recipient of numerous NAACP Image Awards and Black Reel Awards for his screenwriting and directing. He is also a two-time Black Movie Awards nominee for outstanding motion picture for *Diary of a Mad Black Woman* and *Madea's Family Reunion*. His book, *Don't Make a Black Woman Take Off Her Earrings: Madea's Uninhibited Commentaries on Love and Life*, authored by Perry, but written in the voice of his popular character "Madea" Mabel Simmons, received 2006 Quill Awards in the Book of the Year and Best in Humor categories, in addition to being number one on the *New York Times* bestseller list for 12 consecutive weeks. His foray into television has resulted in two award-winning sitcoms on the TBS network, *House of Payne* and *Meet the Browns*,[6] two recent series on BET, *Sistahs* and *The Oval*, which debuted in the Fall of 2019,[7] and two forthcoming series, *Bruh* and *Ruthless,* which are scheduled to air on BET's streaming service BET Plus in 2020.[8]

The appeal of Perry's work to Black audiences of film, theatre, and television has been made apparent by his consistent box office successes and record-breaking ratings, yet his popularity continues to puzzle critics, journalists, and scholars. With the advent of Perry's motion picture films, many African American critics reference the class-based negative portrayals of middle- and/or upper-class African Americans presented in his films. They then use this reading to make assumptions about who attends Perry's work and how the viewing pleasure of this group is derived. For example, in this same article, critical studies scholar Todd Boyd indicates that "Tyler Perry is simply reflecting the thinking of a lot of uneducated, working-class African-Americans." On the other hand, in an extended quote, George attributes Perry's success to his being able to speak to "the most ignored group in Hollywood": African-American women.

> You could see these films as parables or fables. There's a black prince figure who shows up for black women who've been frustrated, unhappy, or abused. . . . Tyler Perry speaks to a constituency that is not cool. . . . There's nothing cutting-edge about the people who like Tyler Perry. So for a lot of other people, it's like, "What is this thing that's representing black people all over the world? I don't like it. It doesn't represent me."[9]

Statements like Boyd's and George's are similar to the assessment that African American theatre practitioners have publicly voiced about Perry's theatrical spectators. In 2006, the BET network aired an entire show about the controversy over Perry's theatre, titled "The New Minstrel Show," as part of the network's now-canceled weekly news show *The Chop Up* (BET, 2006–2007). Their cameras captured moments of the 2005 National Black Theatre (NBT) festival held in Winston-Salem, North Carolina, and collected comments from the late NBT founder, producer, and artistic director Larry Leon Hamlin, actor Malcolm-Jamal

Warner, and performance artist Daniel Beaty regarding the popularity of Perry's plays. The following quotes represent their views on Perry's theatre and his spectators:

LARRY LEON HAMLIN There are people who like that and that's fine, but then there are other people who really just like quality theatre of excellence and that's what we offer. . . . If we look at the profile of those people that attend those productions, I think it's very easily understood. It's the intellect.

MALCOLM-JAMAL WARNER I would really hate for it to come to the point where Tyler Perry type plays become the new Black theatre standard.

DANIEL BEATY: There are definitely things in it, you know, that are kind of low-brow.[10]

Later in the show, Perry is seen giving this response:

> I think traditional Black theatre is suffering because of comments like that one. What makes the people that go to your shows better than the people that go to mine? I don't understand that. . . . It's insulting on so many levels, to, not just to me, but to the millions of Black, the hard-working folk, that want to go out and laugh and have a good time, it's insulting to them as well. So until they start to acknowledge those people and welcome them, then there will be this problem.[11]

As I have contextualized in an earlier publication,

> From George, to Boyd, to Hamlin, to Jamal Warner, and then to Beaty, the above quotes exemplify the disdain for Perry's work by practitioners and critics of African American performance and cultural production who consider Perry's work to be substandard. Yet no matter the points of contention, Perry's defense of his work continues to rest in the never-before-seen theatre attendance numbers and box office film receipts which mark his successful ability to please "millions" of fans.[12]

It was no surprise, then, that many of the spectators I encountered made mention of the fact that not only were they fans of Perry's plays, television shows, and motion pictures but that they and/or their friends were also fans of the book, members of his email LISTSERV, and owners of DVD and VHS versions of the stage productions, which they watch frequently at home with their family and friends. Others, like a husband and wife whom I encountered one evening in the Arie Crown lobby before the beginning of *The Marriage Counselor*, were frequent attendees of more *legitimate* productions of Black theatre in Chicago but had seen Perry's films in the theatre, had enjoyed them, and were curious about seeing one of his plays live. On another evening, I approached a mother in a wheelchair waiting near the entrance of the interior doors to the auditorium with her teen-age son. She told me that although she had seen many African American plays at the Arie Crown and at other theatre houses in the city over the years, this would be the first play for her son. Although her son seemed less than enthused by the conversation that his mother and I were having, he expressed to me that he didn't think he would enjoy the show. Later, we were all surprised when my ticketed seat was right next to them on the main seating level, a few rows from the front of the stage. During intermission, I asked him what he thought of the show so far. He replied by saying he really liked it: the music was good, and the show was funny. His mother then said, speaking to me but really addressing her son, that she hoped this play would encourage him to see this and other types of theatre again.

I continued to encounter spectators who went against the grain of what a Perry spectator *should* be. This is not to say that I did not see large numbers of female spectators in groups or in pairs out for a night/afternoon out, but I also met numerous father–son pairs and an overwhelming amount of dating and mar-ried couples who responded favorably to Perry's productions. Included among what is assumed to be a "working-class" demographic were also teachers, admin-istrators, undergraduate and graduate students, government employees, entrepre-neurs, and MBA degree–holding businesspeople. As visible, paying, and pleased members of the millions, these spectators do not reflect the assumed race, class, gender, and/or type of Perry's viewing theatrical audience. Their presence and enjoyment should not be ignored.

It is my position in this chapter that reducing the widespread appeal of Perry's productions to easily consumable low-aesthetic standards or assumed gender or class appeal simplifies what are in fact more-complex acts of minority spectator-ship and minority consumption of performances that concern and/or feature minorities. Referring again to my discussion of Bobo's notion of "cultural read-ers," discussed in the introductory chapter, I am reminded once again of Perry's spectators being cultural consumers of his material who are engaging with his work in ways that highlight their shared identity and cultural affiliations. There-fore, before launching into a discussion of my selected Perry case studies, I use Bobo's reception study of Steven Spielberg's 1985 film *The Color Purple* to assist in problematizing the appeal of Perry's plays and longitudinally his film and televi-sion work, in spite of their dominant stereotypes.

If we recall, Spielberg's film was an adaptation of Alice Walker's 1982 book of the same name. The film starred Whoopie Goldberg as a forlorn woman named Celie whose stepfather sexually abuses her. The abuse produces two children who are each taken away from her after their birth. Her stepfather eventually gives her away to become the teenage bride of an equally abusive and volatile husband named Mister, played by actor Danny Glover, and the stepmother to his brood of wayward children. Just when Celie seems to have become complacent in her life of destitution, emotional isolation, and forced separation from her sister Nettie, she finds solace in surprising friendships with the women who enter her life. Celie's network of women includes her stepson's wife, Sophia, played by Oprah Winfrey, and her husband's mistress, Shug Avery, played by Margaret Avery. The film documents the bonds of sisterhood that develop between seemingly different women who are commonly burdened by a palpable and intersecting multiple oppression[13] as a result of their class, gender, and race. This triple burden of being *poor* and *female* and *Black* causes their lives to be conditioned and controlled by the demands and desires of the African American men and whites whom they encounter in this early-twentieth-century Southern town.

Bobo's study investigates how many Black female spectators approved of the film despite its negative reviews from critics, Black male spectators, and some Black female academics. "Useful" and "positive" were some of the words used to describe their reactions as the women discussed how they were able to personally identify with the experiences of Celie and the other onscreen women.[14] This led Bobo to surmise that

> This sense of identification with what was in the film . . . provide[d] an impetus for Black women to form an engagement with the film. This engagement could have been either positive or negative. That it was favourable indicates something about the way in which Black women have constructed meaning from the text.[15]

As Bobo accurately asserts, it would be "too easy" to "consider Black women as cultural dupes in the path of a media barrage who cannot figure out when a media product portrays them and their race in a negative manner," especially because "Black women are aware, along with others, of the oppression and harm that comes from a negative media history."[16] The same *easy* mistake of assuming Perry's spectators are wholly ignorant of the examples, causes, and effects of mass media's embattled history of presenting negative, racist, and stereotypical images of African Americans should not be made in discussions of circuit audiences.

In line with Bobo, I consider the varied and multifaceted Perry audience I observed at the Arie Crown and Murat theatres to be little different from her always-already cognizant group of Black women. Thus, I find the meaning making, identification, and receptive processes that I witnessed to be reflective of the broader influences at play in acts of minority spectatorship as identified by Bobo:

> A viewer of a film (reader of a text) comes to the moment of engagement with the work with a knowledge of the world and a knowledge of other texts, or media products. What this means is that when a person comes to view a film, she/he does not leave her/his histories, whether social, cultural, economic, racial, or sexual at the door. An audience member from a marginalized group (people of colour, women, the poor, and so on) has an oppositional stance as they participate in mainstream media.

The motivation for this counter-reception is that we understand that mainstream media has never rendered our segment of the population faithfully. We have as evidence our years of watching films and television programmes and reading plays and books. Out of habit, as readers of mainstream texts, we have learned to ferret out the beneficial and put up blinders against the rest. From this wary viewpoint, a subversive reading of a text can occur.[17]

In other words, we should recognize that although Perry's plays (and their filmic and television offshoots) may not neatly fall into the category of mainstream, as is the case with Spielberg's *The Color Purple*, his minority spectators are similarly bringing their personal and group histories and interpretive skills to bear on his texts. I maintain that their widespread enjoyment is thus derived from the *ferreting out* of stereotypes, negative images, and so on and in their place relating to and identifying with the *positive* and *useful* material that is left behind.

In the sections that follow, I highlight the uniqueness of Perry's theatrical environments and then follow this with an investigation into how Perry's audience engage with his constructions of African American spirituality, blackness, and crossdressing. The totality of this investigation reveals how African American spectators are finding subversive pleasure in Perry's markedly stereotypical representations of African American life, family, culture, and religion.

The "Eventification" of Perry's Theatre: Food, Music, and the Ghosting of the Familiar

Earlier chapters have benefited from minor discussions concerning the particularities of specific theatrical environments. Most of these smaller discussions were either interwoven into direct analyses of performances, highlighted in my ethnographic recounts, or revealed in cited conversations with interviewees. In this chapter, however, I find it important to devote a brief section to the distinct features of Perry theatrical environments because I have found them to be directly related to the appeal of his productions and the expressed and witnessed experiences of his audiences. During my research, these environments became the space in which I was able to collect the most data regarding the methods through which Perry directly attempted to condition the horizons of expectations of his spectators, before they viewed his productions. These environments also allowed me to observe how Perry–specific environments operated in different theatre houses, as I attended his productions in the architecturally distinct spaces of Chicago's Arie Crown Theater and Indianapolis's Murat Theatre.

In Gay McCauley's words, "[m]y interest here, however, is not the place in itself but how space functions in practice in the performance experience and in the construction of meaning by spectators."[18] As Carlson reminds us in his book *Places of Performance: The Semiotics of Theatre Architecture*, "the building or space in which theatre takes place ... [contributes] to the meaning structure of the theatre event as a whole."

> A permanently or temporarily created ludic space, a ground for the encounter of spectator and performer, is a phenomenon found in a wide variety of societies and historical periods, but like any such phenomenon, can carry an almost infinite variety of special meanings according to the usages of those societies.[19]

Unfortunately, however, there are no parallels to be made between the theatrical structures found in Carlson's study and McCormick Place's Arie Crown Theater. Indeed, the only possible link that we might attempt to make would be to compare his brief discussion of massive art complexes, referred to as supermonuments,[20] with the huge 2.7-million-square-feet structures that constitute McCormick Place. However, this comparison soon falls short once we consider the different purposes of these buildings and the different publics that they serve. Instead of being an "artistic enclave," like New York's Lincoln Center or London's South Bank, the Arie Crown Theater is simply the largest of four theatres in this superstructure. Simply stated, the primary purpose of McCormick Place and its interior spaces, as articulated by their website, are to cater to the patrons and guests of trade shows and conventions.[21] Thus, unlike Carlson's supermonuments, it was not built to "demonstrate in a highly visible fashion the public dedication to the arts."[22] Perhaps it is no surprise, then, that in documenting the experiences of theatre spectators in such an unlikely space as the Arie Crown Theater and comparing it with the more traditional theatre house of The Murat, I came into contact with new and exciting information regarding spectatorial activities and the layered construction of theatrical environments in nontraditional and traditional spaces. In retrospect, however, I must admit that although I was well aware of the structural differences and the performance possibilities of different theatre spaces after reading Carlson, I was unprepared for how these Chicago and Indianapolis houses were specifically transformed for Perry events.

Over the years, the Arie Crown has emerged as the premiere destination for African American–centered touring shows that run the gamut from plays and comedy shows to concert events and dance performances. Contemporary circuit touring plays are among the most popular and reoccurring shows produced at the venue. Of course, this is an unsurprising use due to the theatre's large performance space and 4,239-seat auditorium, as well as its proximity to the South Side neighborhoods of Chicago. (As previously mentioned, circuit productions tend to be produced across the country in venues of similar size, capacity, and familiarity with African American patrons.) The areas that came most into view during my Arie Crown research were what Knowles has labeled as *spaces of reception*:

> These spaces include the entrances, foyers, box offices, and lobbies that greet audiences on their arrival, together with the lounges, bars, refreshment

stands, snack bars, and even washrooms, where they gather after admission, at intermissions, and occasionally after the show.[23]

During my first visit to the Arie Crown, I noticed that the convention center layout of McCormick Place creates a movie theatre–like atmosphere for spectators. This is partly due to the two flashing marquees that serve as the awning for the box office ticket window and the façade for the theatre's actual internal entrance. Not only do the marquees provide title and director information about the current production, but they also flash the names of any participating actor celebrities and advertise any upcoming Arie Crown events, such as concerts, comedy shows, and so on, that may be of interest to these spectators. Uniquely, the less sophisticated yet more flexible environment of the theatre's convention hall also engenders a creative use of space that vendors and spectators are able to take advantage of.

For many spectators, an afternoon or evening at the Arie Crown begins a few hours before showtime. An early arrival ensures patrons that they will be able to take advantage of Arie Crown–provided food and fare. During Perry events, the large lobby and the stretch of its wall-to-wall carpet provides a welcome space for the insertion of play-specific materials and non-Perry-related entertainment. This non-Perry-related entertainment includes the standalone shoe-shining stand, whose workers blast R&B and soul music as they shine the shoes of awaiting spectators, and the food vendor area and its accompanying dining area that is also set up for the comfort and convenience of spectators.

I discovered this area on the first evening of my ethnographic research at an Arie Crown Perry event. I walked beyond a floor-to-ceiling partition and noticed 15 large, circle-top tables covered with white table cloths. The seats surrounding the tables were filled with eating ticket holders. There was also a separate section containing standalone circular bar tables. The smell of BBQ chicken and rib dinners was thick in the air. In addition to a red-cloth-covered alcohol and beverage bar that one would normally encounter in many regional and Broadway theatres, there was also a vendor selling warm pretzels and the booth of one of the most popular rib restaurants on the South Side: JJ Robinson's. As I continued to walk, I observed an increasing crowd of Black patrons of all ages and various style of dress—including casual cotton and denim as well as formal suits and dresses—laughing, talking, eating, and greeting each other familiarly from afar. Once the internal theatre doors were opened a half hour before show time, I encountered a smaller lobby that housed the play-specific materials. Behind a built-in counter area, another vendor stood, this time selling t-shirts, CDs, DVDs, binoculars, and $10 glossy color playbooks of that evening's show. The music from the shoeshine stand could no longer be heard from this distance, and in its place, Perry-selected music pumped overhead from unseen speakers that could also be heard loudly in the auditorium seating areas.

As I continued to attend Perry productions at the Arie Crown over the years, scenes like the one just described remained unchanging and, I argue, successful in "impact[ing] . . . the theatrical experience and the spectatorial production of meaning, particularly in their framing and preparing [of] audience horizons of expectations."[24] At all shows, BBQ ribs and soul and R&B music remained a pre-show, intermission, and post-show staple. While inside the internal lobby and auditorium, Perry's tunes were always in line with the most popular songs on the radio. It was within these environments that I encountered spectators who had already begun to enjoy the "show" before the curtain had even risen on the play, becoming themselves part of the performance. These spectators gave rise once again to Schechner's notion of performance in theatrical events as that which consists of the "whole constellation of events, most of them passing unnoticed, that take place in/among both performers and audience from the time the spectator enters the field of performance . . . to the time the last spectator leaves."[25] Singing, dancing, and the eating of good food evoked a different kind of theatre environment that likened itself more to an afternoon in the park, an evening concert event, or a reunion of family and friends.

I continued to observe how the theatre's nontraditional space fell in line with Knowles's sentiments regarding the "architectural features" of these kinds of "alternative spaces." For Knowles, these spaces "figure equally significantly in the ideological coding of productions held in them, though in these cases such coding is more likely to be community-oriented, populist, or even overtly resistant to dominant ideologies."[26] Notably, on occasions when I attended a Madea play, conversations about Madea's antics and advice were plentiful. Later, when I attended his more recent plays, produced after Perry briefly stopped performing as Madea, conversations about his plays *and* his films were more frequent. Different than the other, previously discussed circuit events produced by other playwrights, a greater effort seemed to have been made to cater to Perry spectators. This was evident in the number of vendors (i.e. three for Perry events as opposed to the usual one or none), the presence and/or decorativeness of the dining area, and the constant stream of pre-show, intermission, and post-show in-auditorium music that succeeded in keeping spectators singing, dancing, and/or talking before the play started or while it was in intermission. My observations revealed that pleasing Perry spectators, in particular, was a mutual goal sought out by both Perry and Arie Crown management. For the latter, these efforts were most likely the result of the writer-director-producer's ability to consistently fill seats at high-ranked ticket prices.

Interestingly enough, my research at the Arie Crown revealed a connection to the differently built yet similarly used Murat Theatre in Indianapolis, Indiana. Some of the spectators whom I encountered at the Arie Crown confessed that they drove up to Chicago regularly when they could not make it to a play at The Murat. As I will discuss in my pending discussion of Perry's play *Madea Goes to Jail*, I used The Murat as an alternative field site for this production when my research began after its Chicago production dates. Unlike the Arie Crown, The Murat's structure is of historic significance for the city of Indianapolis. Built in

1907, the Murat Theatre has been the city's primary theatre destination for local and touring productions ever since.[27] Instead of the wide-open spaces boasted by the Arie Crown, the renamed Murat Centre includes an opulent lobby area (that features a grand carpet, gold chandeliers, and gold-plated beverage bars), a concert hall that seats 1,800, and additional rooms sometimes used for meetings and performance spaces. The internally located Murat Theatre has a 2,500-seat capacity.

On the afternoons and evenings that I attended The Murat in mid March of 2006, the winter-chill had not yet left the Midwest. The theatre boasted sold-out crowds of African Americans whose attire matched the opulence of the theatre's interior. Patrons donned their furs, hats, and best tailored suits and evening dresses. Rarely was someone seen wearing a pair of denim jeans or casual clothing. Posters of the production flanked the interior walls, as did pictures of past productions and advertisements of future events. Additional Madea-related posters were also placed on tripods in the lobby. Vested bartenders employed by the center stood behind the gold-plated beverage bars and served customers. An additional table was set up next to the bar, on which lay t-shirts, DVDs, CDs, and posters of Perry-related material. Many patrons stopped and laughed at the funny Madea slogan shirts priced at $15.00 and also considered buying $10.00 soundtracks of his previous plays on CD. On the other side of the lobby, a long line always existed in front of another table that had been set up for a photographer and his team of his assistants. Customers were able to have their picture taken in front of two cloth backdrops that had been affixed to the walls adjacent to the table. Both images had the play title *Madea Goes to Jail* emblazoned in large and bold letters. One picture featured the interior, winding staircase of a mansion. The second picture featured a larger-than-life image of Perry costumed as Madea. I observed the latter picture to be the more popular of the two. Gender-same pairs, gender-mixed couples, and larger groups took advantage of the moment and happily posed in front of the camera. The photographers printed pictures in minutes and placed them inside paper frames. One evening, I stood by myself and posed in front of the mansion's staircase for a $15 4×7 photograph. I must admit to experiencing a feeling of self-consciousness as I stood in front of numerous watching eyes who may have wondered why there wasn't anyone else posing in the picture with me. In other words, it was clear, throughout all the times that I attended them, that these plays were group and/or couple events. This characteristic helped to add to the energy of the environment and was assisted by the Murat Centre, which provided an African American R&B and classic soul soundtrack that pumped through unseen speakers during the pre-show, post-show, and intermission. The Isley Brothers, Kindred and the Family Spirit, and Luther Vandross were among the favorites that I saw elicit singing and dancing instances from patrons in the lobby, in the auditorium, and in the women's restrooms.

Let me refer to another Carlson work here: a discussion of Perry environments would be remiss if it did not mention the ghosting that occurs in these theatrical events that I argue in turn contributes to the feelings of comfort, familiarity, and pleasure that many of my interviewees, such as Melinda and Cheryl, mentioned:

> MELINDA: It reminds me of coming home and being around family or going to the neighborhood. I see a lot of the people I know there from work or where I used to live and it's a good time. Whenever these shows come to town, it's a big deal and we make sure to tell everybody we know to hurry up and buy a ticket. So, I guess it's like a reunion in some ways. We're all coming together.
>
> CHERYL: I like to come with the women from my church group. We come down here and it's something that I look forward to. We know the location so well and we recognize a lot of the people in the plays, so it's like we know them. I feel like I see Tyler Perry on my television all the time, so I feel like I know him too![28]

Carlson's term *ghosting* is linked to his articulation of how reception occurs in relation to a spectator's horizon of expectations:

> The primary tools for audiences confronted with new paintings, pieces of music, books, or pieces of theatre are previous examples of the various arts they have experienced. An audience member, bombarded with a variety of stimuli, processes them by selectively applying reception strategies remembered from previous situations that seem congruent. . . . If a work requires reception techniques outside those provided by an audience's memory, then it falls outside their horizon of expectations, but more commonly it will operate or can be made to operate, within that horizon, thus adding a new experiential memory for future use.[29]

Ghosting, then, explains the recurring, theatre-specific phenomenon in which "audience members encounter a new but distinctly different example of a type of artistic product they have encountered before . . . although now in a different context." As an expansion of my previous discussion of popular secular literature repackaged on Johnson and Guidry circuit stages, I would like to use Carlson's term *ghosting* to account for how Perry's recurring actors and characters help to engender feelings of familiarity, comfort, and pleasure in his spectators. I agree with Carlson's stance:

> The recycled body of an actor, already a complex bearer of semiotic messages, will almost inevitably in a new role evoke the ghost or ghosts of previous roles if they have made any impression whatever on the audience, a phenomenon that often colors and indeed may dominate the reception process.[30]

And if this is true, then ghosting's impact on reception within Perry environments is even more striking. Not only has Perry been successful in attracting audiences to his comedic and headliner characters, Madea and Mr. Brown (played by David Mann), but he has also introduced repeat actors such as Tamela Mann, Cassi Davis, and LaVan Davis. Tamela Mann, in particular, has been cast in the same role in multiple productions. These actors do not bring with them the previously discussed celebrity identity. Unlike the celebrities of Johnson–Guidry or Talbert productions, they do not have prior widely known careers in music, television, or film. Thus, it is only through Perry productions that audiences are able to recognize and identify with them, both as actors and as characters.

My suspicions surrounding the impact of this ghosting effect were confirmed during the run of *The Marriage Counselor*. Without fail, during each intermission of my five viewings of the production, the spectators around me discussed with me their surprise at not seeing Perry's usual cast of actors. Instead of being familiar to them, these actors, though talented, were new, and much time was spent trying to figure out who they were and if anyone knew them from something else (television, film, or music). On a few occasions, I was the only person in close range who had purchased the playbook. I shared with them the information given about the actors and Perry's director's note, which I found interesting:

> Recently, I realized something, over the last few years or so I have been using the same faces over and over again in my plays. I found myself watching a few of my past plays on video and realized that all the faces were the same. While nothing is wrong with that I just began to wonder how many more talented people lay out there waiting for their chance. So I set out and found a new crop of talent . . . people who deserve their shot. And I think I've done just that with this show: The Marriage Counselor.[31]

His new crop of talent included barely known performers and unknown performers who made this production look remarkably similar to any other non-Perry circuit play, except for the fact that this time there were no major celebrities or familiar actor(s) in place to clinch ticket sales. Instead, the cast consisted of a few yet-to-be recognized actors and singers whose claims to fame were varied and/or nonexistent. One had graced the stages of familiar productions such as *Smokey Joe's Café* or *Mama I Want to Sing*. Another was a television extra who had appeared in *The Young & The Restless* and *Girlfriends*. There was also a woman who was both a former Star Search contestant and an American Idol auditioner, and a young man was the season winner of BET's gospel singing contest series *Sunday Best*. A few others had performed in nondescript stage plays, and then there were those who considered themselves to be talented singers in their own rights. Talents and resumes aside, however, none of these 11 performers were recognizable to the spectators I encountered. Yet as evidenced by the sold-out May and October 2008 Chicago runs of this production, Perry had effectively reached a moment in his theatrical career when his plays were *good enough* to stand on his name alone, and he recognized it.

On the last Saturday night of the October run of this play, Perry surprised his audience by appearing onstage after curtain call. Dressed in a hat, casual buttoned shirt, and jeans, he addressed a sold-out crowd who were now standing, cheering, and clapping to welcome him. In his short speech, filled with the words "we," "us," and "you and I," he talked about how coming to Chicago always made him feel like he was loved. He reminisced about his first production in the city, noting how far *we* have come. Apparently, he had watched that night's entire show, sitting four rows behind me, about 16 rows from the front of the stage. Sitting next to him was Cassi Davis, an actor who he had made famous. From the stage, he asked Cassi to stand, and a spotlight revealed her waving to her supportive fans. No longer a part of his theatrical productions, Cassi now played a leading role in his television sitcom *House of Payne*. He then thanked the crowd for supporting his new crop of actors and especially congratulated those among the group with Chicago roots. He ended with a plug for his upcoming movie and then left the stage as quickly as he had entered. The house lights came up on an excited group of almost 5,000 spectators who had just been graced with the presence of a millionaire writer-director-producer who had just talked to them as if they were all old friends. With this final and unexpected act, the eventification of Perry's theatre had come full circle, and patrons were free to purchase any remaining souvenirs on their way out and buy a few meals to go for their rides home.

Case Studies: The Reception of Theatrical Constructions of Spirituality, Blackness, and Crossdressing as Performed on the Perry Stage

Selecting points of analyses in Perry productions is no easy task. Like other circuit writer-director-producers, Perry cleverly portrays varied aspects of so-called urban African American life and repackages familiar modes of African American cultural performance—including song, dance, comedy, and storytelling—for his awaiting audiences. Collectively, his oeuvre can be understood as containing the topics and perspectives that are important to the playwright and, given his popularity, of significance to those in his community of spectators. These factors notwithstanding, my research has revealed that the most interesting discoveries are generated in a consideration of the playwright's construction of African American spirituality, blackness, and femaleness, respectively, and the subsequent reception of these renderings by his African American spectators.

Snapshot No. 1—Constructed African American Spirituality

My first snapshot, also serving as a historical case study, is taken from his year 2000 play *I Can Do Bad All by Myself*. In summary, *I Can Do Bad All by Myself* is the story of two sisters and their conflicting relationships with men. In true soap opera–like form, the wilder sister, Maylee, has begun seeing the ex-husband of her sister Vianne. In the middle of the disputes is Maylee's neglected teenage daughter Keisha, who becomes pregnant by the play's end. Eventually with the help of family, love, and God, the two sisters reconcile their differences. Maylee ends her relationship with her sister's ex-husband, turns to God, and focuses on loving her daughter and taking caring of herself. She realizes that she does not need a no-good man: hence the title, she can do bad all by herself!

The synopsis available on Perry's website at the time of my research directly identified the play's theme as "We Fight So Hard to Hold on to the Things that God, Himself, is Trying to Tear Apart."[32] On the front cover of the production's 8½-inch by 11-inch glossy booklet, distributed during the 2000 tour, I found an extended title of the play: "Tyler Perry's I Can Do Bad All By Myself: Dear God, Are All Men Dogs? The Stage Play." A look inside the program revealed more direct references to God, church, and religion. Contained in each actor bio was either a quote from the Bible, a gospel song, or a familiar religious saying; a personal declaration of one's faith in the Lord; and/or reverence given to one's pastor and place of worship. Different than the more traditional content of actor bios that normally include an actor's past roles, training, and recognition, these bios only briefly mentioned their theatre careers and instead looked more like the following:

KISHA GRANDY (VIANNE): This twenty-something vocal dynamo, grew up in Dallas, TX. Singing since the age of four, Kisha quickly made a name for herself in her hometown. After singing at a local program celebrating Dr. Martin Luther King, Kirk Franklin approached her and told her about this group he was putting together. Thus, becoming one of the original members of The Family, and it was not long before she stepped out from the group and grabbed the lead microphone, much to the delight of everyone fortunate enough to hear her. It is with this group that her voice can be heard in advertisements for The Chrysler Corporation, Church's Chicken, Coca Cola and Cheerios. As a single woman, she realizes that God is in love with her, and His love is unconditional and unwavering. She comes to introduce the Lord as a Comforter, a Healer, and as The Greatest Love to a generation, that [sic] needs assurance. Kisha has been featured in *He Say, She Says, But What Does God Say?* [sic] and The Night I Fell in Love [sic]. Now as a solo artist, Kisha is destined to share her talents with the world.[33]

Grandy's bio notably makes mention of the popular gospel group Kirk Franklin and the Family, whose commercial success as a gospel ensemble group peaked in the early 1990s and continues today with their 2017 Grammy Awards in the categories of Best Gospel Album and Best Gospel Performance/Song and their recent 2019 nominations at the BET Awards in the Dr. Bobby Jones Best Gospel/

Inspirational Award category.[34] She also makes a point to mention her voiceover work in television commercials for popular American food and retail products. Her bio closes with a confirmation of her faith and her previous theatrical work in Talbert's *He Say, She Says, But What Does God Say?* and the lesser-known *The Night I Fell in Love*. The actor bio of her castmate Tyga Graham features a similar blend of personal biography narrative peppered with Black popular culture references from music, film, and television. Like Grandy, he also references his past theatrical work on the circuit and his faith-based philosophy:

TYGA GRAHAM (BOBBY): Tyga's singing roots began in church at the early age of 10. A native of Atlanta, GA, Tyga's destiny as an entertainer began when he was an original member and founder of the group Silk. He went on to form the group Juice and signed a record deal with Mercury Records, which led to a single on the Jason's Lyric soundtrack. Tyga's made his debut as a solo artist when he released the first single "People's Party," during the 1996 Olympics in Atlanta, which gained top spots on radio stations all across the southeast region. Although singing is Tyga's forte he is a prominent songwriter and producer, [sic] and has embarked upon a new career as an actor and model since relocating to Los Angeles. Tyga has headline roles in the plays <u>A Good Man is Hard to Find</u> and <u>Where Have All the Good Men Gone</u> and gained national recognition. He has also made several TV Appearances on such shows as Moesha [sic], The Steve Harvey Show [sic], and MTV [sic]. His first lead in a feature film entitled "Before Now" is slated for release in 2000. He was also featured in the film "Fled" and "Port Chicago Mutiny" both directed by the acclaimed Kevin Hooks. Tyga survives the demands of this business by living his philosophy that "What you are is God's gift to you, and what you do with it is you [sic] gift to God."[35]

Grandy's and Graham's castmate Tosha Moore similarly immerses her performance biography in religion and religious affiliation, with valued acknowledgment given to the pastor and congregation of her hometown church in Chicago, alongside citations of her previous theatrical work on the circuit.

TOSHA [SIC] MOORE (MAYLEE): When you think of an anointed singer and woman of God, you can't help but think of Tasha Amia Moore. Tasha started singing at the age of eight and at the age of sixteen, she was given the opportunity to sing with Chicago's Milton Brunson Thompson community singers. Tosha [sic] proceeded to do a play called Up, Up and Away [sic] featuring Karen Clark and Vanessa Bell Armstrong. Tosha [sic] a powerful singer who is a member of the St. James C.O.G.I.C. in Chicago, Illinois, pastored by Elder James Campbell. She also played the lead role in Bishop T. D. Jakes' <u>Woman Thou Art Loosed</u> and she now plays the role of Maylee in Tyler Perry's new show <u>I can do bad</u> [sic]. Tosha [sic] Moore is one to watch, one to enjoy, and one to love.[36]

Bios such as these not only provided audiences at the time with insight into the prior careers and development of circuit actors but also highlighted information that may have been important and/or recognizable to them on local and national levels.[37] For example, references that included one's involvement in Kirk Franklin's gospel group, advertisements for major corporations, and appearances on MTV and *Moesha* could help to validate an actor's national significance. On the other hand, mentioning one's membership in a particular church or one's participation in an annual city event could help to confirm an actor's local and community import. The more significant attribute of these bios, however, remained in that all information was consistently framed around each actor's personal and long-standing connection to the church.

Once my investigation moved from the playbill to the actual performance as captured on DVD, I became interested in how the actors' bodies in performance became constructed texts and cultural signifiers that denoted African American spirituality. I turn to methodologies of theatre, performance studies, and dance anthropology to exhume the overlapping religious and vernacular content contained in circuit productions. In so doing, this portion of the analysis fulfills dance scholar Jane Desmond's insistence that we "enlarge our studies of bodily 'texts' to include dance in all of its forms," including theatrical performance, to "further our understandings of how social identities are signaled, formed, and negotiated through bodily movement."[38] During multiple viewings of the production, I recognized a connection between the codified movements of Perry's actors and the varying physical movements of worshiping African American congregants found in many Black churches across the country. In my following explication of the first snapshot, I use my developed term *spiritualized vernacular movement* to discuss and emphasize these connections and hypothesize how they were related to Black spectatorial reception during the play's 2000–2001 production run.

Spiritualized vernacular movements, as I am terming them, are spiritually and religiously codified forms of bodily motion that are usually associated with Black worship. Some may describe it as "catching the spirit" or "praising the Lord," and the movements often involve heightened gestures, as the body enacts exaltation and celebratory release. They can be performed when the enraptured is sitting or standing and can be enacted with the accompaniment of music or independently during sermons or songs. In the African American church context, it is what Brenda Dixon Gottschild describes as the "active body-and-soul participation of the communicants."[39] My conception of spiritualized vernacular movement also benefits from the recent scholarship on Black vernacular dance. As described respectively by Jacqui Malone and Anthea Kraut, Black vernacular dance encompasses the varying "multidimensionality," "style," "rhythms," "gestures," "attitudes," and "movement patterns" exhibited by the dancing body which signify African derived "retentions and transformations."[40] My understanding of vernacular practices is generated in large part from Kraut's definition of the phrase as a "set of expressive practices that originate from and thrive in a community whose members constitute both the producers and consumers of those practices."[41] With this in mind, my interest here is not to assert an essentialist understanding of spiritualized vernacular movement but instead to look at how localized movements, as exhibited in the context of the Black church, manifest onstage and, as I argue, are used as performance strategies that seek to entertain and engage African American audiences.

Perry's actors are able to accomplish spectatorial engagement by executing what Paul Carter Harrison refers to as "minting [the] performance strategies [of] the black church."[42] In this dramaturgical technique, the actors perform what I label as their versions of *theatricalized spiritual vernacular movement*, by playing on and exaggerating recognizable and familiar African American gestural tropes of worship. In so doing, they conjure not only the energy but also the memory of actual church worship. Elin Diamond has commented on the duplicitous nature of performative mimesis in action:

> On the one hand, [mimesis] speaks to our desire for universality, coherence, unity, tradition, and on the other, it unravels that unity through improvisations, embodied rhythm, powerful instantiations of subjectivity, and what Plato most dreaded, impersonation, the latter involving outright mimicry. In imitating . . . the model, the *mimos* becomes an other, *is being* an other, thus a shapeshifting Proteus, a panderer of reflections, a destroyer of forms.[43]

If mimesis indeed poses a threat to the model in its imitation of everyday experience, then where is the line drawn between mimesis and mimicry in reenactments of cultural tradition in theatrical pieces that are aimed at producing both recognition and entertainment? In other words, where is the line drawn between the onstage presentation of ritual and the ritualized representation of reality? Evidence of how these issues converge on the circuit stage, in ways that address two of my previously stated questions regarding dramaturgical content, production techniques, and mimetic fidelity, can be found in the following scene that occurs near the end of the production.

Aunt Cora has decided to reconcile the problems between Maylee and Keisha. The opening dialogue of the aunt's heart-to-heart conversation is underscored by the melodic keys of a piano, which preps the audience for the start of yet another musical number, titled "Hallelujah! Thank You Jesus." For the first few minutes of the musical number, Aunt Cora is driven to stand by the power of her words. As she sings, mother and child embrace in a tearful hug while seated on the couch. Then, as the crescendo of the song dramatically increases, a tearful mother and daughter rise from their seats, and all three women begin performing in ways that I find similar to the codified movements of some Black church congregations—particularly those of the Baptist and Pentecostal variety. For example, numerous times in the musical number, Maylee enacts vertical jumping with arms outstretched horizontally and clenched fists. Meanwhile, her daughter Keisha, standing in an unmoving position, repeats the cross-like posture of her mother, displaying her tear-drenched face tilted upward toward the proscenium ceiling. While these movements are being repeated, the aunt, who is now in the middle of her musical number, has begun to punctuate her words with arm movements that end with her fists raised upward toward the ceiling. By the end of the song, all three actors have made their way to downstage center, and as if the living room has been transplanted in an actual church, all three women are seen embracing, jumping, crying, shouting words of praise, and waving with their arms and faces upward toward the heavens.

Although I was not present during the live performance of this production, the recorded audio on the DVD, coupled with my subsequent attendance at other plays produced by Perry and other contemporary circuit producers, leads me to assume that this moment was powerful enough to generate interaction and prompt call-and-response behavior from the attending audience. Contributing to the seemingly realistic depiction of church rituals, we now have not only signs of mimesis and mimicry but also evidence of what Kimberly Benston refers to as methexis. Methexis, according to Benston, is a

> process that could be alternatively described as a shift from display, the spectacle observed, to rite, the event which dissolves traditional divisions between actor and spectator, self and other, enacted text and material context. And through this process, the black beholder has been theoretically transformed from a detached individual whose private consciousness the playwright sought to reform, to a participatory member of a communal ceremony which affirms a shared vision.[44]

Thus, the process of methexis, which I argue occurs seamlessly in the improvisation-laden, participatory space of Chitlin Circuit theatre productions, simultaneously complicates and assists with spectators like the ones in the following quoted material, who are commenting on Perry's theatrical experiences as being so "real."

ROBYN: Tyler Perry is a genius. He's talking about experiences that we, as black people, have been through. I know people like the people he writes about. Those same people are in my family, at work, at church and in my life every day. Sometimes you want to laugh at their problems, but sometimes they are dealing with things in their life that are serious.[45]

JACKIE: I wouldn't be going to his plays if they weren't good. . . . Some people do go for them because they are like church. You get that same feeling and you want to give praise and thanks for His glory after you see those people [onstage] come out the other end of those situations. You can take that with you and sometimes it helps you with your own life. I use these stories all the time when I'm talking to people.[46]

Robyn and Jackie are not alone in their opinions. Jackie's point in particular brings into focus a frequently expressed use of his productions as either a substitute or replacement of church. Across demographics, the self-proclaimed faithful and the wayward continue to find solace and reaffirmation in Perry's packaged renderings of African faith, religion, and the cultural expression of that spirituality.

Snapshots No. 2 and No. 3—White Performances of "Blackness"

Methexis also occurred during my live attendance at two of Perry's productions, *Madea Goes to Jail* and *The Marriage Counselor*, respectively, but this time it was in response to a different kind of representational content that was unique to both productions. During the Murat Theatre's 2006 production run of *Madea Goes to Jail*, I witnessed circuit audiences' introduction to a never-before-seen element of contemporary circuit plays: the inclusion of a white actor-character. Before this and perhaps as a result of the Black-oriented content, narratives, and performance modes contained in circuit productions, white actors playing white characters had never been a part of circuit events. Thus, keeping in line with the characteristically stereotyped content of circuit productions, Perry's new characters were markedly and formulaically coded "white" through their costumes, demeanor, speech, and roles. In *Madea Goes to Jail*, audiences were presented with Jeremy, Madea's probation officer and the prison's chaplain. During the Arie Crown's production of *The Marriage Counselor*, audiences were introduced to Becky, the marriage counselor's office assistant. As the following snapshots will show, interpolated in these "Black" theatrical narratives are moments of white performances of "blackness" that I observed troubling authentic notions of blackness at every show. I witnessed how the staged and reflexive reactions of the Black performers and Black audiences, respectively, challenged the assumed ownership and presupposed qualities of blackness. During these moments, audiences and I were forced to contend with not only our horizons of expectations for circuit events and performances but also the former limitations that we had placed on the voices, abilities, and bodies of whiteactor-characters.

Madea Goes to Jail was advertised as Perry's latest installment in a long line of Madea plays. This time, Perry's trademark grandmother was finally going to have to face the music in prison for one of her many notorious crimes. The slogan "They finally got me," written across the front of the program, spoke volumes. Inside of the Murat lobby, pre-show audiences discussed their growing anticipation and excitement about the production that they were about to see. Everyone I encountered was interested in seeing how Madea, who in previous plays had reminisced about poisoning people with pies and frequently brandished a gun that she was not afraid to use, had finally been caught. Different than the signs of religion and the church first encountered in the program of *I Can Do Bad All by Myself* that I have argued were introductory signposts that clued audiences into the significance of African American spirituality in that production, in *Madea Goes to Jail*'s program, there were no cues that attributed any importance to the inclusion of a white actor-character, Brian Hurst, in the production.

In fact, Hurst's bio looked no different from the bios written by his fellow African American actors. *Madea Goes to Jail*'s program still contained actor bios that linked the performers to the church, community, and recognizable and popular past performances. Since his *I Can Do Bad All by Myself* production, this content had come to be expected in Perry playbills. Hurst's bio appropriately adhered to this standard formula:

> According to Grammy, Dove, and Stellar Award nominated artist, Marvin Sapp, "Brian Hurst is one of the most anointed men of our time and destined to change the direction of gospel music . . ." His desire is to stand in the gap for the unsaved. Brian's music is focused on theses of praise and worship, consecration, faith and deliverance, Brian has been blessed in ministry at various churches and conventions including Pastor Rod Parsleys [*sic*] World Harvest Church; Rev. Clay Evans' A. A. R. C. Convention; Dr. Bobby Jones Gospel; with Bishop Larry Trotter; and others. Brian recently starred in the stageplay "If These Hips Could Talk" with Billy Dee Williams and Robin Givens for 2 years. Born in Toledo, Ohio, Brian resides in Bangor, Maine, with his wife, Katey, and their 3 children.[47]

On the night of my first viewing of the program before the start of the show, I, perhaps like many other audience members, failed to question the similarities in Hurst's bio to those of the other Black actors, nor did I consider the significance of his stated religious affiliations, previous theatre involvement, and recognition by esteemed members of African American gospel and church communities. As a researcher of these plays and as a fellow Black spectator, I found it curious at best that there was a white actor onstage. My initial apathy toward Hurst's involvement was encouraged by the fact that he was not a major character in the narrative and as evidence of this his character faded quickly into the background of the developing plot. It was not until Hurst or Jeremy, as he was called in the play, interrupted a mid-scene performance already underway with his own solo rendition of a popular soul song that I realized the impact that he was making in the production.

Jeremy's moment came near the end of a long "popular song" interlude that took place during the performance. This interlude was the first of its kind for a Perry production, and it occurred midway in the play during a scene that involved most of the play's actors. At the start of the interlude, Madea directs the characters away from the plot and leads them into a discussion about their favorite classic R&B song. The band begins to play as Madea starts to sing a song made popular by the late-1960s to early-1970s soul group The Friends of Distinction, titled "Going in Circles," using his male-sounding voice. This first song simultaneously and smoothly marks a transition onstage as the actors visibly leave their characters behind and participate in the medley as the actors themselves. After the completion of Madea-Perry's solo, each actor takes their turn standing centerstage and sings the song of their choice to, and eventually with, the audience. While this is happening, the other actors dance supportively behind the singer. Throughout the first ten minutes of the medley, Hurst-Jeremy is seen standing separately upstage watching his African American counterparts perform. He then tentatively begins learning the steps of the three-man dance group he has found himself in. The moves of his partners harken back to African American male singing groups like The Four Tops, The Chi-Lites, or, as Madea points out, Gladys Knight's Pips. A patient and willing learner, Jeremy's public dance lesson markedly falls in line with the stereotyped perception that white people or white men, rather, can't dance. Of course, the audience and I easily read this non-fictive interlude, including Hurst-Jeremy's "bad" dancing, as emblematic of a historical and often comedic representation of blackness in performance that is marked authentic especially when juxtaposed next to a lacking or failed attempt at imitation by white performers. Recreated in *Madea Goes to Jail*, this grouping of authentic Black musical performances served to not only signify each actor's seemingly innate talent and skill but also confirm the audiences' expectations that these Black actors are naturally able to sing, dance, and entertain in ways that white performers inside or outside of circuit events cannot. However, this "Black" space becomes exceedingly complicated when Hurst-Jeremy interrupts and announces that he wants to sing his own favorite song.

After hearing endearing and memory-inducing solos of songs like Betty Wright's "Clean Up Woman," Chaka Khan's "Sweet Thing," and Marvin Gaye's "Let's Get It On," the audience is now enraptured by this trip down memory lane via popular 1970s Black soul music. All of a sudden, Hurst-Jeremy interrupts the communal performer–audience party and announces "Hey, guys. I got one." We hear the sound of a drum roll, punctuated by the crash of the symbols, and we see the Black actors looking around at each other and the audience in a mix of disbelief and suspicion. Hurst asks, "What happened?" Madea loudly declares an exaggerated "Hell nah! This is BET!" The crowd erupts with laughter. Hurst responds, "Come on, we're having a good time here, give me a chance." The audience responds positively by clapping encouragingly. With her left hand on her left hip and her right hand holding a cigarette, Madea slowly scans the audience, exhales, and says "Alright, if it's the wrong song, he going home wit y'all!" Hurst-Jeremy then confidently walks downstage center and proceeds to silence the house with his convincing rendition of the song "Before I Let Go," originally sung and produced by the still-performing Black soul band Maze Featuring Frankie Beverly. The audience and his surrounding actors burst into applause with faces of shock and surprise. Hurst-Jeremy punctuates his vocals with well-honed arm movements and gyrations that are in time with the rhythm and beats of the music as he impressively hits all of the notes. On every night of his performance,

I saw Murat audiences consistently voice their approval of Hurst by singing along and confirming to their fellow spectators how excited they were by Hurst's ability to nail the performance. Each night, Madea-Perry marked the end of Hurst's performance with a "Black" and male seal of approval: the handshake commonly referred to as a pound or daps.

In Perry's 2008 production of *The Marriage Counselor*, he decided to challenge his audiences' notion of Black authenticity in performance again, this time with a character that displayed a different kind of whiteness. Actor Stephanie Ferrett played the role of Becky, a blonde, green-eyed, plainly dressed office assistant who laced her conversations with popular African American slangs and expressions much to the comedic delight of the Arie Crown's viewing audience. Ferrett's bio credited her as being a talented singer across "R&B, pop, hip hop, rock, gospel and soul, and Broadway" musical genres.[48] Like Hurst's character Jeremy, Ferrett's Becky spends little time onstage. Similarly, her shining moment comes amid Perry's now-patented "popular song" medley that is used in this production as a vehicle to reminisce about old R&B love songs. This time, however, we see all of the actors remain in character as they serenade each other with Al Green's "Love and Happiness" and The Isley Brothers' "For the Love of You." At this point in the plot, the songs are being used to remind the troubled couples sitting amid their group therapy session at the marriage counselor's office of their love for one another.

Unlike in Hurst's case, Ferrett is not involved in the medley at its start. Instead, Becky enters the office and unknowingly finds herself amid the impromptu concert. Upon her entry, one character annoyingly yells out to her "What is it Becky?! What Becky?!" Another character, by the name of Stanley, pulls her to the side and explains to her that "This is not an affirmative action moment Becky. We don't care to hear anything like," and he completes his thought by singing lyrics from an operatic rendition of "Ave Maria." Stanley then proceeds to show Becky to the door, saying "So God bless your heart and all your parts!" Multiple Arie Crown audiences exploded with laughter during this exchange, while Becky remained unmoved. Instead of leaving, she returns downstage center, faces the audience, and proceeds to belt out the opening notes sung by R&B and soul singer Teena Marie in her famed duet "Fire and Desire" sung with Rick James. Becky continues to sing the lyrics as we see moments of staged surprise expressed by her surrounding characters. Stanley joins her downstage and picks up Rick James's lyrics in time. Night after night, I witnessed this duo bring the house down at the Arie Crown. Audiences consistently jumped from their seats in roaring applause, clapping and swaying to the music with surprised and astonished faces. As the song ends with Ferrett-Becky hitting some of Teena Marie's patented high notes, Stanley asks, "Are you really white?" Each night, the audience exploded with laughter and applause as the stage lights dimmed.

The "Black" performances of Hurst and Ferrett serve as interesting snapshots not only because of how they challenge how circuit audiences have historically comprehended and confirmed performances of blackness on circuit stages and in their everyday lives but also because of what they reveal when compared to each other. Separately considered, Ferrett's performance is markedly different due to the choice of song. Although a renowned and acclaimed R&B and soul singer in her own right, Teena Marie, who passed away in 2010, was considered to be a white American despite her mixed ethnic ancestry of Italian, Irish, Portuguese, and Native American. Her popularity among African Americans, however, is due in large part to the vocal dexterity she shows in her classic R&B songs. In fact, her albums, sound, and visibility in the Black community over the years earned her the title of "No. 1 honorary Soul Sista."[49] In a 2006 interview published in *Jet* magazine, she explained her African American appeal:

> I've always been accepted by the Black community and I think that's a beautiful thing. I wanted to sing R&B. I've just been doing music that I like to do. I only had one big crossover record, which was Lover Girl, but basically my music has always been geared to a Black audience. . . . I think that makes me, me. And I think people can really hear that it is not pretentious, it's not contrived. It's from my heart.[50]

Ferrett's cover of Teena Marie's lyrics, then, was always-already signifying an approved white performance of blackness and/or Black sound. Thus, due to Teena Marie's extraordinary success as a white R&B artist, there were incredible risks involved in Ferrett's performance and a huge potential for failure. She would be judged not only on how "Black" she sounded but also on how close she could come to the Teena Marie register. The eventual success and approval of Ferrett's double-layered white performance of Black sound effectively stood out as a moment in which Black circuit audiences were able to be inclusive of another white body performing Black music. As a result, the original performance as done by Teena Marie's white body was no longer thought to be exclusive to her and perhaps provided an impetus for circuit audiences to begin thinking about the constructed and/or learned nature of blackness.

Extending this last point further, the performances of Hurst and Ferrett collectively fall under E. Patrick Johnson's category of dialogic performances of blackness. Stemming from Dwight Conquergood's understanding of dialogic performance as performances through which "the performer comes to know himself or herself by performing the Other," Johnson uses his category to account for the "possible . . . sharing of ideas, beliefs, and values across barriers of difference" that can occur when white singers perform Black music.[51] In his examination of white Australian gospel singers and their performance of gospel music, Johnson describes one such "performance of possibilities"[52] when this choir performed before an all-Black congregation in Harlem, New York, as part of their tour of Black churches in the United States. As described by Johnson, after a sense of initial and perhaps mutual unease shared by the performers and their audience, the

Café of the Gate of Salvation Choir was able to approvingly engage and connect with the Black congregants during a stirring and convincing rendition of the Clark Sister's song "You Brought the Sunshine." In the following excerpt, Johnson details this moment and explains the dialogic exchange that occurred between all those assembled:

> The performance of "You Brought the Sunshine" tapped into the Others' voice within experience, due in part to the Café's execution of and enjoyment of the song. . . . The choir's competence as performers initiated genuine dialogue in that contested space where identities and subjectivities converse, commune, and contrast. During and after dialogic performance— and specifically within the "performance of possibilities"—performer, subject, and audience are transformed. Each comes away from the performance changed. They traverse the world of the Other, glimpsing its landscape, and this "sighting" leaves a lasting imprint on the consciousness of all who experience this symbolic journey.[53]

I contend that Black audiences at the Murat and Arie Crown theatres witnessed and participated in such "performances of possibilities" during the performances of Hurst and Ferrett. Like gospel music, R&B and soul music are marked in the world as "inextricably linked to black bodies"[54] and as a result are considered to be what Johnson adeptly refers to as "sign[s]/sound[s] of blackness."[55] Consequently, these Black music forms register as "signifier[s] of 'authentic' blackness" and are mistakenly understood to be essentially and biologically Black. Yet as Johnson accurately points out,

> "Blackness" does not belong to any one individual or group. Rather, individuals or groups appropriate it in order to circumscribe its boundaries or to exclude others. . . . Because blackness has no essence, Black authenticity is overdetermined—contingent on the historical, social, and political terms of its production.[56]

Quoting Regina Bendix, Johnson emphasizes this point: "'The notion of [black] authenticity implies the existence of its opposite, the fake, and this dichotomous construct is at the heart of what makes authenticity problematic.'"[57] Through Hurst's and Ferrett's vocal performances, they were "engaging not only in the coproduction of the music, but also of blackness itself," along with their viewing and approving audiences.[58] I therefore highlight the performances of Hurst and Ferrett as two examples of meaning making in circuit events. As Taylor has pointed out, one's "identity crucially depends on [one's] dialogic relations with others."[59] Through conversations and exchanges with those around us, an "inwardly generated identity is formed."[60] Thus, Hurst's and Ferrett's performances of R&B and soul music can be understood as dialogic performances of blackness that forced circuit audiences to confront their assumptions and notions surrounding *blackness* and *blackness in performance* as performed by white singers. In so doing, these moments provided a space and a context for dialogic and identity-forming exchanges to occur.

Snapshot No. 4—Crossdressing Revealed

My last snapshot discussion attempts to effectively condense all of the variety, range, and nuances of Perry's most popular character, Madea, into an analysis of one moment from the production run of *Madea Goes to Jail* which, I argue, features his most complex presentation of the character to-date. This Madea performance not only encompassed the breadth and depth of the character as she was known to audiences up to that point but also represented the most innovative of all Madea-Perry performances aimed at producing audience response and identification. Keeping in line with the focus of this chapter and the project at large, this snapshot also features how Perry's Madea performance challenged his audience's horizons of expectations and achieved relatability or mimetic fidelity to their lived experiences.

Perry's construction of an African American woman through the performative mode of crossdressing is a contemporary strain of a long and winding history in the United States of white men and Black men portraying Black women. Emerging first, the history of white men dressing up and performing as Black women harkens back to the nineteenth-century comedic and stereotypical performances of the minstrel stage that entertained white audiences. As Lott recounts, these blackface minstrel shows were

> organized around the quite explicit "borrowing" of Black cultural materials for white dissemination (and profit), a borrowing that ultimately depended upon the material relations of slavery, the minstrel show obscured these relations by pretending that slavery was amusing, right, and natural.[61]

Although racist and sexualized depictions of Black men were the primary characterizations in blackface minstrel shows, white men soon began caricaturing Black women. References to Black women found in minstrel song lyrics, narratives, and performances included, but were not limited to, images of "castrated," "vulgar," "blind," "engulfing," "gorging," and "grotesque" women:[62]

> On the most immediate level, collective white male violence toward black women in minstrelsy not only tamed an evidently too-powerful object of interest, but contributed (in nineteenth-century white men's terms) to a masculinist enforcement of white male power over the black men to whom the women were supposed to have "belonged."[63]

As Judith Williams discovered in her analysis of nineteenth-century theatrical adaptations of Harriet Beecher Stowe's *Uncle Tom's Cabin*, early American theatre performances were littered with such minstrel depictions that left Black women "displace[d]" and "absen[t]": "The audience sees the image of a black woman but without the presence of a black female body—or even a white female body. The false image of a black woman is instead inscribed on a white male body." Bean extends Williams's view further in the following point:

> The mutability of color coupled with the changeability of gender furthered the white minstrels' promotion of color and gender as being primarily theatrical and of entertainment as a type of mimicry or mimesis, "an almost, not-quite" relationship with the subject, the African American woman.[64]

In my upcoming discussion of Perry's construction and performance of Madea, I address how these issues of displacement, absence, and what Bean correctly identifies as the theatrical and entertainment nature of crossdressing assemble in Perry's contemporary Black male presentation of a Black woman, a performance where gender alone becomes the mutable factor.

As respectively addressed by Bean and Krasner, newly appropriated Black minstrel performances were done with nuanced and intended differences. I have already discussed the nuances of Krasner's *reinscription*[65] term in Chapter 2. Notably, Bean describes a similar process undertaken by the African American actor Andrew Tribble in his impersonations of Black women on minstrel stages. Included in his repertoire of female personalities were characters who went by the names of "Ophelia Snow," "Ophelia, the Village Pride," and "Sis Hopkins." Tribble's take on female impersonation, however, was markedly different from those of his white male counterparts:

> black minstrelsy commented on white minstrelsy's performances of color and gender by narrowing the scope of female impersonation. Gender impersonators such as Tribble were primarily comic in purpose and did not in any way thrive on the ambivalence of whether or not Tribble was truly a man or a woman. Tribble, in his 'screamingly funny' female portrayals, both expanded the importance of humor in his performances and neatly contained the oft-present dual purpose in white minstrelsy of denigrating the subject of the performances—African American women—and the vehicle of the performance: his own African American male body.[66]

Bean likens Tribble's performance to that of the African American comedian Flip Wilson during his crossdressed performances as Geraldine, a fast talking, slender, coiffed, and fashionably dressed African American woman. Geraldine quickly gained popularity, becoming a regular installment on Wilson's televised variety show during the 1970s. Wilson created a well-developed and sophisticated comedic character in the no-nonsense Geraldine who hailed from the streets of New York. Geraldine frequently appeared in skits with Wilson's guests, donning her trendy and color-coordinated ensembles. Bean writes, "[t]he comedy of Wilson's gender impersonation was similar to Tribble's in that it based itself in the social and political satire of gender."[67]

Although stemming from this lineage, the contemporary version of the African American woman as performed by a crossdressed Perry places the comedic execution and the savvy social and political caricaturing of gender that Bean identifies in the performances of Tribble and Wilson into a female body type that seems, on first impression, to *look* similar to the large, bulky, and matronly male impersonation nascent in white minstrelsy. The result is a male impersonated mammy-*looking* figure that has been constructed to entertain contemporary African American spectators. I contend, however, that Perry's Madea signifies not only the mammy figure of minstrelsy and of early American film—described by Donald Bogle as being "big," "fat," "cantankerous," and "fierce[ly] independen[t]"[68]—but also the physical size and presence of many real and loved African American mothers and grandmothers. In fact, Perry attests to the influence of the latter in the opening lines of his Madea book: *Madea's Uninhibited Commentaries on Love and Life: Don't Make A Black Woman Take Off Her Earrings.*

> Whoever came up with the saying that "it takes a village to raise a child" must have been thinking of my friend Madea. In the black community, Madea was the head of that village. Her name is the southern term for 'mother dear.' Madea used to be on every corner in every neighborhood when I was growing up and generations before. She used to be everywhere, but today she is missed. Back in the 1970s, the Madeas in our neighborhoods began to disappear and they have left an unmistakable void.[69]

Perry's theatricalized version of this *dear* African American *mother* comes equipped with her own shotgun, an always-within-reach cigarette, and a vault full of matronly wisdom about men, relationships, and family issues, all of which are made complete by her ironic musings about biblical lessons and churchgoers.

Here I am most interested in Perry's construction and presentation of this African American woman in his theatrical performances and her subsequent reception by African American spectators. At issue for male impersonators like Perry (and others like African American film actors and comedians Eddie Murphy and Martin Lawrence) who re-create African American women in their crossdressed performances is the need to justify such performances when numerous African American actors are readily available to play the part. A questioning parenthetical by *New York Times* film critic Anita Gates in her review of Perry's 2006 movie *Madea's Family Reunion* made this concern clear. Gates pointedly asked, "What is it about fat-lady drag that appeals to so many young black male comedians?"[70]

Perry responds to a similar question posed to him in an interview with *Essence* magazine held a month later:

> Perry decided to play Madea rather than cast a woman in those big shoes, he says, because of the special perspective he brings. "Men watch women all the time. We sleep with you, we love you, we talk to you, we watch you shower," he says. "I don't know if it's a Virgo thing, but I'm tuned in."[71]

In the same article, he traces Madea's personality, virtues, and her positive and negative qualities to the combined influences of his mother and his aunt:

> "The nurturing part of Madea comes from my mother, who would open the doors of our home to you no matter who you were," he recalls. "My aunt inspired the pistol-packing, the wig, and the voice. She overpronounces her words and puts an *r* on everything to make it sound proper."[72]

My conversations with Perry spectators revealed that most of them considered Madea to be a funny and positive character whose antics were not to be taken seriously. Although some recognized the danger in such a representation, many felt that this danger was nullified in an all-Black space because white spectators, who may not be able to recognize that Madea is a caricature, are not present in the theatre. Others compared Perry's crossdressing to the already-mentioned performances of Eddie Murphy, Martin Lawrence, Flip Wilson, and other instances of African American male crossdressing that have appeared in film and/or television. Some interviewees gestured toward making a distinction between the theatrical Madea and the filmic Madea, citing that the Madea of the theatre would always be considered the original Madea since Perry's movies (at that point in time) were not mainly about her. A few were of the opinion that because Madea's primary audience (at the theatre or at the movies) will always be Black people, she will always be understood for what she is meant to represent: a comedic and familiar character. These spectators felt that although Madea represented a stereotype, she did not take away from the positive messages in the play and was there just to be laughed at and/or to laugh with you.

Interestingly enough, I encountered one woman in Arie Crown's lobby who talked to me about how she used the advice written in Madea's book to talk to her teenage daughter about sex and relationships with boys. When I asked her to tell me more about what Madea said, the woman replied: "I told my daughter, Madea said 'klink-klink'! Meaning, she better lock up those legs! We're not having those problems in this family."[73] The woman's friends stood around us laughing in agreement. I noticed that they all had a favorite Madea quote that they interjected into their dialogue. When asked, all of the women confessed to having read the book, and from their conversation, I ascertained that they all seemed to approve of its contents. Strikingly, they talked about Madea as if she were real instead of a character. They used the pronouns "she" or "her" and never referred to Madea as Perry or vice versa. There seemed to be a clear distinction between the two that was immune to the blurring of lines that crossdressing or transvestism can sometimes produce. Examples such as these not only revealed the pedagogical usage of Madea in Black families (specifically by Black women) but also confirmed that Madea's real-life influences and comedic purpose have not gone unnoticed by Perry's fanbase.

On the same night that I witnessed for the first time the transgressive and racialized performance of Brian Hurst as Jeremy, I also witnessed another moment in the production that made me question just how neatly the lines were drawn between Perry and his crossdressed performance as Madea. This brief moment took place a few scenes before the "popular song" medley discussed earlier, in a scene aptly titled on the DVD "Madea vs. Players." In this scene, we find Madea's nephew, Sonny, amid deep reflection over his failed marriage. Before this, the audience witnessed the adulterous behavior of his wife, who cheated on Sonny with his best friend and coworker. A few minutes into the scene, Madea comes down the stairs and finds Sonny in this depressed state. Being the maternal figure and caretaker that she is known to be, Madea proceeds to give Sonny advice on the lessons of love, heartbreak, and how to detect cheating.

At first, Perry's performance during this moment harkened back to the now-classic and traditional Madea performances found in his previous plays. Madea's Southern and aged wisdom to her nephew was expectedly laced with jokes, sarcasm, and storytelling, all of which were told from the gendered perspective of a woman who had experienced her share of trouble with men and could readily pull from her collected examples of other women's dealings with unfaithful men. Keeping in line with her now recognizable style of storytelling, Madea animated her advice and storytelling by inserting popular culture references, as is seen in the following transcribed example.

SONNY I thought I could change her Madea.
MADEA You can't change people Sonny. I don't know what make folk think they can change somebody. You can't change nobody. That is a waste of time sittin around trying to change somebody. Maya Angelou said it best, she said "If someone shows you who they are believe them." You know what that mean? If it walk like a duck and quack like a duck, then guess what?
SONNY It's a duck?
MADEA AFLAC![74]

Similar to the reaction documented on the distributed DVD version of this play, I witnessed several audiences at the Murat Theatre explode with laughter after this exchange, given the reference to the popular AFLAC television commercials,[75] and continue to laugh as Madea continued to disperse her culturally specific and gendered wisdom from her rocking chair.

However, an almost-imperceptible and unexpected shift in Perry's performance mode and line delivery occurred when Madea began to instruct the audience—no longer Sonny—on how to know if a man is cheating. I have tried to re-create this moment, including audience reactions and Perry's physicality, as best I can in the following transcription:

MADEA And if you ever want to know if a man is cheatin ask him to give you one thing. And if he give it to you he ain't cheatin. Ask him . . . (*Madea starts to writhe uncomfortably in her chair*) for . . . (*Madea exhales*) whooooo . . . (*She looks down and says the following lines*) I was getting ready to tell you but I can't. I wanted to, but who I am is conflictin wit this dress I got on!! (*Madea starts laughing uncontrollably and the audience responds by laughing with her*). Nah, nah, nah! Madea's strong, but she can't fight dis playa I'm sorry. (*More laughter by Madea and audience*). Nah. Hell nah! Nah! Tyler spoke up just then. (*Madea speaks in the voice of Perry*) Come on bruh, come on, come on. Too far, you goin too far. (*More writhing. Madea wipes sweat of her face and continues to writhe and also delivers the following line in Perry's voice.*) Let's stay in character. (*More writhing and laughter from Madea who now speaks in her voice.*) Cause I'm tellin you when a man . . . (*in Perry's voice*) when we be cheatin we . . . (*more writhing*) . . . Let me stay in character . . . (*More writhing from Perry who now speaks in his "Madea" voice.*) When a man be cheatin . . . you can catch him cause they give they-self away. Men, just, I don't understand. Men just always give they-self away by doin dumb stuff. But a woman . . . them things is sliiickk. (*Loud audience laughter.*) Personally, I think women cheat more than men . . . (*Perry continues to speak in his "Madea" voice but delivers the following line as if it were an aside, addressing only Sonny and herself.*) Oh, they don got quiet now.
(*Perry turns his head back to the audience and delivers the following lines.*) And the reason they get away wit it is because, you know, they never think, the men never think they woman would cheat on them but aaaahhhhhhhh that's a fool who think that! Never underestimate your opponent! (*Madea, audience, and Sonny explode in laughter.*)[76]

The monologue continues as Madea switches focus back to Sonny and addresses him directly during the remainder of her speech. She now educates him on how to recognize the signs of a cheating woman. Significantly, this transition marks the end of Perry's spirit possession of Madea that arguably does not occur again until, perhaps, during that already-referred-to moment in the popular song medley when Perry briefly sings his favorite songs, in Madea's body, using his own voice.[77]

Madea's spirit possession, masterfully executed in the live theatre event, calls forth issues surrounding the performative nature of gender, the strategies of cooptation that are used in acts of transvestism, and the blurring that occurs in these performed acts. The latter point in particular consciously or unconsciously signifies the conflicts inherent in such performances. In her oft-cited book *Undoing*

Gender, Judith Butler details the reasons why gender should be understood as being performative in composition in ways that I find helpful when analyzing a performance such as Perry's:

> [G]ender is a kind of doing, an incessant activity performed, in part, without one's knowing and without one's willing, it is not . . . automatic or mechanical. On the contrary, it is a practice of improvisation within a scene of constraint. Moreover, one does not "do" one's gender alone. One is always "doing" with or for another even if the other is only imaginary.[78]

This idea that the display of gender is akin to acting pushes Butler's main thesis that gender is socially constructed, learned, and therefore interchangeable among bodies regardless of biological makeup or anatomy. Thus, the terms *masculine* and *feminine* are not fixed modes of being, nor are they predetermined and/or natural biological products, but instead, they have "meanings [that] change radically depending upon geopolitical boundaries and cultural constraints on who is imagining whom, and for what purpose."[79] In deconstructing our entire understanding of gender and how the category has been historically, socially, and culturally produced, Butler seeks to open the door to allow for not only the range in which gender can be displayed but also for the multiple or seemingly contradictory gender performances that can be produced by one body. Conceptualizing gender in this way undoes our preconceived, assumed, and unquestioned notions of gender. It also allows for an understanding of how the practices of crossdressing and transvestism operate. By Butler's framing gender and its subsequent categories as modifiable and boundless, she is also profoundly implying that gender belongs to no sex and therefore can neither be appropriated nor claimed by any sex. Thus, male-as-female gender performances should not be seen as inaccurate or unnatural, because that would incorrectly posit that "every person born with female anatomy is therefore in possession of a proper femininity (whether innate, symbolically assumed, or socially assigned), one that can either be owned or disowned, appropriated or expropriated."[80]

Here again, Collins reminds us that African American femininity has its own unique history of race-specific construction under sociopolitical and historical circumstances attributable to the conditions of American slavery in which neither the women's bodies nor their constructed femininity were their own or of their own making. Stemming from these conditions, African American female bodies and their femininity have a long history of being appropriated for various reasons.[81] Indeed Butler is correct in her statement that gender has become a norm, yet being outside of the norm extends beyond just being "not quite masculine or not quite feminine" enough.[82] With the history of race-based oppression and the dehumanization of racial others in the United States, the situation of being outside of the gender norm can also read as not being *quite white enough* to be considered capable of possessing/performing normative masculine or feminine traits (be they socially constructed or not). As Collins states, "[w]ithin white/black binary thinking, ideas about racial normality and deviancy draw heavily upon ideas about gender and sexuality for meaning."[83] Thus, white people are considered to be "carriers of 'normal' gender ideology and sexual practices" while Black people are considered to be "carriers of 'deviant' gender ideology and sexual practices."[84]

> Moreover, because racial normality has been defined in gender-specific terms, African Americans' progress or lack thereof in achieving the gender norms attributed to Whites has long been used as a marker of racial progress. Stated differently, African Americans have been evaluated within the context of a sex role theory that by its very nature disadvantages Black people.[85]

Therefore, Black sexualities emerge as being always-already non-normative. In the case of Black heterosexually identified men, such as Perry, appropriating the bodies of Black women, this process is already fraught with racial histrionics—as described in my earlier discussion of minstrelsy—that posit both parties as *lesser than* subjects.

Yet according to Marjorie Garber's discussion of transvestism[86] and crossdressing in popular culture performance, it should be no surprise that Perry has chosen to use the African American female body and image as vessels through which he entertains, critiques, and generates income and acknowledgment in theatre.

> The pattern of subjection and subjugation imposed upon African-American cultural representations in the U.S. and in Western Europe through the figure of transvestism (both male-to-female and female-to-male) has been in recent decades strategically appropriated by black artists, with the result that transvestism has become a powerful rhetorical force for intervention *by* blacks in formerly white-dominated cultural arenas like literature, film, and television.[87]

However, Garber emphatically warns that

> The appropriative gestures of black artists towards the specter of black transvestism, however conscious or unconscious, do not always, of course, succeed in vanquishing the unregenerate racism of stereotypes, nor are they always to be found in a political alliance with pro-feminist, anti-sexist attitudes. Some images of black transvestism are racist, some are sexist, some are both. . . . Furthermore, the degree to which such appropriation is deliberate, "intentional," or designed will vary from case to case, and is . . . always at best a matter of hypothetical speculation. (Even if we possess documentary "evidence" that an artist has a certain "meaning" in mind, the unconscious of the text—novel, play, film, historical event—may be in conflict with the

conscious purpose of its maker. In other words, the unconscious as well as the conscious, may have "intentions," and the two sets of intentions might well be expected to come into conflict with one another.)[88]

I find Garber's sentiments helpful in reconciling Perry's stated intentions to pay homage to his mother, his aunt, and the other Black women in his life whom he claims to know and love at the same time that he takes part in a crossdressing performance that silences and denies the voices and experiences of real Black women and Black female actors, alike.

Implications of Performance and Reception

Perry's crossdressed Madea performances continue to be approved and deemed entertaining and relevant by his audiences. As in the other examples presented in this chapter, I hypothesize that Perry strategically uses the image of a crossdressed African American man specifically because it is a recognizable aspect of African American historic and popular culture that he, like other African American male performers, has been able to manipulate. In this complex reception process, audiences are able to see themselves or the people, aspects, and things they hold dear in Perry's crossdressed representation. For Perry, his Madea performances garner him notoriety, recognizability, and a unique performance element that only he and his productions can lay claim to. While other circuit productions incorporate humor and comedic hijinks, as was discussed in previous chapters, the arena of crossdressing in circuit theatre belongs to Perry alone. Through Madea, Perry strategically taps into the power in this crossdressed figure, which Garber accurately identifies as having a "remarkable—and dangerous—history of representation."[89]

Moreover, in the context of his version of circuit theatre, Perry has transmuted this transvestite or crossdressed figure into one that is coded urban, Southern, matriarchal, domestic, strong, experienced, and undeniably Black. Instead of being an afterthought, Madea's gender is used as an enabling pulpit from which Perry pontificates on the social, political, and cultural aspects of being Black in the United States and instructs his audiences on how to survive in spite of these circumstances. He acknowledges this fact in the closing lines of his *Essence* interview, which I present here as an effective summation of Perry's thoughts on his crossgendered performances:

> He says he uses writing to heal divisions—between young and old, men and women, rich and poor—and he believes that these stories can change lives: "It's good to act as a bridge. And who knew that a man in a dress would be the one to do it?"[90]

During the debut airing of the 2019 BET Awards, which aired on June 23 simultaneously on BET, MTV, and MTV2 networks, Perry was the recipient of the 2019 BET Ultimate Icon Award. His award presentation and video tribute were introduced by Taraji P. Henson, an award-winning African American television, film, and theatre actor since 2001. Henson, who has starred in two Perry's films, *The Family that Preys Together* (Tyler Perry, 2008) and *I Can Do Bad All By Myself* (Tyler Perry, 2009), credited Perry for being the first producer to compensate her for her talent and work at a level that matched her peers in Hollywood:

> He isn't solely about representing us onscreen, he does so in a major way behind the scenes. At a time when my counterparts were making way more money than I was, I was only making a fraction of what most of them were making, Tyler Perry was the first to pay me my worth. . . . Giving me my first real quote in Hollywood. A Black man did that and that means the world to me and I will never forget that. That's what . . . makes Tyler Perry iconic.[91]

The montage video that followed Henson's introduction not only provided multiple images and soundscapes of Perry at work but also featured prominent African American cultural makers such as Oprah Winfrey, Cicely Tyson, Whoopi Goldberg, Tiffany Haddish, and Mary J. Blige. Tyson notes, "We have more Black actors and actresses in the building than we have ever had. . . . He has not forgotten where he came from and that's what allows him to be the giver and sharer of what a God has blessed him in."[92]

Perry's acceptance speech picked up on the bridge metaphor that he used in his 2006 interview with *Essence* magazine, again referencing his crossdressed performance of Madea. Referring to his "20,000 square foot film and television studio, equipped with five sound stages . . . in Atlanta, Georgia,"[93] he stated, "Putting on that dress was a means to get to owning the studio, to get to opening the doors to hire more people."[94] He recalled memories of his mother and the women whom she spent her leisure time with in the projects as being the oral history tellers of their truths who used laughter to heal themselves and each other. A five-year-old Perry would soak up these stories, including characters, gestures, and tones and later reenact them for his mother to lift her spirits after she had been beaten by his stepfather. Perry recalls, "I'd walk in and imitate one of those women and she would start laughing. There was a power in that, that I didn't really get until I get older."[95] From Perry's perspective, laughter was the bridge for his mother and others—the catalyst that enabled a biblically invoked "cross[ing]"[96] over a bridge of pain and suffering. Building his studio on land that was once a base for the Confederate army—"now that land is owned by one Negro"[97]—is also his method of healing and enabling, in his mind, a collective and spiritually rooted Black crossing.

He closed his speech by directing attention to April Reign's 2015 protest hashtag #OscarsSoWhite[98]—which I use as a critical anchor in the opening pages of my introduction chapter.

> While everybody was fighting for a seat at the table, talking about "Oscars So White," "Oscars So White," I said y'all go 'head and do that, but while you fighting for a seat at the table, I'll be down in Atlanta building my own. Because what I know for sure, is that if I can just build this table, God would prepare it for me in the presence of my enemies. Rather than being an Icon, I want to be an inspiration.

With these lines, Perry solidified the resounding cultural and political impact of the Black Circuit, as executed by him and his counterparts through their self-produced, Black-centered, and Black-owned Chitlin Circuit theatrical fare and their filmic and television offshoots: politically declaring, in faith-binding Christian-based rhetoric, that there is no need to seek acceptance anywhere, build your own and they will come. For Perry, his audiences have proven the fortitude and utility of his bridge.

Notes

1 Hughes, "Simply Heavenly," 192–93.
2 Benjamin Svetkey, Margeaux Watson, and Alynda Wheat, "How Do You Solve a Problem Like Madea," *Entertainment Weekly*, March 20, 2009, 27.
3 There are numerous books that discuss the performances and damaging representations contained within turn-of-the century American minstrelsy. Notable sources include: Eric Lott, *Love and Theft: Blackface Minstrelsy and the American Working-Class* (New York: Oxford University Press, 1993); and Bean, "Blackface Minstrelsy and Double Inversion, Circa 1890," 171–90.
4 Svetkey, Watson, and Wheat, "How Do You Solve a Problem Like Madea," 28.
5 Like Perry's other filmic adaptations, the film version of *Diary of a Mad Black Woman* differs in varying ways to the stage version, although its plot remains largely similar. Nevertheless, this movie is significant because it was his first adaptation and marks the first of his numerous box office successes. The film broke box office records for several weeks and shocked industry standards, which led to Hollywood's investment in other black films (penned by Perry and other screenwriters) with a gospel and religious focus.
6 Although his movies and television shows are noteworthy because of how they operate as adaptive spinoffs of Perry's theatrical work, any in-depth analysis into their specific content and wide national reception unfortunately falls outside of the established scope of this project. For more information on the impact of Perry work and the awards and nominations that he has achieved as a producer of theater, film, and television, please see Rashida Z. Shaw McMahon, "'I Am Them': Tyler Perry's Black Musical Theater for the Masses," in *Palgrave Handbook of Musical Theatre Producers*, ed. Laura MacDonald and William Everett (New York: Palgrave MacMillan, 2017), 433–39.
7 Smitri Mundhra, "Tyler Perry Celebrates his New Series 'Sistahs' and 'The Oval' with an Emotional Speech to his Fans," *BET.com*, October 22, 2019, https://www.bet.com/celebrities/news/2019/10/22/tyler-perry-sistas-bet.html, accessed December 22, 2019.
8 Breanna Belle, "Tyler Perry Sets Two New Original Series at BET Plus," *Variety.com*, November 7, 2019, https://variety.com/2019/tv/news/tyler-perry-sets-bruh-and-ruthless-as-two-new-original-series-for-bet-plus-exclusive-1203396341/, accessed December 22, 2019.

9 Svetkey, Watson, and Wheat, "How Do You Solve a Problem Like Madea," 31. A similar discussion of this material appears in Shaw, "From the Margins to Center Stage," 46–47.

10 Commentary by Larry Leon Hamlin, Malcolm Jamal-Warner, and Daniel Beaty, *The Chop Up: The New Minstrel Show*, Black Entertainment Television (BET), August 20, 2006. A similar discussion of this episode appears in Shaw, "From the Margins to Center Stage," 46–47.

11 Commentary by Tyler Perry, *The Chop Up: The New Minstrel Show*, Black Entertainment Television (BET), August 20, 2006. A similar discussion of this episode appears in Shaw, "From the Margins to Center Stage," 47.

12 Shaw, "From the Margins to Center Stage," 47–48.

13 My notion of multiple oppression benefits from the writings of Francis Beale and Deborah K. King, respectively. Please see Beale's original 1970 essay for a discussion of the effects of racism and sexism on Black women. Francis Beale, "Double Jeopardy: To Be Black and Female," in *Words of Fire: An Anthology of African American Feminist Thought*, ed. Beverly Guy-Sheftall (New York: The New York Press, 1995), 146–55. Additionally, King's notion of multiple jeopardy was extremely helpful in understanding how "racism, sexism, and classism constitute three interdependent control systems." Deborah K. King, "Multiple Jeopardy, Multiple Consciousness: The Context of a Black Feminist Ideology," in *Words of Fire: An Anthology of African American Feminist Thought*, ed. Beverly Guy-Sheftall (New York: The New York Press, 1995), 297.

14 Bobo, "*The Color Purple*," 101.

15 Bobo, "*The Color Purple*," 101.

16 Bobo, "*The Color Purple*," 101–2.

17 Bobo, "*The Color Purple*," 96.

18 Gay McCauley, *Space in Performance: Making Meaning in the Theatre* (Ann Arbor: The University of Michigan Press, 1999), 8.

19 Marvin Carlson, *Places of Performance: The Semiotics of Theatre Architecture* (Ithaca, NY: Cornell University Press, 1989), 6.

20 Carlson, *Places of Performance*, 92.

21 Metropolitan Pier and Exposition Authority, Chicago, IL, "About Us," McCormick Place Chicago, www.mccormickplace.com/about_us/about_us_01.html, accessed May 26, 2009.

22 Carlson, *Places of Performance*, 92.

23 Knowles, *Reading the Material Theatre*, 70.

24 Knowles, *Reading the Material Theatre*, 71.

25 Schechner, *Performance Theory*, 31.

26 Knowles, *Reading the Material Theatre*, 71.

27 For more information on the history of The Murat Theatre, please see: *The Encyclopedia of Indianapolis*, ed. David J. Bodenhamer, Robert Graham Borrows, and David Gordon Vanderstel (Bloomington, IN: Indiana University Press, 1994), 150.

28 Interviews conducted during May of 2008 in Chicago, IL. Melinda and Cheryl are pseudonyms that are used in place of the actual names of two female respondents based on Institutional Review Board (IRB) stipulations.

29 Carlson, *The Haunted Stage*, 5–6.

30 Carlson, *The Haunted Stage*, 8.

31 Tyler Perry, "A Word from Tyler," *The Marriage Counselor*, Tyler Perry Playbill, May 2008.

32 Tyler Perry Studios, "Stage Plays and Books," *I Can Do Bad All by Myself*, Synopsis, www.tylerperry.com/_Plays/, accessed May 26, 2009.

33 Kisha Grandy, "Kisha Grandy—Vianne," *I Can Do Bad All by Myself*, Tyler Perry Playbill, 2000.

34 "Kirk Franklin: Awards," *IMDb*, www.imdb.com/name/nm0004938/awards, accessed January 22, 2019.

35 Tyga Graham, "Tyga Graham—Bobby," *I Can Do Bad All by Myself*, Tyler Perry Playbill, 2000.

36 Tosha Moore, "Tosha Moore—Maylee," *I Can Do Bad All by Myself*, Tyler Perry Play-bill, 2000. Please note that the correct spelling of the Moore's first name is Tasha; how-ever, her actor bio misspelled her name as "Tosha" in many instances.

37 The three examples I have selected showcase the range of content included in these bio statements and provide insight into previous actor training and performance expe-rience. The bio statements of Kisha Grandy and Tosha Moore also provide further con-text for my upcoming discussion of *spiritualized vernacular movement*, in *I Can Do Bad All by Myself*, that involves their respective characters Vianne and Maylee. Additionally, Tyga Graham's statement is particularly useful as a representative example of the kind of background and training possessed by Perry's male actors.

38 Jane C. Desmond, "Embodying Difference: Issues in Dance and Cultural Studies," in *Performance: Critical Concepts in Literary and Cultural Studies*, ed. Philip Auslander, vol. 2 (London and New York: Routledge, 2003), 334.

39 Brenda Dixon Gottschild, *The Black Dancing Body: A Geography from Coon to Cool* (New York: Palgrave MacMillan, 2003), 228.

40 Please see Jacqui Malone, "'Keep to the Rhythm and You'll Keep to Life' Meaning and Life in African American Vernacular Dance," in *Signifyin(g), Sanctifyin', & Slam Dunking*, ed. Gena Dagel Caponi (Amherst, MA: The University of Massachusetts Press, 1999), 222–23; and Anthea Kraut, "Between Primitivism and Diaspora: The Dance Perfor-mances of Josephine Baker, Zora Neale Hurston, and Katherine Dunham," *Theatre Journal* 55 (2003): 440.

41 Please see Anthea Kraut, "Reframing the Vernacular: The Dance Praxis of Zora Neale Hurston" (PhD dissertation, Northwestern University, 2002), 32.

42 Paul Carter Harrison, "Form and Transformation: Immanence of the Soul in the Per-formance Modes of Black Church and Black Music," in *Black Theatre: Ritual and Per-formance in the African Diaspora*, ed. Paul Carter Harrison, Victor Leo Walker, II, and Gus Edwards (Philadelphia: Temple University Press, 2002), 325.

43 Elin Diamond, *Unmaking Mimesis: Essays on Feminism and Theater* (London: Routledge, 1997), v.

44 Kimberly W. Benston, *Performing Blackness: Enactments of African-American Modernism* (London and New York: Routledge, 2000), 28–29.

45 Anonymous, interview conducted by author, Chicago, IL, May 2008. Robyn is a pseu-donym that is being used in place of the actual name of the female respondent based on IRB stipulations.

46 Anonymous, interview conducted by author, Chicago, IL, May 2008. Jackie is a pseu-donym that is being used in place of the actual name of the female respondent based on IRB stipulations.

47 Brian Hurst, "Brian Hurst as Jeremy," *Madea Goes to Jail*, Tyler Perry Playbill, March 2006.

48 Stephanie Ferrett, "Stephanie Ferrett as Becky," *The Marriage Counselor*, Tyler Perry Playbill, May 2008.

49 "At Home with Teena Marie and Daughter, Alia Rose," *Jet* 110, no. 17 (October 30, 2006): 55.

50 "At Home with Teena Marie and Daughter, Alia Rose," 56.

51 Johnson, "Performing Blackness Down Under," 72.

52 Johnson's "performance of possibilities" is attributed to D. Soyini Madison's explication of the term as it is related to the transformation that can occur between audience and performers during such performances. This transformation has the potential to move all involved participants toward social and/or political action. For a more detailed dis-cussion, please see E. Patrick Johnson, "Performing Blackness Down Under: Gospel Music in Australia," in *Black Cultural Traffic: Crossroads in Global Performance and Popular Culture*, ed. Harry J. Elam, Jr. and Kennell Jackson (Ann Arbor: University of Michigan Press, 2005), 72; and D. Soyini Madison, "Performance, Personal Narratives, and Politics

of Possibility," in *The Future of Performance Studies: The Next Millennium*, ed. Sheron J. Dailey (Annandale, VA: National Communication Association, 1998), 285.

53 Johnson, "Performing Blackness Down Under," 78.

54 Johnson, "Performing Blackness Down Under," 61.

55 Johnson, "Performing Blackness Down Under," 59.

56 Johnson, "Performing Blackness Down Under," 60.

57 Regina Bendix, *In Search of Authenticity: The Formation of Folklore Studies* (Madison: Wisconsin University Press, 1997), 7; quoted in Johnson, "Performing Blackness Down Under," 60.

58 Johnson, "Performing Blackness Down Under," 61.

59 Taylor, "The Politics of Recognition," 80.

60 Taylor, "The Politics of Recognition," 80.

61 Lott, "Love and Theft," 23.

62 Lott, "Love and Theft," 33–35.

63 Lott, "Love and Theft," 35.

64 Bean, "Blackface Minstrelsy and Double Inversion, Circa 1890," 173.

65 Krasner, *Resistance, Parody, and Double-Consciousness in African American Theatre, 1895–1910*, 26.

66 Bean, "Blackface Minstrelsy and Double Inversion, Circa 1890," 180.

67 Bean, "Blackface Minstrelsy and Double Inversion, Circa 1890," 180. For additional information on Flip Wilson and his portrayal of Geraldine, please see Meghan Sutherland, *The Flip Wilson Show* (Detroit, MI: Wayne State University Press, 2008).

68 Donald Bogle, *Toms, Coons, Mulattoes, Mammies, and Bucks: An Interpretive History of Blacks in American Film* (New York: Continuum, 2001), 9.

69 Tyler Perry, *Madea's Uninhibited Commentaries on Love and Life: Don't Make a Black Woman Take Off Her Earrings* (New York: Riverhead Books, 2006), ix.

70 Anita Gates, "Love, Dignity and Angels Hanging on Wires," The Arts/Cultural Desk, *The New York Times*, February 25, 2006, late city final edition, 14, Sec. C.

71 Patricia K. Johnson, "Diary of a Brilliant Black Man," *Essence* 36, no. 11 (March 2006): 123.

72 Johnson, "Diary of a Brilliant Black Man," 123.

73 Anonymous, interview conducted by author, Chicago, IL, October 2008.

74 Transcribed from Tyler Perry, *Madea Goes to Jail*, DVD, dir. Tyler Perry (Santa Monica, CA: The Tyler Perry Company, Inc., 2006).

75 AFLAC is the acronym for the American Family Life Insurance Company of New York. The company's duck commercials have been popular since the late 1990s. Each commercial features a talking duck that repetitively says (or quacks) the word "AFLAC" throughout.

76 Transcribed from Perry, *Madea Goes to Jail*.

77 Another dramatic spirit possession of note within contemporary African American theatre can be found within Christina Anderson's play *Good Goods*. Please see Christina Anderson, "Good Goods," in *The Methuen Drama Book of Post-Black Plays*, eds. Harry J. Elam, Jr. and Douglas A. Jones, Jr. (London: Methuen Drama, 2012), 95–206.

78 Judith Butler, *Undoing Gender* (New York: Routledge, 2004), 1.

79 Butler, *Undoing Gender*, 10.

80 Butler, *Undoing Gender*, 9.

81 Collins, *Black Sexual Politics*.

82 Butler, *Undoing Gender*, 42.

83 Collins, *Black Sexual Politics*, 44.

84 Collins, *Black Sexual Politics*, 44.

85 Collins, *Black Sexual Politics*, 44.

86 Garber's use of the term *transvestism* in her book is similar to my own usage of the term in this chapter. *Transvestism* is the practice of "wearing the clothes of the other

sex" (3). According to Garber, the desire to dress in the clothes of the opposite sex does not automatically indicate that one has homosexual desires, although this is entirely possible. It should also be made clear that transvestites are different from transgender people in that the latter wish to "physically becom[e] a member of [the opposite] sex" (3). See Marjorie Garber, *Vested Interests: Cross-Dressing and Cultural Anxiety* (New York and London: Routledge, 1992).

87 Garber, *Vested Interests*, 274–75.
88 Garber, *Vested Interests*, 275.
89 Garber, *Vested Interests*, 274.
90 Johnson, "Diary of a Brilliant Black Man," 123.
91 *The BET Awards*, Black Entertainment Television, June 23, 2019.
92 *The BET Awards*, Black Entertainment Television, June 23, 2019.
93 Shaw, "I Am Them," 437.
94 *The BET Awards*, Black Entertainment Television, June 23, 2019.
95 *The BET Awards*, Black Entertainment Television, June 23, 2019.
96 *The BET Awards*, Black Entertainment Television, June 23, 2019.
97 *The BET Awards*, Black Entertainment Television, June 23, 2019.
98 Workneh, "Meet April Reign."

7

SMALL ACTS

The Politics of Black Theatrical Pleasure

> But I am not tragically colored. There is no great sorrow dammed up in my
> soul, nor lurking behind my eyes. I do not mind at all. I do not belong to
> the sobbing school of Negrohood who hold that nature, somehow has given
> them a lowdown dirty deal and whose feeling are all hurt about it. Even in
> the helter-skelter skirmish that is my life, I have seen that the world is to the
> strong regardless of a little pigmentation more or less. No, I do not weep at the
> world—I am too busy sharpening my oyster knife.
> —Zora Neale Hurston, "*How it feels to be Colored Me*" (1928)[1]

"Literature and other arts are supposed to hold up the mirror to nature,"[2] a presci-
ent pioneering Zora Neale Hurston intimated in 1950. "With only the fractional
and the 'exceptional' and the 'quaint' portrayed, a true picture of Negro life in
American cannot be. A great principal of national art has been violated."[3] In her
declaration that Black life was important and the ultimate muse for staging and
fictionalizing humanity, Zora would be proven right. Anticipating this affirma-
tion, Hurston poignantly surmised that "[t]hese are the things that publishers and
producers, as the accredited representatives of the American people, have not as
yet taken into consideration sufficiently. Let there be light!"[4]

In its design and in its adherence to Hurston's poignant charge, *The Black
Circuit* challenges us to move away from analyses that would perceive Chitlin
Circuit theatre productions as instances of low culture and thereby assume that
their efforts and objectives were of a lesser significance than those in the domain
of high culture. Drawing from Hall, I have sought to demonstrate that the

> role of the "popular" in popular culture is to fix the authenticity of popu-
> lar forms, rooting them in the experiences of popular communities from

which they draw their strength, allowing us to see them as expressive of a particular subordinate social life that resists its being constantly made over as low and outside.[5]

Indeed, the strength of the Chitlin Circuit theatre is that it has continued to thrive despite its imperfections and marginalization due to the demands of its audiences and the innovative supply of its practitioners. Chitlin Circuit theatre, then, is a spectator-driven mode of dramatic performance.

These dramas are presented as part and parcel of theatrical events in which spectators engage with onstage and offstage materials in ways that relate to their individual experiences and, at times, their overlapping cultural perspectives as Black Americans. In each chapter, I have revealed how four practitioners have left their imprint on Langston Hughes's established form by strategically engaging with their audiences in ways that are unique to their mode of theatre-making. I have accomplished this through a mixed-methods approach that has used performance analyses, ethnographic field work, examinations of African American cultural practices and of African American theatre history, and analyses of practitioner and spectator commentary to determine some of how Black audiences have interacted with production related materials (both onstage and offstage). I have also offered rationales about what keeps some Black audiences coming back to these events.

A look at Talbert's productions revealed that the writer-director-producer crafted his circuit plays and environments with a keen understanding of how the dramatic narrative, supporting music, acting, and direction all contribute to a spectator's experience at his events. Taken together, his principles for cultivating circuit productions offer us a cohesive set of aesthetically motivated principles that detail the mechanics and objectives behind his theatre-making. Moreover, my discovery of Talbert's theatrical connection to Langston Hughes's Black audience–oriented Broadway musicals of the late 1950s and early 1960s not only places this artist in a long-standing tradition of African American playwrights who have melded Christian faith, worshiping practices, and common life experiences into African American drama but also aligns Talbert's work with the even-broader development of African American musical theatre in this country. As was discussed, his political act of relabeling these plays as *inspirational theatre* strives to elevate the form as it simultaneously represses the negative connotations and derivations that the terms *chitlin* and *Chitlin Circuit* bring with them. His inclusion of jazz, combined with his decision to alternatively present productions that showcase narratives in which characters are motivated more by faith-based practices infused in their everyday lives and less on devout and sustained Christian worship, demonstrates Talbert's desire to present a more secular-based world to his audiences, albeit in the always-already religion-framed structure that has become recognized in circuit theatre. The most intriguing discussion in the chapter was, perhaps, the attention given to Talbert's unparalleled ability to control the engagement of his circuit audiences by molding his spectators, through the course of the production, into a collective character who participates with onstage scenic action in moments that were scripted by the writer-director-producer.

The productions of Johnson and Guidry examined the team's distinct approach to theatre-making through an injection of new materials and methods of performance into the established terrain of circuit theatre. I examined the early catalog of Johnson and Guidry plays, which transformed secular Black popular fiction novels into sacred circuit plays. In transforming these literary texts into dramatic and performance texts, Johnson and Guidry had to contend with the mandatory content of circuit productions: religion, comedy, popular culture, and specific African American vernacular expressions and representations. These plays not only launched the duo's success but also continue to serve as the blueprints for the original plays that they now develop. As I discussed in the chapter, in these early plays, Johnson and Guidry successfully adhered to the circuit form and satisfied the engagement of their spectators by not only relying on their familiarity with the original literary text but also strategically infusing religious material into the now-theatrical plot. They also developed onstage performances that took place within fictional environments that mimetically recreated African American religious experiences onstage. Central to this discussion was my use of African American religion scholarship to aid in identifying exactly *how* they were transforming the secular narrative content into sacred dramatic performance elements and *why* the sacred content was of African American religious and cultural import and thereby identifiable and appealing to their attending audiences. The second half of the chapter proposed that Johnson and Guidry have created a production style in which the dramatic arc of the play is intentionally interrupted by vaudeville-like, variety show–styled performance acts that manipulate the plot to offer their Black heterogeneous audience, who come to the theatre with different interests, a more varied form of entertainment. Using ethnographic fieldwork, historical research, and performance reconstruction, I discussed moments in Johnson–Guidry plays in which this was done with dexterity and effectiveness to increase and sustain audience engagement.

My case studies came to an end with a detailed consideration of Perry's theatrical environments, onstage presentation of stereotypes, and his constructed representations of African American spirituality, blackness, and gender (specifically in his crossdressing performances of Madea). This chapter revealed how the engagement of his audiences was shaped by the production-specific materials and culturally specific African American content that his audience encountered in the theatre's auditorium and inside the lobby during pre-show, intermission, and post-show interludes. The findings of my ethnographic field work inside Chicago's Arie Crown Theater and my supplemental data collection during ethnographic visits to Indianapolis's Murat Theatre to see Perry's production of *Madea Goes to Jail* provided the material evidence for this aspect of the discussion. The subsequent sections of the chapter presented four snapshots of Perry production moments in which I analyzed plays that best captured the dramaturgical and performance methods used by Perry to present mimetic representations of culturally and/or historically salient aspects of African American life in his productions. In these sections, the onstage performances of Perry and his actors were analyzed in terms of their content, embodiment, signification, and cultural and/or historical triggers. As in previous chapters, I considered how Perry uniquely challenged the horizons of expectations of his audiences through examples such as his use of white actors to purposefully trouble his attending audience's notions of authentic blackness and his respective gender shifting performance of Madea at the Murat Theatre.

As one who has studied the circuit extensively, I would be remiss if I did not acknowledge how the efforts of its practitioners and the loyal support of its spectators have politically impacted American theatre and, even more impressively, the content and orientation of American culture. Through the unprecedented and unexpected success of Chitlin Circuit theatre, the marginalized experiences and interests of an ignored segment of the United States' Black citizens have emerged and broken through the barriers of recognition. In its totality, *The Black Circuit* has aimed not only to present these experiences and interests as significant but also to unveil the labor, creativity, and motivations that are involved in this undertaking from both sides of the proscenium arch. Additionally, I have strived to understand how the circuit attracts Black spectators and to uncover the use and significance of *the popular* in its theatrical events.[6] As an example of popular American theatre, Chitlin Circuit theatre stands alone as a Black theatrical form that has managed to secure a prominent position in the American mainstream through its film and television offshoots that attract racially diverse consumers despite the fact that they are created and maintained by African American popular culture interests. Like numerous media and cultural studies scholars, Gans, Levine, Stallybrass and White, have respectively asserted, the content, appeal, and longevity of popular culture forms should be recognized as inherently political because of how they produce pleasure for citizens whose interests lie outside of the dominant cultural order.[7] Moreover, Iton reminds us that the "political legitimacy" of the popular lies in its ability to "render the invisible visible," the "unheard audible," the "invisible audible," and the "unheard visible."[8] Resoundingly then, the circuit's popularity should be recognized as having far-reaching implications well beyond the terrains of theatre.

Act 1: Black Theater as Black Public Sphere

In March 2006, I attended the Chicago run of *The Man of Her Dreams*, penned by a lesser-known circuit playwright by the name of Donald Gray. Gray's production was well advertised on local Black radio stations in Chicago months in advance with much attention given to his celebrity cast, which included actors Clifton Powell and Jackee Harry, and respective music artists of gospel, neo soul, and R&B: Shirley Murdock, Musiq Soulchild, and Ralph Tresvant. Gray's musical drama presented a Black romance story made complete by the infusion of slap-stick comedy, gospel music, biblical teachings and religion. Assembled audiences looked on as Louise, a devoted wife, came face to face with the realities of her husband's adulterous and extortionist past. As the plot unfolded, the broken façade of Louise's marriage revealed truths and hidden secrets that even she was keeping, yet the spiritual framework of the production ensured that all were set on a path toward salvation by the play's end. Although this production was not authored by Talbert, Johnson and Guidry, or Perry, *The Man of Her Dreams* represents one of many circuit productions and their environments examined during my ethno-graphic research that did not make it into this book. Importantly, however, Gray's production, along with countless others that are still featured on national circuit stages today, critically adds another political dimension to our understanding of the processes of production and reception within circuit theatre environments.

During multiple live performances of Gray's musical, I witnessed Black Chica-goans engage with his circuit production in complex ways that notably reflected the present and central concerns of their community. Nestled in Gray's produc-tion were moments that allowed spectators to "recall," in Veve Clark's words, shared memories of their collective and local experiences.[9] One such moment arose in the second act, which I present here through a performance reconstruc-tion of my ethnographic field notes:

> The family's pastor finds Louise in a state of confusion. She is in the middle of contemplating about whether she should confess to having an affair with her sister's husband, the Senator (played by Clifton Powell) or continue to live with the lie of her deception. The pastor proceeds to offer Louise advice on how she can get reconnected with God during her time of need. In the midst of his dialogue the pastor smoothly transitions into a gospel song— a performative move that by now the audience is very accustomed with. Yet different than previous songs in the show, this particular song trans-forms from a diegetic and narrative device of the plot, into a conjuring tool that summons the audience's lived and present reality. The pastor directly sings the following lines to the audience: "I don't care what you're going through. I don't care what your situation may be. All you've got to do is lay your burden's down. Down at the feet of Jesus." Simultaneously, the stage has also changed during this transition from dialogue to song. The pastor now stands downstage center, bathed in a bright spotlight, on an otherwise dark stage. He looks out into the audience and says with a booming voice: "Oh I wish I had a witness in here tonight y'all. I wish I had at least about twenty-three people in here that's ever been through something. Do I have a witness?"[10] Within this moment, the issue of adultery seems to fall by the wayside, and as if in response to the call, there is an erosion of the fourth wall. Many audience members rise out of their seats, clapping, cheering and

standing, with arms outstretched over their heads; again, mimicking many Sunday morning worship services and seamlessly becoming a part of the performance.

Although it is likely that this scene and these physicalized audience reactions were created and recreated in multiple theatres across the country, week after week, I would like to push the boundaries of interpretation to consider what this moment may have meant for many Chicago spectators that night. Just one week before this performance event, a second child was murdered in the predominantly Black Southside neighborhood of Englewood. Ten-year-old Siretha White was killed by a stray bullet that entered the window of her parents' home while she sat in front of the dinner table at her own surprise birthday party. On March 3, 2006, a week before Siretha's murder, 14-year-old honor student Starkesia Reed was killed by a stray bullet as she stood in front of the window inside another Englewood home while eating an orange. These two senseless killings received full media attention in the city and prompted community activists, government officials, and religious leaders to work together to end the sale of assault weapons in the state of Illinois.[11] Dozens of marches, vigils, and rallies were held in Black communities across the city. Given that Black radio is the primary mode of advertising for circuit plays, it was nearly impossible to listen to one of these radio stations, read a newspaper, or watch news broadcasts without hearing an update about the victims' families, the hunt for the killers, or the proposed legislation spawned by these events. More importantly, it was almost impossible not to read or hear testimony from Black citizens throughout Chicago expressing their grief for the young girls they never knew. Stated plainly, *The Man of Her Dreams* came to town when many in Chicago's Black communities were in a shared state of trauma.

Given all of these internal community factors, this manufactured moment in the play had the possibility of operating locally for many of the play's spectators. As Carlson discusses in *Theatre Semiotics: Signs of Life*, the semiotics of the theatre experience in the theatrical event includes "what [an audience] brings to the theatre, and how it organizes what it finds there."[12] Indeed, as I make the link between the tragic real-life murders of the young girls and the mimetic and fictionalized call for testimony, I suggest that a sense of community may have arisen in this production, not only from spectators being able to identify the cultural significance held in the act of testimony but also from them grasping how the elements of performance were related to their own lives and recent events.

As stipulated by Wilkerson in her 1979 article "Redefining Black Theatre," any investigation into Black community theatre practices and performances should never be separate from a consideration of its audience. Second, the researcher or critic should always consider the intent and the cultural context in which the theatre exists and is generated. "Without this perspective," says Wilkerson, "groups are judged merely on their end results or 'products.' . . . These judgments are subject to prevailing notions of 'good' theatre or the critic's personal preferences without reference to the cultural context."[13] Although plays on the circuit operate as touring theatre, and thus are not borne of and from the community, this brief example reveals the mutually constitutive relationship between performance, identity, sociocultural contexts and practices, and spectatorship. Gray's production highlights how audiences engage with what are assumed to be generic, standard, and stereotypical representations in ways that, at times, reflect their social identities and experiences in their localized community.

Act 2: Black Theatre as Popular Culture

On Sunday, June 20, 2010, spectators of Aaron McGruder's popular animated series *The Boondocks* discovered that they had been given front-row seats to McGruder's latest dose of African American cultural critique that this time turned its attention toward the Chitlin Circuit. That McGruder used his show as a platform to expose the popularity of these plays was, perhaps, expected. Over the years, episodes from *The Boondocks* series have been the podium from which McGruder has revealed his sentiments about African American consumption, politics, social behaviors, and ideologies through comic yet not always wholly fictional representations of Black American life. In McGruder's animated world, no topic is considered too sacred for critique. The main characters Huey (age 10) and Riley (age 8), along with their grandfather (Robert Freeman), often find themselves encountering Black icons and participating in storylines that are embedded with dominant African American culture signifiers such as hip hop, the BET network, and slavery. Across several seasons, the Freemans' fictional neighborhood of Woodcrest, Maryland has been graced with the presence of Martin Luther King Jr, Rosa Parks, Dr. Cornel West, and even former president Barack Obama. In most cases, the names of his caricatures are altered to protect the innocent (or the accused), and the humor in his satires is often increased when spectators recognize the "real" in his imagination-based illustrations. Once again, as Hall has explained,

> However deformed, incorporated, and inauthentic are the forms in which Black people and Black communities and traditions appear and are represented in popular culture, we continue to see, in the figures and the repertoires on which popular culture draws, the experiences that stand behind them.[14]

Remarkably, the kind of spectator recognition and awareness to which Hall is referring took place that night in front of televisions across the country (and later on Internet replays) when Cartoon Network and their affiliated channels aired *The Boondocks* season three, episode eight, titled "Pause."

For many loyal Boondocks fans, the word *pause* had become a familiar term because of an oft-repeated phrase said by Riley whenever he thought that something or someone was gay or could be perceived as gay. As a means of both separating himself from the alleged homosexual person or act *and* asserting his eight-year-old manhood through homophobic signifiers, Riley would impulsively assert, throughout episodes and without hesitation, his patented interjection: "Pause, no homo." For Riley, a dedicated Black middle-class follower of a marketed and packaged hip hop culture and lifestyle, his statement falls in line with the homophobic tenets of the "gangsta rap" lifestyle that he upholds and dreams to be a part of. Thus, when McGruder chose to use "Pause" as the title for his Chitlin Circuit episode—without actually mentioning the term *Chitlin Circuit* in the episode—his fans were at least given a hint about the content.

In "Pause," McGruder used the thespian aspirations of the boys' grandfather, Robert, to take his spectators on a journey into the world of ever-popular "Black plays." Once Robert finds out that the acclaimed Black playwright-producer-director-actor Winston Jerome is holding auditions for his new play, he decides to go in the hopes of finally getting his chance under the spotlight. Robert gets cast into a production and soon learns that this world is not what he thought it was and that his fame would come at a price. He is cast as "Ma Duke's" love interest in the play titled *Ma Dukes Finds Herself a Man*. As portrayed in McGruder's episode, "Ma Duke" is a gun-toting, no-nonsense Black grandmother who physically and emotionally protects her family by offering her sage advice and physical strength. Just as Madea is performed by a crossdressed Tyler Perry, in "Pause," Ma Duke is performed by a crossdressed Winston Jerome. The similarities do not stop here. McGruder also uses this episode to play on rumored suspicions about the alleged closeted homosexuality of Tyler Perry by surrounding Jerome with an entourage of physically attractive young Black men who display their oiled, muscular, and shirtless bodies at all times. The homosexual undertones of the episode are amplified even further when Jerome casts Robert as Ma Duke's love interest in the play and later decides, after hearing Jesus speak to him during rehearsal, that Ma Duke and Robert need to share a kiss to improve the play. Although there are numerous scenes in which McGruder plays on Jerome's ambiguous sexuality, the true motive behind Jerome's creation of these plays is unveiled in the near-final scene of the episode. In the confines of his private study, Jerome offers Robert a chance to advance his career if Robert would agree to engage in sexual activity with him. In a moment of truth, he confesses to Robert that he creates these plays so that he can sleep with men. Seconds later, viewers see a shocked and disgruntled Robert speeding from the theatre in his car with his grandchildren and an adoring fan of his performance (a large Black woman eating fried chicken) along with him, as the credits start to roll.

Through the comedic presentation of Winston Jerome's theatrical enterprise, McGruder's "Pause" directed a national television audience's attention toward the real, the popular, the controversial, the alleged, and the assumed in Chitlin Circuit theatre. Presented by means of satire, parody, and critique, McGruder shined light on homophobia in circuit representations and narratives; the use and presentation of African American stereotypes; and the persistent use of African American religious content in dramatic narratives framed by Black Baptist and Pentecostal religious ideologies. And through a problematic caricature of an ever-present and looming-large Black female spectator—the same Black woman who closes the episode with a chicken drumstick in hand—McGruder brought the loyal fanbase of Chitlin Circuit plays into direct view. Notably, McGruder's episode brimmed with the sensory trademarks of the circuit's theatrical environments. Whenever television viewers were provided with snippets of Jerome's theatrical production, his audiences were either heard or seen actively engaging with the plays in ways that were similar to my own descriptions of the audible audience responses on circuit DVD recordings. McGruder even made it a point to include soundbites of the loud roars of applause and the seemingly uncontrolled laughter in response to onstage performances. A particularly distinct view of the audience from McGruder's perspective was captured in a scene that illustrated the night of Robert's debut as Ma Duke's leading man. In the scene, an aerial shot of the theatre's lobby showed a packed house of male and female African American spectators either rushing through the theatre's front doors or standing in the lines of the indoor food vendors, before the start of the show. By the time "Pause" aired, the controversial success of the circuit and its producers had already been the subject of many articles and discussions in national press and media outlets; thus, McGruder's interest in the plays was almost predictable. Yet McGruder's artistic and critical rendering in "Pause" effectively cemented the circuit's evolution from marginal Black theatrical fare to a historically marked American cultural phenomenon.[15]

Act 3: Black Theatre as Black Politics

In its foci, coalitions, and articulations, *The Black Circuit: Race, Performance, Spectatorship in Black Popular Theater* has generated a politics of Black theatrical pleasure and complicated our contemporary understanding of "blackness" in performances of Chitlin Circuit theatre, with attention to how this "blackness" is created, performed, received, and circulated—through "marginalization"—who is doing the marginalization, what is being repressed, and what does that repression reveal. With attention to the politics that the circuit has unearthed in our present epoch, Chitlin Circuit theatre directs us to consider how Black pleasure is conditioned by choice, access, space, temporality, history, innovation, identification, and healing. Black popular theatre, as found on the stages of the contemporary Chitlin Circuit, should be considered a necessary and contributing dimension to studies of popular culture, Black politics, and both race and intraracial relations in the United States. Discourses concerned with the politics of minority spectatorship should now pay special and inclusive attention to the politics of Black theatrical pleasure. In these productive arenas, my Black Circuit concept becomes an interpretive methodology, a theoretical frame, and an artistic praxis that shifts our understanding of the relationship between politics and performance and extends the implications of Black performance and reception beyond the terrains of Chitlin Circuit theatre, specifically, and theatre and performance, more broadly, after the houselights have dimmed.[16]

Curtain Call: Some Black Feminist Thoughts

Inserting radical Black feminist voices at the close of a full-length study on the artistic imaginings and articulations of African American male theatre-makers may strike some as uncanny and others as fanciful and egregious. Some readers may find my use of Zora Neale Hurston's fearless statements—which clearly assert her politics as a Black female artist and intellectual—as the critical frame in which I voice my final ruminations on Chitlin Circuit theatre and its embedded politics to be far afoot and out of applicable intellectual utility. However, I implore my readers to walk with me, a Black female artist and scholar, and the circuit, my complicated performance companion, through dense and untraveled terrains across one final bridge of connection.

As guiding beacons through this uncharted stroll, I would like to remind some of and introduce others to the radical Black feminist thoughts of Cheryl Clarke and June Jordan. Cheryl Clarke, in her groundbreaking and unapologetic essay "Lesbianism: An Act of Resistance," published in the immortally powerful anthology *This Bridge Called My Back: Writings of Radical Women of Color*, lambasted racist, sexist, misogynist, and homophobic structures and actions both inside and outside of Black LGBTQ communities that continue to disengage, discriminate against, and disempower Black lesbian women culturally, politically, and sexually. Her essay closes with warning words that I now resurrect and insert in our present conversation about Black representation, Black artistic efforts, and popular Black reception:

> all of us would do well to stop fighting each other for our space at the bottom, because there ain't no more room. We have spent so much time hating ourselves. Time to love ourselves. And that, for all lesbians, as lovers, as comrades, as freedom fighters is the final resistance.[17]

Borrowing, yet not losing, the focus of the context and specificity of Clarke's directive, I ask, what would it look like if the artistic imaginings, embodied voicings, and confirming viewership of Chitlin Circuit theatre were welcomed and valuably recognized in the celebrated arenas of Black cultural production as whole, full, and complex expressions of blackness? As Black artists and cultural critics, who are first and foremost complex people who always-already produce complex art and are aware of our complex histories, should we continue to fight ourselves, our *complex* selves, for recognition in the figurative and literal bottom space of recognition that Black art continues to denounce, counteract, overcome, or altogether work outside of? In this register, June Jordan's "A New Politics of Sexuality" places Black sexual and individual freedom in full light in her stance against discriminatory, reductive, and oppressive acts of disempowerment against bisexuality:

> If you can finally go to the bathroom wherever you find one, if you can finally order a cup of coffee and drink it wherever coffee is available, but you cannot follow your heart—you cannot respect the response of your own honest body in the world—then how much of what kind of freedom does any one of us possess?
>
> Or, conversely, if your heart and your honest body can be controlled by the state, or controlled by community taboo, are you not then, and in that case, no more than a slave ruled by outside force?
>
> *What tyranny could exceed a tyranny that dictates to the human heart, and that attempts to dictate the public career of an honest human body?*
>
> Freedom is indivisible; the Politics of Sexuality is not some optional "special-interest" concern for serious, progressive folk.[18]

A repetition of Jordan's revolutionary refrain is needed here: *Freedom is indivisible. Freedom is indivisible. Freedom is indivisible!* Could we, who work, study, and revel in African American theatre and culture, not learn a thing or two or many from Jordan's call for a politics of sexual inclusivity? Can we conceive of a politics of Black artistic inclusivity wherein Black artistic freedom is understood as indivisible? Artistic freedom is indivisible. Artistic freedom is indivisible. *Black artistic freedom is indivisible!*

As a feminist-practicing womanist who is always and consistently at all times an artist, a scholar, and a whole, complete, and dynamic self, I am indebted and sustained by the Black feminist principles of intersectionality,[19] the contours of Alice Walker's womanism,[20] and global agendas of inclusivity and embrace. I give abundant and pointed thanks to Clarke, Jordan, Walker, and Hurston for emboldening my intellectual steps, here, in the summative thoughts of this study.

Indeed, Zora, let there be light!

Notes

1 Zora Neale Hurston, "How It Feels to Be Colored Me," in *I Love Myself When I Am Laughing: A Zora Neale Hurston Reader*, ed. Alice Walker, 2nd ed. (New York: The Feminist Press, 1993), 152.
2 Zora Neale Hurston, "What White Publishers Won't Print," in *I Love Myself When I Am Laughing: A Zora Neale Hurston Reader*, ed. Alice Walker, 2nd ed. (New York: The Feminist Press, 1993), 172.
3 Hurston, "What White Publishers Won't Print," 172.
4 Hurston, "What White Publishers Won't Print," 172.
5 Hall, "What Is This 'Black' in Black Popular Culture?" 26.

6 John Fiske, *Reading the Popular* (New York and London: Routledge, 1989).

7 Gans, *Popular Culture & High Culture: An Analysis and Evaluation of Taste* (New York: Basic Books, 1999); Levine, *Black Culture and Black Consciousness*; and Stallybrass and White, *The Politics and Poetics of Transgression*.

8 Iton, *In Search of The Black Fantastic*, 19.

9 Clark, "Developing Diaspora Literacy and *Marasa* Consciousness," in *Comparative American Identities: Race, Sex, and Nationality in the Modern Text*, ed. Hortense Spillers (London and New York: Routledge, 1991), 42.

10 *The Man of Her Dreams*, performed at the Arie Crown Theater in Chicago, IL on March 17, 2006 (audiocassette recording).

11 Evelyn Holmes, "Another Girl Killed by Gunfire in Englewood," *ABC News*, March 12, 2006, http://abclocal.go.com/wls/story?section=local&id=3984844, accessed May 5, 2006; Demetrius Patterson, "Second Englewood Girl Killed by Stray Bullet in Little Over a Week," *Chicago Defender*, March 13, 2006, www.chicagodefender.com/page/local.cfm?ArticleID=4347, accessed May 5, 2006.

12 Carlson, *Theatre Semiotics*, xv.

13 Wilkerson, "Redefining Black Theatre," 34.

14 Hall, "What Is This 'Black' in Black Popular Culture?" 27.

15 There have been conflicting reports about Tyler Perry's response to McGruder's episode. First, rumors alleged that Perry had fired some of his staff and was threatening to take legal action as a result of the episode being aired. A June 30, 2010, *Los Angeles Times* article, for example, reported that Perry telephoned the heads of Turner Broadcasting in an outrage. (Turner Broadcasting is the owner of Cartoon Network and its affiliate station Adult Swim which airs *The Boondocks*.) In the weeks that followed, however, Perry did not publicly give a response to the episode. For more details, please see Joe Flint, "Turner Broadcasting Tries to Make Peace with Tyler Perry," *Los Angeles Times*, Business, June 30, 2010, 1, http://latimesblogs.latimes.com/entertainment newsbuzz/2010/06/turner-broadcasting-tries-to-make-peace-with-tyler-perry.html, accessed January 11, 2011.

16 Crucially, the analyses and findings presented in this book are not underestimated as solely of value because the plays and environments of Chitlin Circuit theatre (re) presents marginalized voices, ideologies, customs, and locales onstage and in nontraditional theater auditoriums. As I have demonstrated from the onset of *The Black Circuit*, these facts are indeed important. Yet what is also significant is the circuit's widespread impact of the circuit as a viable American cultural form that does not cease to be culturally, socially, politically, and even economically relevant.

17 Cheryl Clarke, "Lesbianism, an Act of Resistance," in *This Bridge Called My Back: Writings of Radical Women of Color*, ed. Cherríe Moraga and Gloria Anzaldúa (Watertown, MA: Persephone Press, 1981), 137.

18 June Jordan, "A New Politics of Sexuality," in *Words of Fire: An Anthology of African-American Feminist Thought*, ed. Beverly Guy-Sheftall (New York: The New Press, 1995), 409.

19 The Combahee River Collective, "A Black Feminist Statement," in *Words of Fire: An Anthology of African-American Feminist Thought*, ed. Beverly Guy-Sheftall (New York: New Press, Distributed by W.W. Norton & Company, 1995), 232–40.

20 Alice Walker, "Womanist," in *In Search of Our Mothers' Gardens: Womanist Prose* (San Diego: Harcourt Brace Jovanovich, 1983), xi–xii.

INDEX